PENGUIN BOOKS

WHO THE HELL IS
Pansy O'Hara?

Courtesy of the Authors

Jenny Bond and **Chris Sheedy** are based in Sydney, Australia, and run a successful freelance journalism and media consulting company, The Hard Word. They also have worked in London and New York City. Prior to her reinvention as a journalist, Jenny held the position of Head of English at Eaton House The Manor in London's Clapham Common. She also has taught English and drama for eight years at a selective high school in Sydney. Chris is one of Australia's most in demand freelance writers, having had work published regularly in such magazines and newspapers as the *Sydney Morning Herald,* Virgin Blue's *Voyeur,* the *Sunday Telegraph, Australian Good Taste, Australian Penthouse, Cosmopolitan,* and *Management Today.* In London and New York City he was vice president of Guinness World Records.

Chris's most memorable reading experience was sweating it out in the heat of London's Tube with a copy of Dostoevsky's *Crime and Punishment,* often feeling as feverish as the lead character Raskolnikov. He's also a fan of great Australian writers such as Tim Winton (*Cloudstreet*), Peter Carey (*True History of the Kelly Gang*), and Nick Cave (*And the Ass Saw the Angel*). As a boy he was endlessly entertained by Stephen King and Alistair MacLean.

Jenny's favorite reading experience of all time was *Emma* by Jane Austen, as the lead character was so flawed and did such awful things but at the same time was so likeable. This was also the first book that Jenny's students truly enjoyed, and in class she noticed that they discussed the characters as if they were real people. Her other literary loves include F. Scott Fitzgerald's *The Great Gatsby,* Mark Twain's *Adventures of Huckleberry Finn,* A. S. Byatt's *Possession,* and Emily Brontë's *Wuthering Heights*. As a youngster she couldn't resist Agatha Christie and James Herriot.

WHO THE HELL IS
Pansy O'Hara?

THE FASCINATING STORIES
BEHIND 50 OF THE WORLD'S
BEST-LOVED BOOKS

Jenny Bond & Chris Sheedy

PENGUIN BOOKS

PENGUIN BOOKS
Published by the Penguin Group
Penguin Group (USA) Inc., 375 Hudson Street, New York, New York 10014, U.S.A.
Penguin Group (Canada), 90 Eglinton Avenue East, Suite 700, Toronto, Ontario,
Canada M4P 2Y3 (a division of Pearson Penguin Canada Inc.)
Penguin Books Ltd, 80 Strand, London WC2R 0RL, England
Penguin Ireland, 25 St Stephen's Green, Dublin 2, Ireland
(a division of Penguin Books Ltd)
Penguin Group (Australia), 250 Camberwell Road, Camberwell, Victoria 3124,
Australia (a division of Pearson Australia Group Pty Ltd)
Penguin Books India Pvt Ltd, 11 Community Centre, Panchsheel Park,
New Delhi – 110 017, India
Penguin Group (NZ), 67 Apollo Drive, Rosedale, North Shore 0632, New Zealand
(a division of Pearson New Zealand Ltd)
Penguin Books (South Africa) (Pty) Ltd, 24 Sturdee Avenue,
Rosebank, Johannesburg 2196, South Africa

Penguin Books Ltd, Registered Offices: 80 Strand, London WC2R 0RL, England

First published in Penguin Books 2008

3 5 7 9 10 8 6 4 2

Copyright © Jenny Bond and Chris Sheedy, 2008
All rights reserved

Library of Congress Cataloging in Publication Data

Bond, Jenny.
Who the hell is Pansy O'Hara? : the fascinating stories behind 50 of the world's best-
loved books / Jenny Bond and Chris Sheedy.
p. cm.
ISBN 978-0-14-311364-5
1. Authors, English—20th century—Biography. 2. Authors, American—20th century—
Biography. 3. Authors, English—19th century—Biography. 4. Authors, American—19th
century—Biography. 5. Authorship. 6. Best sellers. I. Sheedy, Chris. II. Title.
PR106.B66 2008
820.9—dc22 [B] 2007039840

Printed in the United States of America

Set in Granjon • Designed by Elke Sigal

To the greatest character we know—
a beautiful little man by the name of Sam
who entered our lives halfway through
the writing of this book.

Contents

Nonfiction

Introduction

"We're writing a book about books," was our response when people wondered out loud why they hadn't seen us for the eighteen months it took to produce the fifty fascinating chapters into which you are about to delve. But really we were enjoying a journey deep into the lives of some of the world's most talented authors, people who with the simple act of writing have filled our lives, and yours, with excitement, sadness, tension, horror, joy, love, and so much more.

It began as a discussion over dinner. What is the special ingredient, we wondered, that creates a truly spectacular piece of literature or a work with enduring appeal? It's too easy to analyze the work itself—the language, the story lines, the characters—experience told us the answer lay deeper. We would only discover the secret to an unforgettable read by uncovering what it was that occurred in each author's life to propel her or him toward penning the book in the first place.

The list of books began taking shape from our own bookcase, then from those of friends and colleagues, before being argued and discussed with professionals in the world of publishing and with other book specialists and finally finessed by a large amount of research into book sales and awareness figures in various countries. Then began the all-consuming task of researching each of the writers, but rather than a chore it became a joy, an enthralling expedition into the lives of some surprisingly heroic people.

Fyodor Dostoevsky, for instance, faced death in front of a firing squad before being given a reprieve and sent to a hard labor prison in Siberia for four years—all because he was an intellectual. George Orwell was a Brit whose political views were so strong that he voluntarily traveled to serve on the front line during the Spanish Civil War, only to be shot in the neck after ten days. Stephen King lived in poverty from the age of two, when his father walked out, and produced *Carrie* on a typewriter in the trailer in which his family lived. After writing *All Quiet on the Western Front,* Erich Maria Remarque had his German citizenship revoked and his books burned.

So what is the special ingredient? The answer, we discovered, is passion and struggle. J. K. Rowling hardly had two pennies to rub together when she introduced Harry Potter to the world. As a young child Charles Dickens was forced to work in a rat-infested factory as his father served a prison sentence. Charlotte Brontë lived her life completely surrounded by sickness and death. And Stephen Hawking was diagnosed with a life-threatening, crippling disease a week after his twenty-first birthday and told he had three years to live.

But it's not all doom and gloom—these stories are more about triumph over tragedy. Through their struggle and passion most of the writers created lifestyles and levels of wealth and celebrity beyond even their own fertile imaginations. And perhaps most important, their work will forever provide moments of quiet pleasure for millions of readers around the globe.

It's been a true pleasure getting to know them. We hope it is for you, too.

WHO THE HELL IS
Pansy O'Hara?

Fiction

PRIDE AND PREJUDICE,
Jane Austen, 1813

I had not known you a month before I felt that you were the last man in the world whom I could ever be prevailed upon to marry.

Jane Austen's biographer, her nephew J. E. Austen-Leigh, wrote the following of his subject in the opening of his *A Memoir of Jane Austen:* "Of events her life was singularly barren: few changes and no great crisis ever broke the smooth current of its course." Statements such as these have led many critics and readers to assume that nothing significant or untoward ever happened in Jane Austen's world, and that for this very reason the action in her novels largely revolved around the trivial pursuits of dances, letter writing, visiting friends, and domestic affairs. But in reality Austen's existence was filled with trials and tribulations.

For most of Austen's life England was at war with France. In the year she was born the American Revolution erupted and James Watt invented the steam engine, a machine that would herald in the industrial age. The author witnessed the French Revolution from the safe side of the English Channel and saw her own country defeated in the American colonies. Meanwhile, the First Fleet sailed to Botany Bay in Australia and England established a new colony in the remote outpost of New South Wales.

On a personal level Austen's own family should have been fodder enough for her fiction. Two of her brothers saw action against Napoleon's forces, her mother was related to a duke, her aunt was once wrongly imprisoned for theft, and her cousin fled the Reign of Terror in France after her husband met his fate at the guillotine, later marrying Austen's brother Henry. A handicapped brother was sent away to live with another family and was never spoken of again and yet another brother, Edward, was adopted by a wealthy couple unable to have children and made heir to their substantial fortune.

Jane Austen was not deprived of exciting subject matter but chose to write instead about the goings-on in her imagination. The year she penned her most famous novel, *Pride and Prejudice,* was a miserable year for the author. Consequently, it is not surprising she turned away from world events and the affairs of her own family to a world inhabited by a bright and confident heroine, her comical family and thoughtful friends, caddish militia officers, arrogant suitors, overbearing grand dames, and the often-harrowing journey of love.

Jane Austen was born in Steventon, Hampshire, England, into a largely male family on December 16, 1775. She was the second daughter born to George and Cassandra Austen, who also had five sons. Their eighth and final child was a boy. As a result of this imbalance, Jane and her sister, Cassandra, were inseparable. George Austen worked as a vicar and to supplement the meager stipend he received from the church he and his wife tutored students. Reverend Austen was a relatively poor member of the landed gentry and, as such, had no way of providing his two daughters with dowries.

Although Jane and Cassandra did spend a short period away from home at boarding school, they primarily were educated at the rectory. Reverend Austen was well aware of his financial restrictions and realized that his daughters, without dowries, likely would have to make their own way in the world as governesses. Jane had a precocious mind and, by the age of eight, she was able to read most of the books in her father's library. Moreover, she could speak some French, Latin, and Italian, play the pianoforte, and sing.

Her preferred writers were Dr. Samuel Johnson, the poet William Cowper, Henry Fielding, and Laurence Sterne, while her favorite author was Samuel Richardson. According to her brother Henry, Austen had read Richardson's epistolary novel *History of Sir Charles Grandison* so many times that she had almost committed the words to heart. Austen also read the popular female authors of the era, such as Fanny Burney, Maria Edgeworth, and Charlotte Smith, all of whose writing strongly influenced her own.

The Austens were a literary family, and from an early age Jane was encouraged to write, especially by her father. Reverend Austen soon thought his daughter's work good enough to warrant the purchase of expensive notebooks. It was on the opening page in one of these books that her father wrote the dedication "Effusions of Fancy by a very Young Lady Consisting of Tales in a Style entirely new." To amuse themselves the Austen children frequently performed plays in the rectory's barn, with Jane's brother James writing the prologues and epilogues. James also wrote poetry and was responsible for writing and editing his own weekly magazine, called the *Loiterer,* which he sold for threepence.

By the time Austen was eleven years old she was penning short satirical sketches for the amusement of her family. By the age of fourteen she had written her first novel, *Love and Friendship,* and when she was sixteen she wrote the comical *A History of England by a partial, preju-diced and ignorant Historian. Lesley Castle* followed in 1792, and between 1793 and 1794 Austen wrote *Lady Susan.* Although Austen was not yet out of her teenage years, her writing demonstrated enormous promise. Sat-irizing social conventions, this early work showed a sharp observation of human behavior, immense wit, a sense of the ridiculous, and the writer's trademark use of irony.

In 1795 the war intruded very directly into the lives of the Austen family when Cassandra's fiancé, Tom Fowles, became the chaplain to a regiment fighting the French in the West Indies. Cassandra was devastated when he died overseas of fever in February 1797. Jane Austen's own love life also was not without incident. During the Christ-mas of 1795 a visiting Irish law student, Tom Lefroy, stole the twenty-year-old's heart. After a few dances and meetings it was clear the couple had formed a strong bond. However, Lefroy soon was encouraged to depart Hampshire by his family, who was not willing to have their son attach himself to the penniless daughter of a clergyman. Although the flirtation was brief, Austen now knew the feeling of heartbreak. At the same time, England was nearing breaking point—the winter of 1795 seemed to last an eternity, with the price of food ris-ing and no end in sight to the war with the French. There was the prospect of riots, and the king himself faced crit-icism and attack.

It was under these circumstances that Austen ven-tured into her most productive period as a writer and began her first full-length novel in the same style as her idol Samuel Richardson. *Elinor and Marianne* was drafted in epistolary form in 1795. The novel explored feminine behavior through two sisters, one levelheaded and discreet, the other romantic and imprudent. In October of the following year the author began her first draft of *First Impressions*. This work told the story of twenty-year-old Elizabeth Bennet, the daughter of a country gentleman not unlike George Austen. When the intelligent and witty Elizabeth meets the landowning aristocrat Mr. Darcy, they dislike each other immediately. But as the story progresses a series of incidents changes their opinion of each other, and the pair finally discover their love for each other.

Many similarities are apparent between the worlds of Jane Austen and Elizabeth Bennet. The two women were the same age and shared close relationships with their fathers. They were without dowries but known for their intellect and sharp wit. The Bennets and the Austens were of equal social and economic standing, with the financial welfare of females of the family left to the mercy and charity of the males. However, *First Impressions* was first and foremost a romance. All the characters achieved marriage and some degree of happiness by the end of the book, no matter how insecure the foundations on which they were built. Apart from the dances, the gossip, and the domestic affairs of daily life, Jane Austen's future looked nothing like that of Elizabeth Bennet!

The novel was completed in August 1797. Austen made a practice of reading her work aloud to her family, and *First Impressions* delighted her father so much that he took the liberty of sending it to the publisher Thomas Cadell in London, offering to pay for the printing costs. The manuscript promptly was returned to Steventon with the words "Declined by Return of Post" written on the envelope.

The rejection did not dishearten the author; in fact, it had the opposite effect. She became determined to have her work published. Austen also decided to rework *Elinor and Marianne,* as she was not happy with its style. She chose to rewrite it in direct narrative form, and this considerable work was carried out in the winter and spring of 1798. At the same time Austen began a third novel, called *Susan,* a work that parodied Gothic fiction. This was sent by her brother Henry to the publishers Richard Crosby and Son in 1803. The company bought the manuscript for £10 but failed to publish it, perhaps because it lampooned a very popular genre. Six years later Henry bought the manuscript back. It was not to be published until 1818 (after the author's death), as *Northanger Abbey.*

In 1801, without warning, George Austen retired from his parish and moved his wife and daughters to the cosmopolitan city of Bath. But Austen was unhappy with the move—she disliked the busy town and, as a consequence, her writing ceased. Four years later, in 1805, George Austen died, leaving his wife and daughters in financial disarray. But Austen's brothers came to the rescue and pooled funds enough for the trio to enjoy a yearly income of £600 and a home with Austen's brother Frank in Southampton. The women lived there for four years until Edward offered the ladies a permanent home on his Chawton estate in 1809.

Settled once more in her dearly beloved Hampshire, Austen returned to writing and immediately began revisions on *Elinor and Marianne,* now titled *Sense and Sensibility.* When completed, *Sense and Sensibility* was sent to publishers T. Egerton of Whitehall by Henry Austen, who had become his sister's unofficial book agent. Henry, now a prosperous London banker, paid for the printing, and the novel was published in 1811 without revealing the author's name—it simply stated that it was by "A Lady." *Sense and Sensibility* was an immediate success, with the first edition selling out. Reviews were excellent and the author made the handsome sum of £140. At the age of thirty-six, Jane Austen was financially independent.

By the time *Sense and Sensibility* reached the shelves, Austen was already undertaking revisions of *First Impressions,* now titled *Pride and Prejudice.* Austen wrote that she "lop't and crop't" the first lengthy version of the work. In 1813 it was sold to T. Egerton for £110 and once again was not advertised as a book by Jane Austen but instead as a novel by the author of *Sense and Sensibility.* Like her previous endeavor, *Pride and Prejudice* was well received, garnered the praise of the Prince Regent, and required a second print run that same year. Poet/ playwright Richard Sheridan said that it was one of the most clever pieces he had ever read, and a literary critic told Henry Austen that it was far too good to be the work of a woman.

In *Pride and Prejudice* Jane Austen showcased her stunning observation of character. Her superb use of irony to highlight the often quirky and ridiculous foibles of her characters was made possible by her employment of an omniscient narrator. This allowed the author to tell the story with seeming objectivity while suggesting an ironic incongruity between what is happening and what is being read. Moreover, the dialogue sparkled, the romance between Elizabeth and Darcy was shaped to perfection, and each character was made memorable in his or her own right.

Austen once referred to *Pride and Prejudice* as her own darling child, and with it she achieved everything a mother would hope to for her offspring. But it had been a long and arduous journey, with the writer beginning the novel when she was twenty and not seeing it published until she was thirty-seven. Written in a period when there was very little light in Austen's life, the goings-on in the world of Elizabeth Bennet provided the author with much-needed joy and fulfillment.

FRANKENSTEIN,
Mary Shelley, 1818

✦

*Every where I see bliss, from which I alone am irrevoca-
bly excluded. I was benevolent and good; misery made me
a fiend. Make me happy, and I shall again be virtuous.*

In May 1816, Mary Godwin and her soon-to-be husband,
the poet Percy Bysshe Shelley, vacationed in Switzerland
by Lake Geneva. One night during this idyllic summer
vacation, when Mary was in a deep slumber, she was visited by a disturbing dream that was to alter her life, her
career, and eventually the entire literary landscape. It
was a dream of a hideous creature that had been put together from several body parts and into which life had
been breathed, as she herself would soon breathe literary
life into that very character.

Mary Shelley was born Mary Wollstonecraft Godwin
in London in August 1797, to two of Britain's most
radical thinkers and writers of the eighteenth century:
the feminist Mary Wollstonecraft and the philosopher
William Godwin. With two such powerful influences it
was not surprising that her own life was to follow a similar path. Mary wrote in 1831, "It is not singular that, as
the daughter of two persons of distinguished literary
celebrity, I should very early in life have thought of writing." She goes on to describe a childhood spent scribbling
and writing stories, but she says, "I had a clearer pleasure

than this, which was the formation of castles in the air—the indulging in waking dreams . . ."

Mary's mother died from puerperal fever ten days after giving birth. Suddenly Godwin became the chief caregiver for his child and for his wife's child from a previous relationship, Fanny Imlay. Having studied the progressive educational theories of French philosopher Jean-Jacques Rousseau, Godwin schooled both children at home with the aid of a governess named Louisa Jones. Godwin called his daughter "pretty little Mary" and took great delight in her obvious superiority over the older Fanny. A sensitive, intelligent, and beautiful young girl, her attachment to her father was powerful and her feelings for the mother she never knew bordered on idolatry. She would often sit by her mother's grave in St. Pancras Cemetery and read her works.

When Mary was three Louisa Jones left the household and Godwin decided the best solution was to remarry. Surrendering to the flattery of the widow Mary Jane Clairmont, Godwin and she were married in 1801. Clairmont was described by James Marshall, one of Godwin's close friends, as a "clever, bustling, second-rate woman, glib of tongue and pen, with a temper undisciplined and uncontrolled; not bad-hearted, but with a complete absence of the finer sensibilities."

All at once the quiescent life Mary had led with her father, half-sister, and their beloved governess was over, replaced by an expanded household and a severely strained relationship with her new stepmother. Clairmont resented Mary's close relationship with Godwin, who objected when it was suggested that Mary be sent to boarding school to further her education. Instead Clairmont's own daughter, Jane (later Claire), was sent away to further her education, while Mary and Fanny were left to their own devices at home.

Although offered no formal schooling, the girls received the best education possible by utilizing their father's extensive library and by spending time with those within his circle of intellectual friends. Frequent guests to the Godwin home were Charles and Mary Lamb, Samuel Taylor Coleridge, William Wordsworth, and William Hazlitt. One evening when Mary was just nine years old, she hid under the sofa and listened to Coleridge recite *The Rime of the Ancient Mariner,* a poem that was to echo throughout her first great work. Such was the influence and guidance she received that, when she was eleven years old, she had her first written work appear in print. Published by the Godwin Juvenile Library, it was a poem entitled *Mounseer Nongtongpaw,* a humorous reworking of a famous song of the time.

But as Mary approached womanhood the conflict with her stepmother became too great, and the teenager was sent to live with family friends in Dundee, Scotland, in 1812. She enjoyed the time she spent in the north and regarded it as an important catalyst to her creativity. She later wrote of her adopted home, "Blank and dreary on retrospection I call them; they were not so to me then. They were the eyry of freedom, and the pleasant region where unheeded I could commune with the creatures of my fancy. I wrote then—but in a most common-place style. It was beneath the trees of the grounds belonging to our house, or on the bleak sides of the woodless mountains near, that my true compositions, the airy lights of my imagination, were born and fostered."

On a brief visit back to London that year the fifteen-year-old met Percy Bysshe Shelley, another frequent visitor to her father's home. Two years later she began an intellectual and sexual relationship with the twenty-two-year-old poet. In a loveless relationship with his wife, Harriet, Percy found in his mentor's daughter exactly what was lacking in his life. Mary was beautiful, vibrant, and intellectual, and she was the child of two of the country's most brilliant writers. The poet wrote of Mary in the dedication for his poem *The Revolt of Islam* (1817), "They saw that thou wert lovely from thy birth, / Of glorious parents, thou aspiring Child."

Conversely, Percy was everything Mary was looking for in a partner—he was a free-thinking, passionate poet who shared a deep respect for her father. Percy had in fact grown very important to the Godwin household by this time as by 1814 Godwin's debts had skyrocketed and Percy was supporting the family financially.

Despite this, when Godwin discovered the relationship between his daughter and Percy, he forbade the union, while continuing to accept Percy's charity. Mary originally obeyed her father, but when Percy threatened to commit suicide, she gave in to her heart. The two eloped to France in July 1814, but their mission was aborted when authorities discovered Percy was still married. On returning home, Godwin would not see the couple and refused to speak with his daughter for more than three years. Mary and Percy eventually were married in December 1816, after Harriet committed suicide.

Percy, however, was a nonconformist and a believer in free love, and he openly pursued a relationship with Mary's half-sister Claire Clairmont. He also encouraged Mary to bed his good friend Thomas Hogg, a suggestion she refused to act on. But Percy was also an excellent tutor and mentor for Mary. Taking over where her father left off, the young poet drew up a schedule of study for his wife that included literature and languages. He respected and encouraged Mary's thinking by discussing poetry, politics, and philosophy with her on a regular basis.

In May 1816, Mary, Percy, and Claire Clairmont decided to spend the summer in Switzerland. Renting a villa on the banks of Lake Geneva, they were happy to discover the poet Lord Byron was staying only minutes away at the Villa Diodati with his physician Dr. Polidori. Once they'd managed to make his acquaintance, Byron struck up a relationship with Claire and the group spent many hours boating, picnicking, and discussing poetry and philosophy.

As a result of a particularly wet summer they were regularly confined to their houses. One dreary evening the group was entertaining themselves by reading aloud from a compendium of German ghost stories entitled *Fantasmagoriana*. When they reached the conclusion, Lord Byron suggested they each write their own ghost story. Mary later wrote of the evening, "The noble author began a tale, a fragment of which he printed at the end of his poem Mazeppa. Shelley, more apt to embody ideas and sentiments in the radiance of brilliant imagery, and in the music of the most melodious verse that adorns our language, than to invent the machinery of a story, commenced one founded on the experiences of his early life. Poor Polidori had some terrible idea about a skull-headed lady, who was so punished for peeping through a keyhole . . ."

Mary herself could not think of an idea on which to base her tale. Each morning when she awoke she would be asked if she had thought of a story. On each occasion she replied in the negative. Then one evening she sat listening as the men in the party discussed the work of Dr. Erasmus Darwin and Luigi Galvani. The former had preserved a piece of vermicelli until it moved voluntarily by some extraordinary means and the latter had investigated the effects of electricity on dead animals in the 1790s. Mary later described what happened when she went to sleep that night:

"When I placed my head on the pillow, I did not sleep, nor could I be said to think. My imagination, unbidden, possessed, and guided me gifting me successive images that arose in my mind with a vividness far beyond the usual bounds of reverie . . . I saw the pale student of unhallowed arts kneeling beside the thing he had put together. I saw the hideous phantasm of a man stretched out, and then, on the working of some powerful engine show signs of life, and stir with an uneasy, half vital motion."

The next morning Mary began writing her tale with the words "It was on a dreary night in November . . ." The author originally intended the story to be but a few pages, but under Percy's encouragement and guidance she developed the ghost story into a striking tale of death, rebirth, and the disastrous consequences of one man's struggle to overcome human limitations.

The result, completed in 1817 and published in 1818, was *Frankenstein, or, The Modern Prometheus*. The novel, originally published anonymously, tells the story of an overreaching scientist, Victor Frankenstein, who builds a man from body parts scavenged from graveyards, slaughterhouses, and dissecting rooms, and gives life to his creation. Described as "a spark of life," Mary suggests animation was given through some electrical process similar to the experiments carried out by Galvani. Frankenstein is compared to the mythological figure Prometheus, who stole fire from the gods to give life to a man of clay. However, rejected by his creator and everyone he comes in contact with because of his hideous appearance, Frankenstein's creature becomes a malevolent killer. When Frankenstein realizes the consequences of his ambition, he sets out to track down the monster and destroy it.

At the novel's core is the theme of creation, highlighted in the opening quote from Milton's *Paradise Lost:* "Did I request thee, Maker, from my clay / To mould Me man? Did I solicit thee / From darkness to promote me?" The novel also acts as a warning against pride, obsession, and single-minded ambition.

So powerful was its premise that the novel, and its lead characters, went on to become some of popular culture's most instantly recognizable icons. No less than a dozen films have been produced around the theme of Frankenstein's monster, starring such greats as Boris Karloff, Gene Wilder, Robert De Niro, Kenneth Branagh, and Ian McKellen.

While unpopular with critics, who labeled the novel "a tissue of horrible and disgusting absurdity," the work itself was an outstanding success with the public. And most important, the writer, who was still in her teens when the book was completed, transformed the genre in which she was writing—the gothic novel. Mary rejected the stock characters and formulaic plots of gothic fiction and instead wove a rich tapestry of terror that reflected the power, complexity, and darkness of the human mind.

OLIVER TWIST,
Charles Dickens, 1838

❧

*The fact is, there was considerable difficulty in inducing
Oliver to take upon himself the office of respiration, a
troublesome practice, but one which custom has ren-
dered necessary to our easy existence; and for some time
he lay gasping on a little flock mattress, rather unequally
poised between this world and the next, the balance being decidedly in favour of the latter.*

When Charles Dickens was twelve years old an extraordinary incident occurred, an event so disturbing
and profound that it was to shape the rest of his life. In
1824 the well-educated boy of middle-class birth was
separated from his family and sent to work in a blacking
factory, a business that produced shoe polish. Not only
did this situation open the child's eyes to the putrid un-
derbelly of society and the many ills that plagued London's lower classes, it also burned into his soul a deep
sense of abandonment. Out of this experience Dickens
gained an empathy with the weak, neglected, and impoverished, but more importantly, it sparked in him a
determination and ambition to be successful in an effort
to guard against ever falling into such depths of despair
again.

Charles John Huffman Dickens was born on February 7, 1812, in Portsmouth, Hampshire, England, the
second of John and Elizabeth Dickens's eight children.

John worked as a clerk at the navy pay office and provided his family with a moderately comfortable existence. Humorous, theatrical, larger than life, and optimistic, Dickens Sr. possessed many admirable qualities. The author later said of his father, "He was like a cork—if he was pushed under water in one place, he always 'bobbed up to time' cheerfully in another, and felt none the worst for the dip." Despite this resilience, however, John had one fatal flaw that was to lead to his eventual downfall. John Dickens enjoyed leading a life far above his class, and in an endeavor to live like a gentleman on a clerk's income, he amassed massive debts.

Nevertheless, in his early childhood young Charles enjoyed an idyllic life. In 1817 John was transferred to Chatham, Kent, on England's southeast coast, and the boy spent many hours outdoors. The countryside surrounding Chatham was sprawling and wondrous and Charles often would go walking with his father in this glorious landscape. One day the pair came across a great manor house called Gad's Hill Place standing on a high point on the road. Charles immediately dreamed of one day becoming the owner. When he expressed this desire to his father, John assuredly replied, "If you were to be very persevering, and were to work hard, you might some day come to live in it." Charles took John's words to heart. It was also at this time that Charles began to read voraciously. His favorite authors were Henry Fielding, Tobias Smollett, Daniel Defoe, Cervantes, and Oliver Goldsmith—all whose influences are reflected in Dickens's later works.

Initially Charles's education was provided by his mother, although while in Chatham Charles did attend school briefly. Elizabeth possessed a fine sense of humor and a fondness for the ridiculous and entertained her children with vivid stories from her imagination. But she also was hard-minded and practical—she had to be. Married to a man like John meant she was constantly attempting to shore up the family's unstable finances.

By the time John was transferred to London in 1822, the family's situation had grown dire. With creditors demanding payment, the family took inexpensive lodgings in a small tenement in Camden Town, one of the worst suburbs of the capital. Charles missed Chatham desperately and began to believe his parents were growing neglectful of their children. Dickens missed most his education, he later recalled: "As I thought in the little back garret in Bayham Street, of all I had lost in losing Chatham, what would I have given, if I had anything to give, to have been sent back to any other school, to be taught something, anywhere!"

The family's finances reached crisis point in 1824 and, in desperation, twelve-year-old Charles was sent to work at Warren's Blacking Factory on the banks of the Thames. It was there that Charles worked in decaying, rat-infested conditions pasting labels onto shoe polish jars from eight in the morning until eight at night, six days a week, earning six shillings a week. The writer later reflected on the experience: "It is wonderful to me how I could have been so easily cast away at such an age. It is wonderful to me that, even after my descent into the poor little drudge I had been since we came to London, no one had compassion enough on me—a child of singular abilities, quick, eager, delicate, and soon hurt, bodily or mentally—to suggest that something might have been spared, as certainly it might have been, to place me at any common school. Our friends, I take it, were tired out. No one made any sign. My father and mother were quite satisfied. They could hardly have been more so, if I had been twenty years of age, distinguished at a grammar-school, and going to Cambridge." But the situation soon was to grow even worse.

Not long after Charles began work at Warren's, John was sent to Marshalsea Debtor's Prison. As was the practice at the time, the entire family, excluding Charles and his sister Fanny, who was attending the Royal Academy of Music, joined him in jail. Consequently, Charles was forced to take lodgings in Camden Town, a three-mile walk from Warren's. Completely alone in London and forced to fend for himself, Dickens later recalled feeling that there was ". . . no advice, no counsel, no encouragement, no consolation, no support, from anyone that I can call to mind, so help me God." Combined with this was the feeling of humiliation at being forced by circumstances beyond his control into this pitiful state.

Without friends or family in London, Charles came to know the city itself intimately, spending his spare time wandering its streets, becoming familiar with every twist, turn, and hidden corner. This was reflected in Dickens's later fiction in which London, in all its beauty and ugliness, very much became a character in its own right. After about a year John was released from prison and Charles retired from his job at the blacking factory, even though his mother saw no reason why he couldn't go on working there. Dickens later wrote of the incident, "I never afterwards forgot, I never can forget, that my mother was warm for sending me back."

Once the family was reunited, Charles was enrolled at Wellington House Academy and life returned to seeming normality. However, the impact of the previous year was immense and played a major role in shaping Charles's future character. All the boy's expectations regarding education, social class, and worthwhile employment in the future had been swept away. Likewise, any sense of love and security had vanished. Instead of revealing his obvious pain, though, Charles came to recognize it in others, especially children, and developed a gentleness and empathy for which he became renowned. The seeds of his success had been sown during his time in the factory, and the teenager developed an iron-willed determination never to fall victim to his father's careless habits.

In 1827, at the age of fifteen, Charles left Wellington House and found employment as a lawyer's clerk in the hope of one day joining the legal profession. Realizing quickly that law was not his calling, Dickens often entertained coworkers by mimicking the practice's clients and passersby on the street. But he soon grew to dislike the law and its practitioners, an aversion mirrored in his later fiction, and embarked on a project of self-education. Aware that his formal schooling had been random and sketchy, Dickens taught himself shorthand in his spare time in an effort to become a parliamentary reporter—he believed many notable men in London had begun their careers in this way. He also became a regular visitor to the British Museum's reading room. He later referred to the time spent with his head buried in books as some of the most useful days of his life.

In 1831, at nineteen years of age, Dickens's ambition was fulfilled when he became a parliamentary reporter for the *Mirror of Parliament*. He later moved on to the *True Sun,* then the *Morning Chronicle,* where he began to publish short, humorous articles on London life under the pseudonym Boz. Seeking a memorable pen name, Dickens had turned to a childhood nickname of his brother, derived from one of his favorite characters in Oliver Goldsmith's *Vicar of Wakefield*. Boz's first published work was entitled "A Dinner at Poplar Walk" (1833). Enormously popular with the public, three years later these sketches were collected and published in a book called *Sketches by Boz*.

In the same year Dickens was hired to write short captions for a series of comical sporting illustrations by the artist Robert Seymour. Two months into the newspaper serial Seymour committed suicide and Dickens was left to complete the commission. With the words now taking precedence, twenty-four-year-old Dickens transformed the original concept into *The Pickwick Papers*. A popular success, the story was published in nineteen monthly parts and paved the way for Dickens to become England's favorite serial novelist. Once it was published in book form it became one of the biggest sellers in English literature and gained Dickens great fame.

It is important to remember that Dickens was a serial novelist who wrote his books without prior knowledge of how they would develop over the subsequent months. Consequently, public opinion often contributed to the outcome of a story line and collaborators such as illustrators often might motivate Dickens to change his original ideas through, or for the sake of, their art. Likewise, serials, although fictional, also were very timely and, as a result, were swayed in their themes and plots by current events such as crime, the poor, and the law. This was the case with the author's second literary effort, *Oliver Twist*.

The amended Poor Laws of 1834, which strengthened the workhouse as the only means of relief for the impoverished, proved to be a massive failure of legislation and led to discrimination, crime, and increased poverty. Frustrated and angered at what he was witnessing and harboring strong resentment toward his own past ill treatment, Dickens decided to change tack with his next work and launched an attack on the social injustices caused by this law. The rollicking fun and humor of *The Pickwick Papers* was gone. In its place was a gritty and harrowing tale of the London underworld and an orphan who'd been forgotten by society.

Dickens was passionately committed to this story, writing day and night to meet each monthly deadline while also employed as the editor of the magazine *Bentley's Miscellany.* Although the grim reality of Dickens's text shocked readers, *Oliver Twist, or, The Parish Boy's Progress,* was a huge success. Memorable characters such as Fagin, Bill Sykes, the Artful Dodger, Nancy, and Oliver not only brought the reality of Victorian London's impoverished to the fore, it also acted as an outlet for Dickens's long-held feelings of abandonment and rejection.

The success of *Oliver Twist* cemented Dickens as Victorian England's most popular novelist and spurred an additional eighteen novels and numerous short stories and collected works. And, in 1856, when Dickens, then one of the world's most renowned authors, returned to Chatham, he purchased Gad's Hill Place and, four years later, made it his permanent residence.

JANE EYRE,
Charlotte Brontë, 1847

❦

> *Do you think, because I am poor, obscure, plain, and lit-*
> *tle, I am soulless and heartless? You think wrong!*

According to literary legend, the critic George Lewes once remarked to his mistress, the author George Eliot, that Charlotte Brontë was "a little, plain, provincial, sickly-looking old maid." Eliot had not yet read Brontë's *Jane Eyre* but, once she had, she was said to have exclaimed to her lover, "Yet what passion, what fire in her!"

Like her most famous heroine, Charlotte Brontë was a complicated woman. Fearlessly stubborn and full of integrity, she was also sensitive and possessed a paralyzing shyness. Passionate and steadfastly independent, she was also painfully insecure and obsessed with her lack of physical beauty. *Jane Eyre* was only partly a product of the author's imagination—Charlotte Brontë delved into the deepest areas of her own soul to create her most memorable novel and most unforgettable character.

Born in 1816 in Thornton, Yorkshire, England, Charlotte was the third of Patrick and Maria Brontë's six children. An Anglican clergyman, Irish-born Patrick was appointed curate in Haworth, a small and remote village set on the Yorkshire moors, when Charlotte was four. It was a bleak landscape and, although the new position offered a higher income, the family did not leave the prettier outlook of their Thornton home enthusiastically.

When his wife died in 1821, Patrick found life difficult. Taking over the education of his children and running the parish was too much for one man. Consequently, his sister-in-law moved in with the family. When Charlotte was eight years old she was sent with her two older sisters, Maria and Elizabeth, to a school for the daughters of poor evangelical clergymen at Cowan Bridge in Lancashire, about fifty miles away. This was to be a significant life-shaping experience for the child.

The director of the school, Carus Wilson, was a wealthy and successful clergyman and seemed well suited to running a school. Unfortunately, he embodied the worst qualities of evangelicalism. Wilson was dour and strict and possessed a stern and unyielding attitude toward children. Under his reign Cowan Bridge was no better than a death trap for the weak and helpless.

More than two decades later, when Charlotte was asked her opinion of the school, she replied, "The establishment was at that time in its infancy, and a sad, rickety infancy it was. Typhus fever decimated the school periodically, and consumption and scrofula in every variety of form, which bad air and water, and bad, insufficient diet, can generate, preyed on the ill-fated pupils." Combining these conditions with an uncaring staff and a heartless director made for a crucible of misery and disease. Consequently, before long both Maria and Elizabeth were removed from the school and sent home suffering from tuberculosis, or consumption, as it was known at the time. Both died shortly after, in 1825. Patrick promptly removed Charlotte from the school while still healthy.

Before her tenth birthday Charlotte was motherless and had endured the loss of two sisters. But at home in

Haworth, she and her younger sisters, Emily and Anne, and their brother, Branwell, comforted themselves with books and a rich fantasy life. The children discussed politics with their father, read the newspaper with him, and took delight in reading books from his extensive library. Their favorites were the historical adventures of Walter Scott, *Arabian Nights,* and the poetry of Lord Byron. They wrote stories, poems, journals, and serials and published their own monthly magazine.

In 1826 Mr. Brontë bought his children a box of wooden soldiers. Possessing amazingly vivid imaginations, the four used these soldiers as the foundation for two extraordinary worlds. Emily and Anne immersed themselves in the land of Gondal, while Charlotte and Branwell became obsessed with the kingdom of Angria.

These fantasy lands provided the four with exactly what was lacking in Haworth, and the young writers scribbled tirelessly of villains, heroes, and the gallant deeds they performed. Many children create imaginary worlds and stories, but for the Brontës this pastime continued into adulthood.

When in 1835 Charlotte became a teacher at Roe Head School, a school she had attended briefly in 1831, she and Branwell had been writing about Angria for many years. Without the creative freedom Haworth provided her, Charlotte grew increasingly anxious and disappeared even further into her imagination.

Charlotte disliked her new position at Roe Head and described herself as being "chained to this chair prisoned within these four bare walls." Consequently, Angria became even more real to her and if a student or a fellow teacher dared to wrench her from her daydreams, she became furious.

The twenty-two-year-old left Roe Head in 1838 and begrudgingly took a series of positions as a governess to families. It was during this time she gave up Angria, stating, ". . . I long to quit for a while the burning clime where we have sojourned too long . . . The mind would cease from excitement and turn now to a cooler region, where the dawn breaks grey and sober and the coming day, for a time at least, is subdued in clouds."

Despite sacrificing her beloved Angria, Charlotte was ill-suited to the role of governess. Her paralyzing shyness, her inability to interact with children, and her debilitating homesickness led her once and for all to return to Haworth in 1841.

The following year Charlotte, along with Emily and Anne, decided they should open their own school at Haworth. But lacking the necessary skills, Charlotte and Emily decided to enroll in the Heger School in Brussels and learn French and German.

The Heger School was run by Monsieur Constantin Heger. The thirty-three-year-old teacher was charismatic, talented, and passionate about education, and he possessed an intensely magnetic personality. Heger recognized that the Brontë sisters were of a much higher intellectual standard than his other students and decided to take the introverted pair under his wing. Tutoring them separately, Heger introduced Charlotte and Emily to France's greatest literature. Charlotte couldn't have been happier. She wrote in a letter to a friend, "My present life is so delightful, so congenial to my own nature . . ." Impressed with his two young charges, Heger often boasted of their achievements and read their work aloud to the rest of his pupils. At twenty-six years of age, Charlotte had never met anyone like the handsome and fiery Belgian, and she fell deeply in love with him. Although Heger did not discourage her feelings, he was married with a large family, and Charlotte's love remained unrequited.

After completing her studies, Charlotte became an English teacher at the school. Emily had left in 1842 and it is believed Charlotte stayed on because of her attachment to Monsieur Heger, but she was miserable. Yearning for her family and with her emotions in tatters, Charlotte finally returned to Haworth in 1844 to open her own school. But once home she was anything but settled. In a series of letters to Heger, Charlotte poured out her feelings to him. Upon reading her correspondence, Heger tore the letters to pieces. His wife, who is said to have been a suspicious woman with little trust for her husband, discovered the fragments and pieced the sordid jigsaw together (the patched-together pages are still in existence today). On top of this unrequited love from Heger, further disappointment arose when an advertisement the sisters placed for the new school received not a single response.

With this career path blocked, Charlotte turned to her first love, writing. Years before, on her twenty-first birthday, in 1837, she had written to poet laureate Robert Southey to ask his advice on her prospects in this endeavor. He replied, "Literature cannot be the business of a woman's life and it ought not to be." Charlotte's response was meek in the extreme: "I trust I shall never more feel ambitious to see my name in print; if the wish should rise, I'll look at Southey's letter, and suppress it."

By 1845 Charlotte was not so humble. With her father going blind and her brother a hopeless drunk, it was up to the remaining sisters to keep the household solvent. As the eldest, Charlotte convinced Anne and Emily that they should publish a selection of their poetry. Keeping South-ey's sage words in mind, the poems were written under the pseudonyms of Currer, Ellis, and Acton Bell. Although not particularly masculine, the names successfully cloaked the gender of the authors. The sisters had their combined efforts published in a single volume of poetry, but unfortunately they only managed to sell two copies.

In the meantime each sister had undertaken the immense task of writing a novel. Charlotte, inspired by her time in Brussels, penned *The Professor*. Emily, influenced by the wilds of the moors, had written *Wuthering Heights*. Anne had produced *Agnes Grey,* a story based on her experiences as a governess. When the novels were completed, they began the exhaustive mission of sending the manuscripts to publishers.

In 1846, Charlotte escorted her invalid father to Manchester, where he was undergoing cataract surgery. While in the northern metropolis, she received news of another rejection of *The Professor*. At this time Charlotte described herself as being "depressed" and "weary," but it was under these conditions, in the shabby rooms of a boarding house, that she began writing *Jane Eyre*.

The product of her time at Cowan Bridge and her love for Monsieur Heger, several manuscript fragments that survive suggest *Jane Eyre* had been long in development. But it was the enforced imprisonment in Manchester and sheer desperation at her situation that spurred Charlotte to write. As she was severely shortsighted, she wrote with a pencil in little square books held close to her face. Rarely leaving the boarding house, she wrote for three weeks straight while her father recovered.

On her return to Haworth, *Jane Eyre* was not yet finished. In a last-ditch effort, *The Professor, Agnes Grey,* and

Wuthering Heights were sent to a publisher in London called Newby. While the latter two works were accepted, *The Professor* was rejected yet again.

The tenacious author then tracked down an obscure publishing house in London, Smith, Elder and Company, the sixth to receive the book. While they weren't willing to publish *The Professor,* they were impressed with the passion and flair in her writing. Charlotte remarked enthusiastically of the rejection letter, "This very refusal cheered the author better than a vulgarly expressed acceptance would have done. It was added that a work of three volumes would meet with careful attention." So encouraging were these words that Charlotte decided to complete *Jane Eyre* and find out whether this novel was more to their liking.

The result was the tale of the orphan Jane Eyre. Having been sent to Lowood, a school run by the inhumane Mr. Brocklehurst, Jane becomes a teacher and takes on the position of governess at Thornfield Hall, the home of the dark and passionate Mr. Rochester.

The couple fall in love and decide to wed, but, at the nuptials, she discovers Rochester is already married. His wife, now insane, resides in the attic. Jane leaves Thornfield Hall but eventually returns to find it destroyed by fire. In the blaze Rochester had lost an eye and a hand in an unsuccessful attempt to rescue his wife. With his wife dead, the pair reunite and marry.

Because of its unorthodox heroine, when the novel was published in 1847 it fueled great debate and controversy. Through her work Charlotte criticized the inadequate options open to impoverished women. Jane's passionate desire for fulfilment, her desperation to be loved, and her defiance in the face of convention reflected the author's own opinions and ideas. Jane was an unattractive, poverty-stricken teacher who defied the odds to realize her dreams and find love and fulfillment. The dark and moody Rochester was Heger and all her Angrian heroes rolled into one. The book was an outpouring of Charlotte's life up to that point.

Jane Eyre: An Autobiography, by Currer Bell, was an immediate success—critics were positive and sales soared. Charlotte's good friend Ellen Nussey visited London shortly after the novel was published and remarked, "When I reached London I found there was quite a fureur about the authorship of the new novel. The work was quickly obtained, and as soon as it arrived it was seized upon and the first half page read aloud. It was as though Charlotte Brontë herself was present in every word, her voice and spirit thrilling through and through."

The reviews were outstanding. Never had a first novel been received with such favor. The very first review, appearing in the newspaper the *Atlas,* read, "This is not merely a work of great promise, it is one of absolute performance. It is one of the most powerful domestic romances which has been published in many years." Hailed as "powerful," "fresh," and "original," readers raved, and the novel was an immediate bestseller.

Vanity Fair,
William Makepeace Thackeray, 1847

Those who like may peep down under waves that are pretty transparent, and see it writhing and twirling, diabolically hideous and slimy, flapping amongst bones, or curling round corpses; but above the water-line, I ask, has not everything been proper, agreeable, and decorous, and has any the most squeamish immoralist in Vanity Fair a right to cry fie?

When William Makepeace Thackeray's *Vanity Fair* first appeared in serial form in the satirical magazine *Punch,* it was subtitled *Pen and Pencil Sketches of English Society.* For eleven years Thackeray had been one of the hardest working freelance journalists in England, and the subtitle suggests *Vanity Fair* was originally intended to be a series of comical articles lampooning society. When it appeared in book form a year later, the subtitle had changed to *A Novel without a Hero.*

What lay behind Thackeray's intentions with *Vanity Fair* remains a mystery. Academics suggest that during the process Thackeray's original idea evolved into a novel of such breadth and scope that it has become one of literature's most brilliantly conceived and constructed social satires. Moreover, it catapulted Thackeray to fame and fortune, placing him second only to Charles Dickens in the league of great Victorian writers. Yet at its heart lay little more than a journalist's need to earn a living while maintaining a bleak view of human nature.

It is not surprising that William Makepeace Thackeray possessed a skewed view of the world, as the very foundations of his background were unstable. His mother, Anne Becher, had been sent to Calcutta, India, in 1809, where her father was employed by the British East India Company. While on the subcontinent she was informed by her family that the man with whom she was in love at home in England, Henry Carmichael-Smyth, had died. She eventually recovered from her heartbreak and married Richmond Thackeray (William's father), also employed by the British East India Company, the following year. So it was quite a shock when, a year into their marriage, Richmond invited an unexpected guest to dinner, a military man stationed in Calcutta named Henry Carmichael-Smyth. Legend says Anne's parents had concocted the story of Carmichael-Smyth's death to prevent her from marrying a soldier who had few prospects. After Richmond died in 1818, when William was seven years old, Anne finally married Carmichael-Smyth and returned to England. By this time William already had been in England for two years attending school.

Thackeray was not an outstanding student, and he hated his time at school. The six years he spent at Charterhouse School, an establishment later to become known as "Slaughterhouse" in his satirical writings, was characterized by brutal canings from the teachers and physical abuse from the boys. In class he found the lessons dry and boring. But his years at one of England's most prestigious private schools were not all wasted, for at Charterhouse Thackeray escaped the horridness of his situation by sketching and reading.

Thackeray had a sharp and precocious mind and enrolled at Trinity College at Cambridge University in 1828, but after spending too much time partying and gambling, and not enough time studying, Thackeray left the university two years later without a degree. The following years were spent traveling abroad to locations such as Paris and to the home of the German intelligentsia, Weimar, where he met Johann Wolfgang von Goethe. Back in England he began studying law but soon ceased his studies in this field as well. In 1832, when Thackeray turned twenty-one, he received his inheritance.

Unsure of where life was taking him, Thackeray decided to invest in the media industry of magazines and newspapers that was blossoming in England at the time. After an unsuccessful attempt to purchase a newspaper business, Thackeray bought a literary magazine, the *National Standard,* in 1833. He not only edited the magazine himself but also wrote comic prose and sketched and penned satirical verse. Sadly, because of competition in the field and the volatile nature of the industry, the magazine collapsed the following year. Despite its failure, this experience gave Thackeray a taste for journalism and the media. More hard times were to hit Thackeray with the crash of the Indian banks, institutions in which much of his and his family's money were invested. By this stage Thackeray's finances were in bad shape, with much of his inheritance squandered on gambling, alcohol, and women.

The twenty-two-year-old took refuge in Paris, where he lived with his grandmother for several years. There he studied art, wrote for various magazines and newspapers, and met his future wife—an Irish woman named Isabella Shawe. The couple married in 1836, and once

Isabella became pregnant Thackeray realized he would have to get serious about providing an income.

Thackeray and Isabella returned to England, and the writer immediately established himself as a freelance journalist and artist, working for a number of titles, including *Fraser's Magazine,* the *Morning Chronicle,* and the *Times.* He wrote under pen names such as George Savage Fitz-Boodle, Michael Angelo Titmarsh, Théophile Wagstaff, and C. J. Yellowplush, Esq. As a writer, Thackeray soon earned a reputation as an intelligent and skillful humorist.

He wrote travel articles on France that were collected as *The Paris Sketch Book* in 1840. This was followed by a commission for an Irish Sketch Book in 1843, as well as an Eastern travel book called *A Journey from Cornhill to Grand Cairo* in 1846. He also moved into fiction, writing serials for magazines, such as the parodic *Catherine: A Story* (1839) and *The Luck of Barry Lyndon* (1844) as well as satires on modern life such as *The Ravenswing* (1843). But his finest accomplishment came in 1842 when he began writing for *Punch,* a satirical magazine launched in the previous year, which was attracting some of the country's best writers. Thackeray's *Snob Papers* were received with great praise, popularizing the word *snob* in the English language.

As Thackeray's career thrived, his personal life suffered. Isabella had fallen into a depression after the birth of their third child in 1840 (their second child had died at eight months of age). On a trip to Ireland later that year Isabella threw herself off the boat in a suicide attempt. Although she was rescued, Isabella needed constant observation from then on. Thackeray deeply loved his wife and traveled with her all over Europe, attempting to find a cure for the mental imbalance to which she had fallen victim, all the while caring for his two daughters. Soon Isabella no longer responded to her children or recognized her husband. In debt and at his wit's end, Thackeray eventually resigned himself to his wife's condition and placed her in the care of an institution. For the rest of his life Thackeray faced a crisis of conscience whenever he was attracted to another woman. He undertook the raising of his daughters with the help of his mother. Based on the memories of his daughter Anne, he was a loving, if busy, father.

It's entirely possible Thackeray originally conceived the idea of *Vanity Fair* as a novel but because of financial and time constraints decided instead to sell it to *Punch* as a series of articles. The flamboyant, carefree style in which it is written and the occasional error in continuity would suggest the story was not planned in its entirety but instead written on the run, a few steps ahead of each monthly deadline. Nevertheless, the story was published in serial form over twenty monthly parts, beginning in 1847. It was Thackeray's first work published under his own name and the author himself produced the illustrations.

The title is derived from the book of Ecclesiastes and John Bunyan's *The Pilgrim's Progress*. Bunyon described Vanity Fair in 1678 thus: "Therefore at this Fair are all such merchandise sold, as houses, lands, trades, places, honours, preferments, titles, countries, kingdoms, lusts, pleasures, and delights of all sorts, as whores, bawds, wives, husbands, children, masters, servants, lives, blood, bodies, souls, silver, gold, pearls, precious stones, and what not." A multitude of exchanges, bargains and interactions take place in Thackeray's novel and the author concludes his work with the words "Ah! Vanitas Vanitatum! Which of us are happy in this world? Which of us has his desire? Or, having it, is satisfied?—Come, children, let us shut up the box and the puppets, for our play is played out."

Thackeray believed the majority of people were abominably selfish and foolish, that they lived for themselves alone, were morally barren, and lacked a sense of responsibility for their actions. Thackeray's brilliance lies in taking these beliefs and employing satire to expose the moral bankruptcy of society.

Although *Vanity Fair* is vast in its scope, set in the United Kingdom and greater Europe and casting its sharp eye across all of Victorian England's social classes, at its core is the story of two childhood friends—the manipulative Becky Sharp and the good-natured Amelia Sedley—whose fortunes are contrasted throughout the novel. Painting a very bleak view of the human condition, it is a novel about greed, idleness, opportunism, and hypocrisy. It is not an instructive knowledge—Thackeray, acting as omniscient narrator, makes no suggestion that society will ever change.

Vanity Fair was an immediate success, and reviewers took special note of the novel's principal character, Becky Sharp. The *Examiner* wrote in 1848, "She commits every conceivable wickedness; dishonours her husband, betrays her friend, degrades and embrutes herself, and finally commits a murder; without in the least losing those smart, good-tempered, sensible manners and ways, which ingratiate her with the reader in spite of all these atrocities." In Becky Sharp, Thackeray drew a complex and detailed portrait of a woman whom it was difficult to dislike despite her many disgusting traits.

Following the success of *Vanity Fair,* Thackeray moved principally into novel writing, living the life of a celebrity author and enjoying the fruits of his labor. He died at the age of fifty-two as a result of overeating, drinking, getting no exercise, and a complication thought to have resulted from a case of gonorrhea in his youth. Although Isabella Thackeray spent her days in a mental hospital, she outlived her husband by thirty years.

CRIME AND PUNISHMENT,
Fyodor Dostoevsky, 1866

> *... if he had only been able to realize all the difficulties of his situation, all the despair, all the hideousness, all the absurdity of it, and to understand, besides, how many more difficulties and perhaps evildoings he still had to overcome or commit in order to get out of there and reach home, he might very well have dropped everything and gone at once to denounce himself, and not even out of fear for himself, but solely out of horror and loathing for what he had done.*

More than any of his characters and perhaps more than any other literary figure, the life of Fyodor Dostoevsky prior to writing *Crime and Punishment*—considered one of the greatest novels of all time—was an astounding chain of tragedies, mind-boggling events, and life-altering experiences. These collective experiences, and the belief system the author developed as a result, came together to form the characters, the story lines, and the themes within this masterful novel.

One of the major themes in this story of depravity, murder, and redemption is the idea that despair leads to tragic acts, and that for many it is only through tragedy and anguish that they truly can learn to appreciate life. Such was the path to enlightenment for the book's protagonist, Rodion Romanovich Raskolnikov, as it was in the real life of Dostoevsky, who suffered much more than his fair share of despair, anguish, and tragedy.

Born in Moscow in 1821, Fyodor was the second son of a doctor, Mikhail Andreevich, and Maria Fedorovna Dostoevsky. His father was overbearing, intolerant, and strict with his children and with the serfs who worked on the family estate. Fyodor's closest companion during his childhood was his older brother Mikhail, with whom he used to read Pushkin. But the brothers were separated when their long-suffering mother died in 1837. Sixteen-year-old Fyodor was sent to boarding school, a military engineering college in St. Petersburg.

While he was away the young Fyodor often wrote home asking for money, but his access to financial assistance ended when his father died suddenly in 1839. The cause of Mikhail Andreevich's death was said to have been some form of stroke, but strong rumors abounded that he was murdered by his serfs during a violent argument.

Suddenly Dostoevsky was on his own, an orphan in St. Petersburg, a city with both a sense of grandeur and of cancerous deterioration. He graduated from college, was commissioned as an officer, and spent two years as a draftsman in the War Ministry. But having fallen in love with the written word long before, he resigned his post in 1844 and spent the next nine months living off his inheritance, crammed into a small room writing his first novel, *Poor Folk*. This and his second work, *The Double,* both were released in 1846 and were warmly received in the Russian literary world—some critics even dared to compare the young author to Gogol. By the age of twenty-five the writer had become somewhat of a celebrity in literary circles, but soon life would take a disastrous turn that would land him in front of a firing squad.

Dostoevsky's literary connections saw him mixing with young intellectuals and liberal thinkers, many of

whom would meet regularly at the home of Mikhail Petrashevsky (who would go on to become a well-known
Russian thinker) to discuss political issues. High on their
agenda was democratization of the Russian government,
or at least some sort of utopian socialism, and specifically
the liberation of the serfs. As he had seen how the serfs
on his father's estate were treated, this was a topic very
close to Dostoevsky's heart.

A government secret agent, however, had infiltrated
the group and, in April of 1849, the meeting was raided
and all of its members arrested by tsarist police. Imprisoned in the Peter and Paul Fortress, Dostoevsky and his
friends originally believed they would be released quickly
with the equivalent of a slap on the wrist, but days turned
into weeks, and weeks into months, and soon the group
wondered whether they'd ever be released from the dark
cells, straw beds, and squalid conditions of the bleak
prison. At first books and writing materials were not allowed, but after a few months a batch of books, all with
spiritual and religious themes, were delivered to the prisoners. Dostoevsky spent his days delving into these works,
including the Bible.

In October of that year they were taken from their
cells and loaded into carriages. Assuming they finally
were being released, they instead were transported to Se-
menovsky Platz, a public square in St. Petersburg where
hangings took place, and were read their sentences—all
twenty members of the group were to die there and then,
in front of a firing squad.

The first three, including Petrashevsky, had hoods
pulled over their heads (Petrashevsky asked for his to be
removed) and were tied to poles on a scaffold as the soldiers raised their rifles. Dostoevsky, in the second group

of three, watched and waited for his friends to be executed before he, too, suffered the same fate. But at the last moment an official intervened and read their new sentence, an amnesty from Tsar Nicholas I. Saved at the last moment from death by firing squad, the group was instead sentenced to four years hard labor in Siberia, followed by four years as common soldiers in the Russian army.

In a letter to his brother Dostoevsky told how the near-death experience affected him, how it shook him to the core and changed his outlook on life. "When I look back on my past and think how much time I wasted on nothing, how much time has been lost in futilities, errors, laziness, incapacity to live; how little I appreciated it, how many times I sinned against my heart and soul—then my heart bleeds. Life is a gift, life is happiness, every minute can be an eternity of happiness."

In another letter to Mikhail, two months after the near execution, he wrote more of his thoughts: "Life is in ourselves and not in the external. To be a human being among human beings, and remain one forever, no matter what misfortunes befall, not to become depressed, and not to falter—this is what life is, herein lies its task."

Forced to work in the mines of Siberia, Dostoevsky found himself shackled and chained to murderers, rapists, and thieves. But with his new outlook he searched for the positive, and came to realize that these people, because of their situations of despair, had been led to commit tragic acts. Through their suffering they would be redeemed, the writer believed. Through his own suffering, he would learn to live again.

In 1857 Dostoevsky married twenty-nine-year-old Maria Isaev. Twelve months later, when he was finally allowed to resign from the army, Dostoevsky made up for lost time by entering a phase of prolific writing in which many of his greatest works were written—including *The House of the Dead* (1862), *Notes from the Underground* (1864), *Crime and Punishment* (1866), *The Idiot* (1868), and *Devils* (1871). But tragically, Dostoevsky's wife and his beloved brother Mikhail would die from illness by 1865, leaving him truly alone. The epilepsy from which he'd suffered for most of his life began to cause more regular seizures, and whatever money the author made was just as quickly thrown away, as he had become obsessed with gambling.

Crime and Punishment originally was published over twelve issues in a monthly journal called *Russkii Vestnik* (*The Russian Messenger*). The story centered around Raskolnikov, a resentful college dropout with no money, no job, and who lives in a one-room apartment the size of a closet on the fifth floor of a run-down building in the slums of St. Petersburg. When his parents stop sending money, he goes into debt by borrowing from a "dried-up old crone" pawnbroker, and soon decides to solve his problems, and to rid the world of a pest, by smashing her skull in with the blunt edge of an ax. When the woman's stepsister walks in at the wrong time, she becomes Raskolnikov's second victim, and suddenly life goes from bad to worse as the student attempts, and fails, to justify the despicable crime to himself. Like the prisoners Dostoevsky had met while doing hard labor in Siberia, the character Raskolnikov had committed a tragic act as a result of his desperate circumstances, and only through suffering for this act would he find redemption.

Despite his literary success, Dostoevsky's life continued on its downhill course. His gambling left him deeply in debt, and in the late 1860s he left Russia to avoid creditors, living in Switzerland, Italy, and Germany with his new wife, his twenty-two-year-old stenographer, Anna Grigorevna Snitkina, whom he'd married in 1867. He was only able to return to Russia once his next novel, *The Possessed,* was a success and he was able to repay his debts.

After writing his final novel, *The Brothers Karamazov* (1880)—a book about the murder of a father—Dostoevsky passed away in his beloved St. Petersburg on February 9, 1881. His novels, with their stunning insights into politics, society, human nature, and human behavior, went on to influence the writings and teachings of some of modern history's greatest philosophers, including Friedrich Nietzsche and Sigmund Freud.

WAR AND PEACE,
Leo Tolstoy, 1867–1869

*They were all impelled by fear or vanity, enjoyment, in-
dignation, or national consideration, supposing that they
knew what they were about and that they were acting
independently, while they were all the involuntary tools
of history and were working out a result concealed from
themselves but comprehensible to us.*

Since the 1860s two Russian authors have vied for the
title of their nation's most distinguished writer. First
there is Fyodor Dostoevsky who was, at this time, at his
most productive, publishing *Notes from the Underground,
Crime and Punishment,* and *The Idiot* between 1864 and
1868 and beginning work on *The Devils* in 1869. But despite Dostoevsky's immense body of work during this
decade and his undisputed talent, he often has been overshadowed by another great Russian wordsmith. While
Dostoevsky was prolific, his contemporary Leo Tolstoy
wrote and published only one work during this time. As
a result of that single book he is often regarded not only
as Russia's greatest novelist but also as the world's finest
writer.

Tolstoy's epic masterpiece, *War and Peace,* is often
heralded as the world's greatest novel. Spanning fifteen
years and incorporating 580 characters, it's no wonder it
took the author, who was often uninspired and restless,
almost six years to complete. Thanks to a talented and

business-minded wife, and a deep yearning within the writer himself to document a significant period in his nation's history, the first edition of the six-volume tour de force sold out and saw Tolstoy reveling in a level of national and international acclaim that would place him in the pantheon of literature's immortals.

Lev (Anglicised to "Leo") Nikolayevich Tolstoy was born on August 28, 1828, into an aristocratic family whose noble roots stretched back to the 1600s. The fourth of Countess Maria's and Count Nikolay Ilyich's five children, the young Tolstoy enjoyed the privileges of his aristocratic birth as well as the harmony and security of a loving home. The count was a gentle, easygoing man who was kind to the serfs who worked on the vast estate. He disliked hunting and wolf-baiting (two popular aristocratic pursuits), preferring instead to walk with his children in the forest. The countess, who died when Tolstoy was two, was remembered by the author with a saintlike reverence. Despite her early death, Tolstoy's childhood was idyllic.

The family's estate Yasnaya Polyana (Clear Glade) in Russia's Tula region lay approximately 130 miles southwest of Moscow. The estate was an adventure playground for Tolstoy and his siblings, who enjoyed riding, tobogganing, bathing, and boating. Indoors the children were nestled in a loving and nurturing family environment by their ever-present extended family. Music and stories were a constant pleasure in the household and Tolstoy, who was a voracious reader, could often be found snug in his father's study among the family's extensive library. The count would often have the boy recite poetry of Russia's premier poet, Alexander Pushkin.

When Tolstoy was nine years old his beloved father passed away, which affected the boy very deeply. Now orphaned, the children became wards of their father's sister, Aunt Aline. When she died four years later, guardianship passed to other relatives. Despite the series of different homes in which the children grew up, they always were nurtured in a caring environment.

At sixteen years of age Tolstoy enrolled at Kazan University to study Oriental languages, but he was a poor student and left without graduating three years later, but taking with him a working knowledge of over a dozen languages. Retreating to Yasnaya Polyana, the nineteen-year-old attempted to manage the business of the large estate. Blessed with substantial wealth but plagued with a lack of ambition and direction, Tolstoy led a hedonistic lifestyle common among young men of noble birth. Indulging in women and gambling, he soon accrued massive gambling debts that he honored by selling the estate's serfs. But he was conflicted. His diaries from the time show that he despised himself for leading such a life. He wrote, "I am living a completely brutish life . . . I have abandoned almost all my occupations and have greatly fallen in spirit."

His diaries were full of unrealized thoughts, ideas, and resolutions to change his path. For example, in 1849 Tolstoy decided to study law in St. Petersburg. But before long he had accumulated more gambling debts, which were resolved by selling more of Yasnaya Polyana's acreage and serfs. Similarly, in the following year, Tolstoy moved to Moscow carrying more high-minded ideas about changing his life. This, too, came to nothing and the twenty-two-year-old ran into further debt.

Finally, Tolstoy decided to separate himself from temptation. He joined the Caucasian Army, in which his brother Nicolay was an officer, and in 1851 the two left for the Caucus region of Russia, where they saw action against the Chechens. Still keeping meticulous diaries, it was during this time that Tolstoy developed the urge to write fiction. His first effort, *Childhood* (1852), a story that fictionalized the author's early life, was published in the literary magazine the *Contemporary*. So popular was this story with the reading public that Tolstoy followed it up with two similar works, *Boyhood* (1854) and *Youth* (1857). Even more popular with readers was his work called *Sevastopol Sketches,* published between 1855 and 1856. Chronicling the author's experiences during the Crimean War, the work was an authentic, firsthand account that subverted popular notions of war as heroic and glamorous.

By 1855 Tolstoy had become a well-known author, but when he left the army that year, despite his fame and recognition among the St. Petersburg literati, he was at a loss as what to do with his life. Once again Tolstoy was torn between the debauched life he'd been living before joining the army and settling down as a writer. In 1857 he departed for Europe and traveled intermittently until 1861, falling back into old habits. By this time *Childhood* had been translated into English and the author had achieved a level of international fame, but still he gambled incessantly, drank excessively, and kept company with prostitutes. So debauched was his life that, after losing a game of billiards and hence losing a bet, he sold his unfinished manuscript of *The Cossacks* for 1,000 rubles to the game's victor, a publisher. It was published incomplete in 1863.

Still he questioned his role in life. He wrote in his diaries, "I put men to death in war, I fought duels to slay others. I lost at cards, wasted the substance wrung from the sweat of peasants, punished the latter cruelly, rioted with loose women, and deceived men. Lying, robbery, adultery of all kinds, drunkenness, violence, and murder, all were committed by me, not one crime omitted, and yet I was not the less considered by my equals to be a comparatively moral man."

In a drastic final attempt to achieve a semblance of stability in his tumultuous life, Tolstoy married eighteen-year-old Sofya Andreyevna Bers in 1862. Like most events in the author's life, the union was not without emotional anguish. Insisting that their marriage be based on honesty, Tolstoy asked Sofya to read his diaries. Detailing his whoring, gambling, and countless affairs with peasant women, the journals shocked the teenager, but she agreed to go through with the marriage anyway. For Tolstoy marriage achieved exactly what he had hoped for, and for several years Sofya managed to give Tolstoy the happiness he had been searching for.

Sofya, who had attended university and earned a teaching diploma, soon took over the running of the estate, transcribed messy drafts of her husband's works, edited and corrected spelling and grammar in his manuscripts, and discussed story ideas with him. According to her brother, she copied out *War and Peace* no fewer than seven times. The couple bore thirteen children together, but over the years the relationship would decline to the point where the pair could barely tolerate each other. Tolstoy's moods, tempers, and passions eventually were to ostracize most of his family.

The domestic tranquility Tolstoy originally found after marriage, though, had a double effect. While it provided the necessary environment for him to pen a novel of the scale of *War and Peace,* it also served as a distraction from his writing, and there were often long periods of inactivity. As Sofya noted in her diary, "We are on good terms. Lyovochka is very busy with the dairy yard and is writing his novel without much enthusiasm. He is bursting with ideas, but when will he ever write them all down?" Unlike Dostoevsky, Tolstoy was under no financial pressure to write. Although previously a compulsive gambler, this habit had ceased when he married and, after the death of his two brothers, the writer had inherited their land.

At the outset Tolstoy had in mind a historical novel set in the 1850s, but after an intensive year of research he moved the setting back in time to Napoleon's invasion of Russia in 1812 and then even further back to 1805, when Napoleon moved against the Austrian-Russian coalition. Tolstoy initially envisaged a short work and writing began in earnest in 1862. Katkov, the publisher to whom Tolstoy previously had sold his unfinished manuscript of *The Cossacks,* agreed to publish the first thirty-eight chapters of the novel in the February 1865 issue of *Russkii Vestnik* under the title *1805*. Working solidly through the Christmas and New Year of 1864–1865, Sofya busily corrected and copied three drafts of her husband's work to have the manuscript ready for publication. Tolstoy's penmanship was indecipherable to all but Sofya, and often the scribble couldn't even be read by the author himself! Meanwhile, Sofya still was performing the duties of a wife and mother, and in the time it took Tolstoy to write and publish *War and Peace* the couple produced four offspring. But her hard work was rewarded and the patriotic *1805* was a success with readers, who found the battle scenes inspirational.

As Tolstoy's research continued, the story expanded in breadth. As a result of introducing new ideas and constant redrafting, the author frustrated Katkov with his irregular contributions. In fact, between April and November 1865 Tolstoy, under no financial pressure, ceased writing altogether. Angry with Tolstoy's inactivity, Katkov accepted the work of a financially desperate writer to fill the blank pages Tolstoy's idleness had left in his magazine. As a result, Dostoevsky's *Crime and Punishment* was printed. Dostoevsky wrote, "Later I found out that he was only too glad to accept my offer because he had nothing else for that year. Turgenev has not written anything and he has quarreled with Lev Tolstoy."

Meanwhile, Sofya insisted on abandoning serial publication. Tolstoy's savvy wife knew there was more money to be made from publishing in book form than from serializing in a magazine and she believed a writer's income was dependent on volume publication. Tolstoy was happy to sell the rights to his works, but Sofya urged him to rethink and, as a result, the novel was published in six volumes between 1868 and 1869.

Extending his work to 600,000 words (in English), Tolstoy originally had chosen the seemingly lighthearted title of *All's Well That Ends Well*. However, to reflect the historical context of the book, the final title of *War and Peace* was agreed upon in 1867. The excruciatingly detailed story is set against the backdrop of the Napoleonic Wars. Anonymously narrated, the novel examines the absurdity of war and the superficiality of aristocratic society while concentrating on the events in the lives of five families. On publication the novel was praised for its vivid descriptions of war as well as the authentic portrayal of Russian family life. Delving into the diaries he had painstakingly kept since 1847, Tolstoy drew heavily on his own military experience to bring honesty to the war scenes, while memories of his own family and home life at Yasnaya Polyana had much to contribute to the drawing of the novel's long cast of characters. One critic has said of the author, "The artistic work of Leo Tolstoy is at bottom nothing less than one tremendous diary, kept for fifty years, one endless, explicit confession."

ADVENTURES OF HUCKLEBERRY FINN,
Mark Twain, 1885

You don't know about me, without you have read a book by the name of The Adventures of Tom Sawyer, *but that ain't no matter. The book was made by Mr. Mark Twain, and he told the truth, mainly.*

If Mark Twain told the truth "mainly" in *The Adventures of Tom Sawyer,* then he set out to tell the truth wholly with *Adventures of Huckleberry Finn.* The author hoped to write a book to please himself, one that would "say my say, right out of my heart, taking into account no-one's feelings and no-one's prejudices." For many years Twain believed he had compromised his artistic integrity and become a "mere buffoon" through his desire to write popular stories. But in 1876 he resolved to do away with "literature wherewith to please the general public" and set about writing the whole truth about the exploits of a thirteen-year-old boy from the lowest levels of society.

Mark Twain was born Samuel Langhorne Clemens in Florida, Missouri, in 1835. His parents, John, an attorney, and Jane were both from Virginia, and despite a solid financial start to their married life, by the time they had six children the couple decided to relocate in search of better prospects. In 1839 the family moved to the newly-built town of Hannibal, Missouri, on the Mississippi River. Although the author later would be open-minded, his family was deeply southern in their values and, as Missouri was a slave state, both his parents and his uncle kept slaves.

Although their move was forced by hardship, Clemens fell in love with Hannibal and the Mississippi River and spent long, lazy days on Hannibal's stretch of the river fishing and watching the steamboats cruise by. He dreamed of one day becoming a river boat captain. Clemens did not do well at school, later saying that he excelled only at spelling. When his father died in 1847, the eleven-year-old had no complaints when he was forced to leave school and work as a printer's apprentice. By 1851 Clemens was working as a typesetter for the *Hannibal Journal* and also contributed humorous pieces to the newspaper, which was owned by his brother Orion.

Two years later, when he was eighteen years old, Clemens departed Hannibal and, in the following years, worked for a variety of newspapers in New York, Philadelphia, St. Louis, and Cincinnati. In 1857 he returned to Hannibal to pursue his childhood dream of becoming a river boat pilot. Inspired by a recent voyage to New Orleans (he had been heading to South America, chasing a get-rich-quick scheme) and the fact that boat captains were extremely well paid, Clemens studied and apprenticed for two years before earning his license in 1859. Consequently, he gained a knowledge of every twist, turn, ebb, and flow of the mighty river, but his career in the captain's seat would be short-lived. The Civil War erupted in 1861, causing river traffic on the Mississippi to come to a standstill.

After a brief stint in the local militia (Clemens quit after two weeks after witnessing a man's death), he headed to Nevada with his brother Orion. Attracted by the recent silver mining boom in the state, the pair spent two weeks traveling by stagecoach across the Great

Plains and the Rocky Mountains. Meeting many and varied characters along the route, these experiences later were to become the basis for his novel *Roughing It* in 1872. After arriving in Virginia City, Clemens had failed to strike it rich and instead turned to writing to earn a living. He worked on the newspaper the *Territorial Enterprise,* and it was there, in February 1863, that Clemens signed his first article "Mark Twain," a name derived from his steamboat days, meaning two fathoms deep.

Before long Twain's humorous observations elevated him to the status of one of the region's most respected journalists, and in 1865 his short story "The Celebrated Jumping Frog of Calaveras County" was published widely throughout the country. The comical piece about a frog-jumping contest that goes wrong was inspired by a tale he'd heard while traveling to Nevada. Within months the story had become a national sensation and Mark Twain a household name.

In the following year Twain's reports on his visit to the Sandwich Islands became equally popular and formed the foundation of a two-month lecture series on which he embarked the same year. With his clever turn of phrase, an interesting and comical perspective on life, and a talent for performance, Twain was in demand for speaking engagements for the rest of his life. The writer continued to travel the world, and his experiences and observations became the basis of his very successful first book, *The Innocents Abroad,* in 1869. By 1870, after a unique and varied career and years of travel, Twain was established as one of the country's foremost writers and decided to finally settle down and marry.

The woman who won Twain's heart was Olivia Langdon, the daughter of a wealthy merchant from

Elmira, New York. For their family home he commissioned a spectacular Victorian mansion in Hartford, Connecticut, which cost the outrageous (at the time) amount of $40,000. Twain's humble background became a distant reality as he rose higher up the social scale. But this journey, and his extravagant lifestyle, never rested easy with the down-to-earth southerner.

Twain was conflicted. Although he was one of the world's most popular writers and enjoyed the fruits of his success, deep inside him lay an abhorrence of everything this success represented. Twain perceived nineteenth-century American civilization as greedy, corrupted, and materialistic—an argument he developed in his 1873 satirical novel *The Gilded Age*. Rejecting the materialism of his age, the writer yearned to return to his roots and write honestly and openly about a time that he said was "as clear and vivid as a photograph."

For the next seventeen years, Twain completed some of his most famous novels in his Hartford residence and at Quarry Farm, his Elmira home. *The Adventures of Tom Sawyer* (1876) celebrated his boyhood in Hannibal, Missouri, telling the story of a mischievous orphan's adventures in St. Petersburg (a fictionalized Hannibal). Initially the picaresque children's book was not a great success and sold fewer copies than *The Innocents Abroad*. As a celebration of childhood exploits and adventures on the Mississippi River, the novel did not deal with any significant issues, but it was notable for one memorable character, Tom's friend Huckleberry Finn.

Immediately after publishing *Tom Sawyer,* Twain began work on another book for boys. Completing four hundred pages of Huckleberry Finn's story in less than a month, Twain stopped writing at the end of chapter 16, claiming he liked it only "tolerably well." Twain said his "tank had run dry" and believed "as long as a book would write itself I was a faithful and interested amanuensis . . . but the minute that the book tried to shift to my head the labor of contriving its situations . . . I put it away." The author put the book away for close to three years, resuming writing in 1879 for a few months before abandoning it again, this time at chapter 21.

During the spring of 1882 Twain traveled back to Hannibal for his first extended stay in the area since the outbreak of the Civil War. Returning to the location of his boyhood had a powerful effect on him. He wrote that the experience made him feel like "some banished Adam, revisiting his half-forgotten Paradise and wondering how the arid world could ever have seemed green and fair to him." He confided in a letter to a close friend, "The fountains of my great deep are broken up and I have rained reminiscences . . . The old life has swept before me . . . the old faces have looked out of the mists of the past . . . and the songs I loved ages and ages ago have come wailing down the centuries." The overwhelming nostalgia rushing over Twain, plus his sorrow at the direction in which he saw American society to be moving, was ammunition enough for the author to complete *Adventures of Huckleberry Finn* on his return.

Back home Twain wrote in a frenzy and finally completed the novel in 1883. The adventurous tale concerns the events in the life of adolescent Huckleberry Finn. Escaping the brutalities of his drunken father, Huck befriends a runaway slave and the pair journey by raft along the Mississippi River in search of freedom. The story was simple enough and, at a surface level, could have been misconstrued as simply another book for boys. But where *Huckleberry Finn* differed from *Tom Sawyer* was in the depth of its themes and character development and the deeper-level messages about society. Huck and Jim's harmonious journey down the river was contrasted with the violence, corruption, and materialism the pair encountered when they came in contact with civilization.

Mark Twain believed in the book and went to great lengths with its promotion. In 1884 he decided to arrange a lecture tour to correspond with the book's publication and he negotiated for the *Century Magazine* to publish extracts from the novel before its release. When *Adventures of Huckleberry Finn* (subtitled *Tom Sawyer's Comrade*) was published in 1885, it became Twain's greatest success.

Although passionate about the novel, the author had no idea of the impact his work would have. It quickly earned a place in American mythology and spurred Ernest Hemingway to gush, "All modern American literature comes from one book by Mark Twain called *Huckleberry Finn* . . . It's the best book we've had. All American writing comes from that. There was nothing before. There has been nothing as good since."

THE WAR OF THE WORLDS,
H. G. Wells, 1897

❦

> *I remember I felt an extraordinary persuasion that I was*
> *being played with, that presently, when I was upon the*
> *very verge of safety, this mysterious death—as swift as*
> *the passage of light—would leap after me from the pit*
> *about the cylinder and strike me down.*

On the far side of the moon yawns a crater so battered that its outer rim has been reduced to a series of jagged peaks and valleys created by other, more recent impacts. The pockmarked landscape hints at a terrible, ancient intergalactic battle so fierce and explosive that the moon's surface forever bears its scars. It's quite fitting then, that this crater has been named after H. G. Wells, whose terrifying nineteenth-century vision of interplanetary warfare is even now, more than 110 years since the publication of *The War of the Worlds,* a familiar and frightening piece of popular culture. Some call the author the father of science fiction, and although he passed away in 1946 his name will live on, in literature and astronomy, forever.

It has been said that while writing *The War of the Worlds* Wells thoroughly enjoyed fictionally destroying parts of London that he remembered from the many unhappy years of his childhood. But the inspiration behind the book came from a far deeper, and often darker, place. Over the years Wells had developed a unique and controversial view of society. It was one that involved improving humankind by selective breeding and possibly by sterilization of those who were below par. He saw in the future a world-state that rejected democracy for the simple fact that most members of the public were not educated well enough to take part in the making of major decisions. He looked upon humanity simply as one of many species involved in a constant and merciless battle for survival. These views were nurtured over years of personal struggle, failure, and disappointment throughout his childhood, leading up to his rebirth as a writer.

Herbert George Wells was born on September 21, 1866, in Bromley in the English county of Kent. The youngest of four children, his impoverished family struggled to make ends meet. His father, Joseph Wells, was an owner of a china shop that did very little business. Joseph was also an excellent cricket player, although there was no such thing as a professional paid cricket player at the time. Joseph's wife, Sarah Neal, was a former domestic servant who would soon return to her servile duties, forever leaving the father of her children, a man with whom she had had a relatively loveless relationship.

In order to supplement the family's meager income Joseph sold cricket equipment to players and fans after matches, but money was never a constant in the Wells household. Young H. G. Wells was sent to a school for the sons of tradesmen, where he proved to be a star pupil, even producing his very own comic strip, called "The Desert Daisy," by the time he was thirteen years old. But when his father had an accident and broke his leg, meaning he could no longer play cricket, no longer earn extra money through equipment sales, and therefore no longer pay the school fees, Wells was dragged out of school in 1880 at the age of fourteen and sent to work.

His first job was as a draper's assistant at the Southsea Drapery Emporium. It was an unhappy experience that he later utilized in several novels. That same year he also spent time as a pupil teacher (pupil teachers assisted with teaching duties as part of their training to become teachers), a job he enjoyed but was forced to leave when the teacher who employed him was sacked. His next role was as an assistant in a pharmacy, for which he also took lessons in Latin and science. The education in science would begin to shape his future view of the world, but once again financial problems came between Wells and a continuing education. When his family could no longer afford the tutorials, he was forced to leave the pharmacy.

In between bouts of employment Wells often moved in with his mother in the large country house in Sussex where she was employed as a maid to the lady of the estate. There he would spend time in the well-stocked library, escaping his life of labor into a world of fiction. By 1883 he'd been through several low-paying jobs, often involving extremely long hours and tedious work. But in September of that year a glimmer of light finally shone into his life of poverty and despair when he returned to assistant teaching at Midhurst Grammar School in West Sussex.

In 1884 a scholarship for teachers in training meant he finally could afford to study without worrying about dropping out halfway through his course. He had enjoyed his taste of the science world while working in the pharmacy several years earlier, so he took a place in a biology course at the Normal School of Science in central London. One of his lecturers was Thomas Huxley, whose famously strong support of Darwin's theory of evolution would further color Wells's views on society and humanity, and would help develop his ideas about humanity's role in the greater scheme. Huxley was a key player in the wider science world's, and the public's, acceptance of theories of evolution.

Wells's college years truly brought him out of his shell. He joined the school's debating society and soon began using this public forum to preach his still forming, socialist-leaning ideas on the future of society, greatly influenced by the survival-of-the-fittest theme in Darwin's works. During the mid–1880s he was also a founding member of the left-wing Fabian Society, a socialist group committed to gradual social reform. The society still exists today, and other founding members, along with Wells, included playwright George Bernard Shaw, British suffrage leader Emmeline Pankhurst, and famous economists/reformers Sidney and Beatrice Webb.

Wells's passion for the written word was rediscovered when he also joined a group of students who launched the science school's journal. This college newspaper not only offered him another outlet for his personal views on politics and society but, perhaps more important, also allowed him to begin experimenting with fictional work. During the final years of his studies, 1886 and 1887, Wells published several short stories in the *Science School Journal,* pieces of literature that eventually would be rewritten and repurposed for use in his novel *The Time Machine.*

Popular fiction in the United Kingdom at this time included a genre that became known as "invasion literature," illustrated by such novels as *The Battle of Dorking,* an 1871 work by George Tomkyns Chesney about a German invasion of England. The popularity of this book led to a rash of similar, invasion-themed novels that have been credited with affecting the nation's psyche and shaping its politics in the lead up to World War I. Wells was undoubtedly a fan of the genre, but his fiction writing at college was more an early attempt at science fiction. His great invasion novel, the first to mix the genre with science fiction, was still more than a decade away.

Although college was good to Wells, the hard times unfortunately were not yet over. As a result of his lack of interest in sciences such as geology, Wells failed his final exams. Rather than spend another term at the college to complete his degree, he instead took a teaching role in a Welsh boarding school and, like most of his previous jobs, this ended in disaster. During a school rugby match in 1888, Wells suffered a vicious tackle, resulting in serious damage to several internal organs, including his lungs. Tuberculosis resulted, and the young teacher was forced to leave his job to recuperate, once again returning to the estate on which his mother was a servant.

For several months, when his health allowed, Wells read and sketched—for the budding writer drawing pictures was another way he'd found to express his thoughts and to pass time. As soon as his health recovered to a degree where he could travel and work safely, he headed back to London and found a job in 1888 as a teacher at Henley House School, where a young A. A. Milne, future author of the *Winnie-the-Pooh* books, would be one of his students. During this time he began writing again, submitting various articles and stories to university magazines and newspapers. Having continued his studies, he also finally earned his bachelor of science degree in 1890 by correspondence. As a twenty-four-year-old Wells finally had finished something rather than flunking out or being forced to withdraw due to lack of income. But in what had become a very familiar pattern, Wells was to suffer further setbacks before finally tasting true success.

Health problems continued to dog Wells, but a lung infection that forced him out of his teaching job in 1893 turned out to be a blessing in disguise, as it influenced him to take up freelance journalism. He may not have been able to stand up in front of a class and teach, but from his sickbed he was still able to write, so write he did. He began to find success by publishing short stories and reviews in newspapers. His time travel tale from the student newspaper years ago in college was rewritten and given another outing, first as a series of extracts in newspapers, then, in 1895, as the book *The Time Machine*. Where most aspiring writers have problems finishing a novel, Wells finally had found his niche and, turning his back on a lifetime of failed promises, had produced a book that earned rave reviews and impressive sales.

The next few years were spent writing novels, including the 1896 classic *The Island of Dr. Moreau,* another science-fiction tale, this time about a scientist who creates macabre man/beasts. But it would be his next release, first published in 1897 in serial form in *Pearson's Magazine,* that would forever place his name in the annals of literature and popular culture.

The War of the Worlds was an invasion story with a difference—rather than an invasion coming from a militarized Germany or from other neighbors across the seas, this time it came from Mars. One of the first alien invasion novels to be written, *The War of the Worlds* told the frightening tale of towering Martian tripods, equipped with deadly heat rays and poisonous gas, attempting to take over the world literally by sucking the lifeblood out of the human population. A new twist on Darwin's theories about survival of the fittest, the bleak tale was told in a dry, almost documentary-like style, which lent the book's anonymous narrator great authority.

Famously in 1938 a public outcry was caused when a sixty-minute radio version of the novel went to air in New York on the CBS radio show known as *The Mercury Theatre on the Air.* It was presented as a music show being interrupted by a series of news bulletins reporting that an alien invasion was taking place. The media was whipped into a frenzy, claiming the radio show had caused wide-spread panic across the United States. While it was true that it had caused some confusion among listeners, the reports of panic were greatly exaggerated, and when the dust finally settled the entertainment world had a new star—radio host, actor, and director of the show, Orson Welles.

THE HOUND OF THE BASKERVILLES,
Arthur Conan Doyle, 1902

❦

> *What it all means I cannot guess, but there is some secret business going on in this house of gloom which sooner or later we shall get to the bottom of.*

In March 1901, medical doctor, author, and keen sportsman Arthur Conan Doyle was vacationing in Norfolk with his good friend Bertram Fletcher Robinson. Robinson had been raised in Devonshire, and on this particular day, while enjoying a round of golf with Conan Doyle, he regaled his companion with stories of Devon legends from his childhood. Conan Doyle was transfixed by the tales of the pixies who inhabited Dartmoor, the headless horsemen who ruled the windswept moors, and the many ghosts who struck fear into the locals. But most fascinating to the forty-two-year-old were the myths concerning ghostly demon dogs.

At the urging of his friend, Robinson took Conan Doyle on a visit to Dartmoor later that month. The area of moorland in the center of Devon, with its tors and rivers, seemed to the author an excellent setting for a novel. Furthermore, the tales Robinson had told of mystic hell hounds would provide him with exceptional subject matter. By the time Conan Doyle had returned to London, all but one of the elements were in place to begin his moody mystery story—all he needed was the book's hero.

Although he was loath to admit it, the author eventually conceded that the only possible protagonist for his story was his most famous creation, Sherlock Holmes. Yet Conan Doyle faced a seemingly insurmountable obstacle—the writer had killed off the detective eight years earlier. He would have to call on all of his creative abilities from his entire career as a writer to solve this problem.

Arthur Ignatius Conan Doyle was born in Edinburgh, Scotland. Despite being prosperous, the Doyle family's curse was an alcoholic father who made the lives of his wife and children a misery. As a result, young Arthur escaped into the books that his mother, Mary, encouraged him to read. She also regularly invented stories for her son—she was an excellent storyteller. Years later the author described his mother's extraordinary talents, saying, "In my early childhood, as far as I can remember anything at all, the vivid stories she would tell me stand out so clearly that they obscure the real facts of my life."

When Arthur was nine he was sent to boarding school in England, but despite being an excellent scholar and sportsman he despised the strict Jesuit regime and the brutal corporal punishment the order meted out. The only bright spot in the child's bleak stint away from home was correspondence with his mother, from whom he had inherited a valuable gift—young Arthur often could be found surrounded by a crowd of wide-eyed students as he entertained them with incredible stories.

Despite an unstable home life, by the time he graduated in 1876, at the age of seventeen, Arthur Doyle was an extremely well-adjusted young man. With a lively sense of humor, great sporting talent, and a strong sense of adventure, he embarked into adulthood, giving credit to his mother for providing the most secure upbringing she could. He later wrote, "Perhaps it was good for me that the times were hard, for I was wild, full-blooded and a trifle reckless. But the situation called for energy and application so that one was bound to try and meet it. My mother had been so splendid that I could not fail her."

At Edinburgh University, while studying medicine, Conan Doyle (it is unclear when he changed "Conan" from a middle name to a part of his last name) mixed with brilliant young writers such as J. M. Barrie and Robert Louis Stevenson. Under the influence of such an artistic crowd the medico penned a short story called "The Mystery of Sasassa Valley" (1879). The work, evocative of the writing of one of Conan Doyle's favorite writers, Edgar Allan Poe, was accepted for publication by *Chambers's Journal*. In the same year a second story, "The American's Tale," was published in *London Society*. Conan Doyle later remarked that this was when ". . . I first learned that shillings might be earned in other ways than by filling phials."

In 1881 Conan Doyle graduated and, armed with a degree he jokingly called his Licence to Kill, he found employment as the medical officer on a steamer sailing between Liverpool and Africa. On returning to England he opened his own clinic in Portsmouth, on the country's southern coast. Despite a rocky start, with little business for a short while, after three years of hard work his practice began to earn him a comfortable living. With his career under control, Conan Doyle decided to pursue a passion he had placed on the back burner for some years—writing.

In March of 1886 Conan Doyle began a novel called *A Tangled Skein*. The story's two main characters were named Sheridan Hope and Ormond Sacker. One year later, however, when the crime story was published in *Beeton's Christmas Annual,* the title had become *A Study in Scarlet* and the novel's heroes were Sherlock Holmes and Dr. John Watson. Conan Doyle received a fee from *Beeton's Christmas Annual* of £25 for his first major work.

Written in just three weeks, *A Study in Scarlet* was a great popular success and skyrocketed Conan Doyle to fame as a writer, and Sherlock Holmes to fame as a character. The author based the unique detective on a teacher he'd had at college, Dr. Joseph Bell. Years later Conan Doyle described his mentor as a thin, wiry, dark man, "with a high-nosed acute face, penetrating gray eyes, angular shoulders." He would "sit in his receiving room with a face like a Red Indian, and diagnose the people as they came in, before they even opened their mouths. He would tell them details of their past life; and hardly would he ever make a mistake." Bell's powers of deduction were based on his patient's mannerisms, dress, speech patterns, and body language.

With *A Study in Scarlet* Conan Doyle not only created literature's most famous detective, he also gave birth to one of the most inspired partnerships in the literary world. Not only is Dr. Watson a friend and confidante of Holmes, he also acts as the novel's narrator and is a contrast to the detective. Watson plays the "everyman" opposite the intellectually brilliant, scrupulously methodical, emotionally cold, and justifiably arrogant hero.

Sherlock Holmes was a commercial hit, but the character created a conflict that was to plague the author for years to come. Conan Doyle wanted to be recognized for what he considered serious writing—histories, plays, and poetry. In many ways his was a love-hate relationship with Holmes. While giving him great success in

Britain and the United States, the fictional detective also kept Conan Doyle from writing works of more intellectual depth. In 1890 the second Holmes novel, *The Sign of Four,* was published in Britain and the United States.

The author relocated his practice from Portsmouth to London's Wimpole Street, and once again business was slow. The cash-strapped doctor had to make ends meet, so he decided to write a short story featuring Holmes. He negotiated a deal with *The Strand* magazine to publish the tale, and he eventually would pen another fifty-five short stories featuring Holmes and Watson. The image we have today of Holmes with his beaklike nose, deerstalker hat, and calabash pipe is thanks to Sidney Paget, an artist who used his brother Walter as the model.

The following year, while busily producing a steady stream of Holmes stories, Conan Doyle was struck down by a near-lethal bout of influenza. Having hovered close to death for several days, when the author recovered he decided to abandon medicine for the life of a full-time writer.

By the early 1890s Conan Doyle had become a prolific and wealthy author, but the means to his success frustrated him. While churning out Holmes mysteries, he worried he would never be considered a serious writer, and in 1893 he made the very bold move of killing off the detective. He wrote to his mother, "I think of slaying Holmes . . . and winding him up for good and all. He takes my mind from better things." In *The Final Problem* Sherlock Holmes and his archrival Moriarty fall to their deaths at the Reichenbach Falls in Switzerland. As a result, 20,000 readers cancelled their subscription to *The Strand*.

Finally liberated from Holmes, Conan Doyle embarked on a lecture tour of the United States and in 1900 spent time in South Africa working as a doctor during the Boer War. On returning to England he wrote a five hundred page chronicle of the conflict called *The Great Boer War*, which was considered by many to be a masterpiece. Conan Doyle also attempted to enter politics but failed miserably.

Perhaps to recover from his dismal spell in politics, Conan Doyle went on vacation to Norfolk with Robinson. Meanwhile, the writer was being pestered by *The Strand*, which offered him a handsome financial incentive to bring Holmes back from the dead. Whatever his motive, the trip inspired the author to resurrect the detective in the novel *The Hound of the Baskervilles*. However, so as not to be chained to Holmes for the rest of his career, he set events at a time previous to the detective's death.

In *The Hound of the Baskervilles* Holmes and Watson are invited to Devon to investigate the death of Sir Charles Baskerville. Although he had died from a heart attack, the locals are suspicious because of a legend of a vicious demon dog that wanders the moors seeking revenge on the Baskerville clan. Published in serial form by *The Strand* in 1901 and 1902, the novel is considered to be Conan Doyle's finest Holmes story. Conan Doyle had not only matured as a writer, but the myths and legends of Dartmoor had truly inspired him. His interest in the genre and in the character of Holmes had returned.

Sales of *The Strand* shot upward once again, and when the novel was released it soon became a worldwide sensation, helping to make Arthur Conan Doyle, by 1920, one of the most highly paid writers in the world.

PETER PAN,
J. M. Barrie, 1904

*Of course it was great fun to be really flying, to be able
to go round church steeples or high chimneys, just as if
one were a swallow. But it's rather shivery in nighties.*

Kensington Gardens in London is renowned throughout the world for its many significant historical landmarks.
There's the Christopher Wren–designed Kensington Palace that lies in its grounds, the Albert Memorial that stands
gleaming, ever-watchful of the Royal Albert Hall across
the road, and there's a huge wooden pirate ship that is the
centerpiece for the Diana, Princess of Wales' Memorial
Playground. But for children visiting the Gardens the
most exciting discovery is often the magical statue of Peter
Pan, a boy who refused to ever grow up.

One day in 1898, long before the statue ever appeared,
journalist, playwright, and author J. M. Barrie was walking Porthos, his St. Bernard, in Kensington Gardens
when he came upon two young boys. On an outing with
their nanny, five-year-old George and four-year-old Jack
Llewellyn-Davies were amused by this peculiar little
man with his huge dog. Striking up a conversation, the
three immediately became friends. Although childless,
the thirty-eight-year-old Scottish writer loved children
and had the rare ability to relate to them on their level.

Born in 1860 in Kirriemuir, Scotland, James Matthew
Barrie was the ninth of ten children. When James was six

his thirteen-year-old brother, David, died in a skating accident. His mother fell into a depression and would never recover from the loss of her son. James later wrote of his mother, "She lived twenty-nine years after his death. But I had not made her forget the bit of her that was dead . . . In those nine-and-twenty years he was not removed one day farther from her. Many a time she fell asleep speaking to him, and even while she slept her lips moved and she smiled as if he had come back to her. . . ."

James, too, had a hard time coming to terms with the loss of a brother who'd been handsome and talented and adored by his family. The memory of the young boy whose life had been cruelly taken meant he remained forever young—David's death guaranteed that he would never grow up. It struck James that there must be something perfect and magical about remaining a child forever.

James's father was a handloom weaver and his mother the daughter of a stonemason. Despite their humble lives, the couple held very high expectations for their children, and education was seen as the path to achieving success. Consequently, at the age of thirteen James left home to pursue his studies at Dumfries Academy. As a student he was an avid reader of fiction and especially loved the fantastic tales of Jules Verne and the adventure yarns of James Fenimore Cooper. While at Dumfries he also developed a love for the theater.

After graduation from Edinburgh University in 1882, the twenty-two-year-old found work at the *Nottingham Journal,* but he moved to London in 1885 to try his hand at freelance writing. Arriving in the capital penniless, Barrie landed on his feet and sold his humorous tales to highly regarded titles such as the *Pall Mall Gazette.*

Barrie was difficult to categorize as a wordsmith—he was capable of writing with great depth and emotion but was equally at home satirizing the celebrities of the day, as he did in his 1887 mystery novel *Better Dead*. Likewise, the behavior of the diminutive, pipe-smoking Scotsman was a puzzle to many. Good friends with popular literary figures such as George Bernard Shaw, P. G. Wodehouse, and H. G. Wells, he frequently surprised them with his childlike conduct. For instance, on one occasion he is said to have remarked to Wells, "It is all very well to be able to write books, but can you waggle your ears?"

Within a few years after the publication of his first novel, *Better Dead,* Barrie had produced a string of highly successful books, mostly set in Scotland. By the early 1890s he'd grown into a prolific and well-known writer and decided to return to a passion he discovered as a boy, the theater. As a playwright, Barrie achieved great fame and praise in England and the United States.

Then came the meeting in Kensington Gardens with the Llewellyn-Davies family, consisting of parents Arthur and Sylvia and their five sons, George, Jack, Peter, Michael, and Nicholas. Barrie nurtured this relationship and soon became a frequent guest of the family. The Llewellyn-Davies family would also often stay in Barrie's country home for summer vacations. The writer became such a fixture in the family's life that before long he simply became known as Uncle Jim.

In 1902 Barrie penned a book for adults called *The Little White Bird,* the story of a friendship between a man and a boy. At the heart of the novel is a fantastical story the protagonist invents for the child about a boy called Peter Pan who lives in Kensington Gardens. After the publication of *The Little White Bird,* Barrie realized that Peter Pan was much more than a supporting character.

The writer revised, reworked, and extended the character's appearances in *The Little White Bird* into a play called *Peter Pan, or The Boy Who Wouldn't Grow Up.* The play was dedicated "To the Five." The writer explained in the preface: "I always knew that I made Peter by rubbing the five of you violently together, as savages with two sticks produce a flame . . . That is all he is, the spark I got from you."

Premiering in London in December 1904, the play concerned the adventures of a boy who as a baby escapes from his parents and pursues a life of endless pleasure. Peter Pan flies into the Bloomsbury home of the three Darling children—Wendy, John, and Michael— wearing clothes made from leaves, cobwebs, and the juices that run from trees. Peter is cocky, mischievous, and hates all adults, and he is the only boy who is able to fly without the help of fairy dust. The three accompany him to Never-Land, a mythical island inhabited by fairies, pirates, and a rag-tag bunch called the Lost Boys. Wendy becomes a surrogate mother to the whole tribe but is soon kidnapped by Peter's nemesis Captain Hook, who is constantly being chased by a crocodile. Fortunately, Peter saves them from walking the plank and the evil Captain Hook is eaten alive by the crocodile. Returning to London, Mrs. Darling offers to adopt Peter. But Peter declines, preferring to be a boy forever, seeking fun and adventure.

After a successful London season, the play made an equally triumphant debut in New York in 1905 and, in the following year, Barrie published the section of *The Little White Bird* that featured Peter as *Peter Pan in*

Kensington Gardens. The final reworking of the tale came in 1911 when Barrie adapted the play into a novel for children called *Peter and Wendy*.

Finally, on May 1, 1912, a bronze statue of Peter Pan mysteriously appeared in Kensington Gardens. No publicity surrounded the event, but on the day Barrie simply placed this announcement in the *Times:* "There is a surprise in store for the children who go to Kensington Gardens to feed the ducks in the Serpentine this morning. Down by the little bay on the south-western side of the tail of the Serpentine they will find a May-day gift by Mr. J. M. Barrie, a figure of Peter Pan blowing his pipe on the stump of a tree, with fairies and mice and squirrels all around. It is the work of Sir George Frampton, and the bronze figure of the boy who would never grow up is delightfully conceived."

THE GREAT GATSBY,
F. Scott Fitzgerald, 1925

❧

Gatsby believed in the green light, the orgastic future that year by year recedes before us. It eluded us then, but that's no matter—to-morrow we will run faster, stretch out our arms further . . .

Few authors have defined their generations more succinctly than F. Scott Fitzgerald. From the point of view of a participant and chronicler of his time, Fitzgerald was able to step outside his world skillfully and report on it truthfully and critically. As one of the greatest American writers he steadfastly believed in documenting what he knew—not from any lack of imagination but from a belief that experience could only be conveyed with emotional intensity and accuracy if the author was writing from a firsthand perspective.

Born in 1896 in St. Paul, Minnesota, Francis Scott Fitzgerald (known as Scott) grew up with the belief that the United States was the land of opportunity. His boyhood in the late nineteenth and early twentieth centuries was a time of great fortune for the United States—it was the era of the self-made man. It was an era where rags-to-riches stories of the likes of John D. Rockefeller and Andrew Carnegie reached iconic status. People believed that despite birth, race, and religion, if one possessed talent, intelligence, and the willingness to work hard, then a successful and prosperous life would be forthcoming.

Although the term was not coined until the 1930s, it was the era of the American Dream.

Fitzgerald had personal experience of this. His grandfather was an Irish immigrant who became wealthy as a wholesale grocer. Living on his mother's inheritance, the Fitzgeralds, while not wealthy, lived a comfortable middle-class existence. In St. Paul the budding author attended St. Paul Academy, and it was there that his first writing appeared in print—a detective story the thirteen-year-old wrote for the school newspaper.

The budding writer attended Princeton University in 1913 but neglected his studies as his passion for writing grew more fervent. He busily penned scripts and lyrics for the theater troupe the Princeton Triangle Club, and was a regular contributor to the *Princeton Tiger* and the *Nassau Literary Magazine*. When the United States entered World War I in 1917, Fitzgerald joined the army as much to escape his academic challenges as to travel the world.

Although he never saw action, the twenty-one-year-old realized there was a chance that he could be killed during the war so, deciding to seize the day, he wrote his first novel, titled *The Romantic Egoist*. On completion the young writer sent the manuscript to Charles Scribner's Sons. While the publishers applauded the novel's originality and energy, it was rejected. But encouragement came in the form of a note asking Fitzgerald to submit the novel again once it had been revised. So began a pattern of revision that was to characterize Fitzgerald's writing for the rest of his career.

The Romantic Egoist was not Fitzgerald's only endeavor during the war. While in Camp Sheridan, Alabama, he met the youngest daughter of a Supreme Court judge, eighteen-year-old Zelda Zayre. Beautiful and rebellious, Zelda had earned a reputation for her wild ways. Fitzgerald fell in love with her immediately and the pair very quickly became engaged. But Zelda would not marry the young soldier until he had made his fortune. Fitzgerald hastily revised his novel, but it was rejected for a second time.

In 1919 the author was discharged from the army and moved to New York, hoping to find success in the advertising world. But Zelda was unwilling to wait and broke their engagement. With nothing to lose, Fitzgerald left New York in July of the same year and returned to St. Paul, determined to rewrite his novel one final time.

The Romantic Egoist was transformed into *This Side of Paradise* and was accepted by Charles Scribner's Sons in September 1919. Set at Princeton, the novel concentrates on the career and loves of Amory Blaine, a character bearing remarkable similarities to the author. Once the novel was accepted, Scott and Zelda resumed their plans for marriage and the novel was published in March 1920.

Becoming one of the most popular books in the market, *This Side of Paradise* sold more than 40,000 copies in its first year. The book made Fitzgerald a celebrity overnight and within a week of its publication he and his fiancée were married.

Emerging from the war, the U.S. economy was booming. As the stock market soared and general prosperity reigned, a get-rich-quick mentality gripped the nation and stories abounded of Average Joes making their fortunes overnight by playing the market. The Fitzgeralds, enjoying Scott's new success and fame, participated in this nationwide euphoria and embarked on the extravagant life of young celebrities. But Fitzgerald's view of the time was double-edged—he recognized the glamour and charm of the parties and drinking, but he also recognized the hedonism, waste, and often personal destruction the period brought with it.

Scott and Zelda spent the first few years of their marriage living in and around New York City while also traveling frequently to Europe. Never stopping anywhere long enough to call home, the couple made themselves notorious for their partying and unconventional lifestyle. Fitzgerald inadvertently became a living symbol of the Jazz Age, a reputation he struggled against for the rest of his life. His regular partying and drinking inspired the myth that he was a careless writer, yet he was a meticulous revisor who worked through many drafts of each manuscript.

Unable to support their opulent lifestyle by writing novels, Fitzgerald began churning out popular fiction for well-paying publications such as the *Saturday Evening Post, Collier's Weekly,* and *Esquire* magazine. But still the couple continued to suffer financial troubles.

The Beautiful and the Damned, Fitzgerald's second novel, was published in 1922. Far less well-received than the author's first effort, the novel tells the story of a young couple who are destroyed in their desperate grab for wealth. In this book themes emerge that were to become prominent in Fitzgerald's writing for the rest of his career, including the disastrous consequences of money and power on the individual and the predicament of the young man in love with an ostensibly perfect girl—a perception that was often an illusion.

In 1924 the Fitzgeralds moved to France, where Scott began the first draft of *The Great Gatsby.* This work was different from anything he'd done in the past. Through his main character, Jay Gatsby, Fitzgerald delved deeper into the malaise of American culture than with his previous male protagonists. What drove Gatsby was the delusion that money, a grand house, and lavish parties would recapture the past and the heart of the girl of his dreams—Daisy Buchanan.

Echoing the relationship of Scott and Zelda, Daisy and Gatsby met and fell in love during the war when Gatsby was a poor young soldier. Daisy "vanished into her rich house, into her rich, full life, leaving Gatsby—nothing" and married the newly rich Tom Buchanan. The book traces Gatsby's attempts to win Daisy back four years later. In the meantime, he makes his fortune through various means, including bootlegging liquor. Although nothing extraordinary lies in the plot, Fitzgerald makes the story outstanding by telling it from the point of view of Gatsby's neighbor, Nick Carraway—possibly literature's most perfect narrator.

If Gatsby represented one side of Fitzgerald's personality, then Nick Carraway represented the other. Originally from Minnesota, the character of Nick attended Yale, then fought in World War I. After the war he moved to New York to learn the bond business. He was also Daisy's cousin. By using Carraway as a medium, Fitzgerald was able to distance himself from the material—to be at once inside Gatsby's world, identifying with Gatsby's dream, and also looking at the world from an outsider's perspective, with the ability to view events with a critical eye.

Published in 1925, *The Great Gatsby* was praised by critics, who proclaimed Fitzgerald had "mastered his talents and gone soaring into a beautiful light, leaving behind him everything dubious and tricky in his earlier work, and leaving even further behind all the men of his own generation and most of his elders." While his career may have been booming, sadly his relationship with Zelda was coming to an end, and the onset of schizophrenia would see her hospitalized from the early 1930s.

WINNIE-THE-POOH,
A. A. Milne, 1926

Here is Edward Bear, coming downstairs now, bump, bump, bump, on the back of his head, behind Christopher Robin. It is, as far as he knows, the only way of coming downstairs, but sometimes he feels that there really is another way, if only he could stop bumping for a moment and think of it.

In the 1920s children around the globe fell in love with an English bear called Winnie-the-Pooh and his good friend Christopher Robin. Very few, though, realized that Pooh was based on a very real bear, also called Winnie, who had traveled all the way from Canada before finding a home in London Zoo.

The saga began during the opening stages of World War I. Canada's 34th Fort Garry Horse division recently had begun the long journey to the Western Front, and during a stop in Ontario, Lieutenant Harry Colebourn, the regiment's vet, stepped from the train and immediately noticed a man on the platform with a female black bear cub.

Enquiring after the bear's welfare, Colebourn discovered she was an orphan and the man, a trapper, had killed her mother. After agreeing on a price for the cub, Colebourn smuggled the bear onto the train, where she immediately became the regiment's unofficial mascot. Colebourn named his charge "Winnipeg," after his home town.

Soon after the soldiers arrived in England, their regiment was posted to the battlefields of France and Colebourn knew Winnie could go no farther, so he found a home for her at the London Zoo. The original agreement was that the bear would stay at the zoo as a long loan, and once the regiment returned they would take her back. At the zoo, Winnie quickly became the most popular attraction, drawing children from all over England. One of her biggest fans was a shy four-year-old by the name of Christopher Robin Milne. As the bear had been tamed by her time around humans, children sometimes were allowed into her enclosure during feeding times. Christopher was one of the lucky youngsters who was allowed to hand feed condensed milk to the friendly black bear.

Christopher, from the upper class London suburb of Chelsea, loved the bear so much he renamed his teddy bear, originally known as Edward Bear, after the zoo's live version. He also added "the Pooh" to the teddy's name, after a swan in his father's 1924 book of children's verse, *When We Were Very Young*. Christopher's father was the prolific playwright, author, and poet Alan Alexander Milne.

Alan Milne was born in Scotland in 1882 and moved with his family to London at a very young age. His father was a schoolmaster at Henley House in London, the school Alan attended before moving to Westminster School. At Henley House, one of Alan's teachers and mentors was the young H. G. Wells, whose talents and teachings were never lost on the student. Alan continued on to college and, in 1903, graduated with a mathematics degree from Trinity College in Cambridge.

But it was words, not numbers, that were his true love, and in 1906, having had several articles published in the humorous magazine *Punch,* he joined their staff as an assistant editor. In 1913 he married Dorothy de Selincourt, and in 1920 their only child, Christopher Robin, was born. In the years preceding Christopher's birth Alan had served in France during World War I with the Royal Warwickshire Regiment.

Alan also had developed a reputation as a prolific playwright. In fact, on top of the children's books, collections of verse, a detective novel, and an autobiography, by the end of his career he had written more than twenty-five plays, several of which were performed, to great acclaim, in Europe and the United States. But it would be the books he wrote about the Bear of Very Little Brain that would guarantee his place in history.

Although Christopher spent most of his time with his mother and nanny, Alan couldn't help but notice his son's love of the bear at London Zoo. When Christopher told him he'd changed his teddy's name to Winnie-the-Pooh, Alan was inspired to write a book about the adventures of a chubby bear called Winnie-the-Pooh and his friend Christopher Robin. Alan chose other characters for the book from Christopher's collection of stuffed animals, including Eeyore, Piglet, Tigger, Kanga, and Roo. Even the setting of the book, the Hundred Acre Wood, would be modeled on the Ashdown Forest, the wood near Cotchford Farm in Sussex, the Milne family's country home to which they moved to live in 1925.

On a daily basis Alan spent little time with his son, but the quality time they did enjoy together usually was taken up with long walks through the Ashdown Forest. It was here that Alan devised further plots and adventures for the fictional version of his son, although he rarely discussed his story ideas with Christopher. Alan was not writing the stories to read to Christopher (he preferred to read tales by P. G. Wodehouse to his only child), nor was he writing for an audience of children. He was instead writing, so literary historians say, for the child in us all.

Winnie-the-Pooh was first released by London publishers Methuen in 1926, but this was not Winnie's first literary outing. In the book *When We Were Very Young,* Milne had written of a tubby bear who couldn't help putting on weight, and in the Christmas Eve 1925 edition of the *London Evening News* he had published a bedtime story about his son's adventures with his teddy bear.

When *Winnie-the-Pooh* was released, it was an immediate commercial success. The illustrations of Pooh, by artist Ernest Shepard (who had knocked on Milne's door one Saturday morning to show his portfolio to the author and convince Milne he was the right man for the job) were not inspired by Christopher's bear, but rather by his own son Graham's favorite teddy. The partnership between Milne and Shepard would carry over another two bestsellers.

Milne followed *Winnie-the-Pooh* in 1927 with *Now We Are Six,* a book of verse containing the same characters, and *The House at Pooh Corner* in 1928. In an attempt to protect his shy son from the publicity storm created by the international success of the Pooh books, Milne announced, after the publication of *The House at Pooh Corner,* that it would be the final adventure Christopher Robin and Winnie-the-Pooh would share. Milne was also bitter that, despite all of the writing he had done, he had become famous only for a small series of children's books.

In 1952 Alan Milne had an operation on his brain, leaving him an invalid. He retired to the country house in

Sussex and passed away in 1956. By this time his four Pooh books, including *When We Were Very Young,* had sold an estimated seven million copies around the world.

Throughout his life Christopher found it difficult to escape his unwanted fame. As the owner of a bookshop in the 1950s, he constantly was approached by parents bringing their offspring to shake hands with the real Christopher Robin. While he had become quite close to his father during his teenage years, he had fallen away from his mother, and the last time he saw her was at his father's funeral, although she lived another fifteen years.

When Christopher finally came to terms with the fame that had been forced upon him by his father's books, he wrote a few autobiographical books of his own, including *The Enchanted Places* and *The Path Through the Trees,* all of which were critically acclaimed. Christopher married, had one daughter, and in 1996 passed away after suffering from a neurological disease for several years.

And what of the bear that befriended the boy? After the war Winnie's home remained the London Zoo, and Milne's books only increased her popularity. The celebrity bear died in the zoo in 1934 when her friend Christopher Robin Milne was just fourteen.

ALL QUIET ON THE WESTERN FRONT,
Erich María Remarque, 1929

We were eighteen years old, and we had just begun to love the world and to love being in it; but we had to shoot at it. The first shell to land went straight for our hearts.

May 10, 1933, was a dark day in the history of literature. On this day in Germany—particularly in a Berlin public square then known as Opernplatz (now known as Bebelplatz), but also mimicked in about thirty-five town squares across the nation—ultranationalist Nazi youth groups carried out action against what they referred to as "un-German Spirit." This culminated in the burning of tens of thousands of books written by Jews and others they found artistically suspicious, including Karl Marx, Thomas Mann, Bertolt Brecht, Ernest Hemingway, and Heinrich Heine.

Near the top of many of the right wing students' lists, though, was a book written by a German author who had, in fact, put his life on the line and been seriously wounded in the name of his country during World War I. The book they threw into the flames with such hatred was called *Im Westen nichts Neues,* which had been roughly translated for English-speaking markets as *All Quiet on the Western Front,* and its author was Erich Maria Remarque.

Many around the globe found it surprising that this work of fiction, which essentially was a war story, could cause such anger and hatred among the young followers of Adolf Hitler's regime. But at its heart the book was a powerful statement against the violent results of nationalism, which the author had experienced firsthand during World War I. This artful blend of fact and fiction was a very convincing argument against those politicians who would readily send thousands of young men to be slaughtered in battle and, unfortunately for the politicians, the book was also a bestseller. Through its graphic description of the horrifyingly brutal nature of life on the front line, as well as the humanization of the people who'd been sent to die on a hellish battlefield, the book had succeeded in reaching a massive audience without ever once glorifying the idea of war.

The book's author, who eventually would have his German citizenship revoked, was born Erich Paul Remark on June 22, 1898, in Osnabrück, Germany, into a working-class Catholic family. His father, Peter Franz Remark, was a printer and his mother, Anna Maria Stallknecht, would suffer from cancer during Erich's teen years. Erich's childhood was a healthy and happy one—he developed a love of nature through the hobbies of butterfly collecting and fishing, and of music when he threw himself into learning to play the piano. At his Catholic school he was known as a gifted student, often coming in first in his class, but a student whose talents sometimes were challenged by the fact that he was easily discouraged.

Whatever career Erich was dreaming of chasing (some believe he was hoping to become a concert pianist), his plans were shattered when he was drafted into the German army during World War I. Several friends from his school were also sent to training camp alongside the sometimes naive eighteen-year-old. Soon they would find themselves in a hell of man's creation, on the western front where, thanks to poison gas, machine guns, heavy artillery shells, and disease, life was cheap and the threat of death was an ever-present reality. With no respect for the politicians who had sent them to war, no interest in the politics that had led up to the war, and even less interest in killing people from countries that they had never even visited, Erich and his friends were unwilling participants in the slaughter that they witnessed and that ultimately took several of their young lives.

While on the front line Erich and his fellow soldiers regularly were informed of the content of the reports that were sent back to his homeland. They were amazed and disturbed to discover that, after a battle where hundreds of men on both sides had lost their lives or been wounded, but in which neither side had earned an advantage over the other, the report often would simply state "Im westen nichts neues," meaning "nothing new in the west." Their deaths, they realized, would count for nothing.

The war took the lives of over nine million soldiers, but Erich was one of the survivors. Working immediately behind the front lines, one day his arm was wounded by an artillery shell and he was sent home to recuperate. During his stay in the hospital Erich's mother died from cancer and one of his best friends was killed on the front line. The young man struggled, through the dark fog of the horrific and tragic experiences life had thrown at him, to find meaning. Although eventually he recovered to a degree where he was once again considered fit for battle, the war ended soon after, so he never again saw action.

After the war, his injuries dashed any hopes of a career as a musician, so Erich trained as a teacher and in 1919 worked in a school for a year. But he soon found himself searching for purpose. Like the characters in the book he would become famous for writing, the war had cut him off from getting on with life. In search of his place in the world he took jobs as varied as stonecutter, copywriter, race car test driver, picture editor, and clerk. Throughout this time he also wrote poems, short stories, and novels, with little publishing success. He wrote under the name Erich Maria Remarque—"Maria" is understood to have been in memory of his mother and "Remarque" was the original spelling of his family's name.

Remarque's urge to write led to him getting a position as a journalist, and by 1928 he was a successful magazine editor in Berlin. Here he had a taste of big city nightlife and found it very much to his liking. He quickly developed a reputation as a ladies' man and became a regular in bars, cafés, and cabarets.

At this point having had little luck with novels, in 1929 he gave it one more shot with a book that was a mix of reportage and fiction. The work gave voice to the horrifying experiences Remarque had suffered on the battlefield and described in great detail the utter destruction of man, society, and nature that comes with war. It highlighted the cruelty and futility of war and the absurd nature of the nationalism that feeds the war machine. The book, of course, came to be known in the English-speaking world by a title readers would realize was filled with terrible irony—*All Quiet on the Western Front*—and within 18 months it had sold 3.5 million copies.

The writer was now rich beyond his dreams and his life would never be the same again. He was hailed internationally as the spokesperson for the pacifist movement, and his fame grew by the day. Remarque's German citizenship was revoked nine years after the book's release as a direct result of its content. He was welcomed into the United States, where he was granted citizenship, but he had also purchased a house in Switzerland, where he ended up spending most of his life. He was famously married three times, twice to the same woman, and was known to have had several affairs—one with actress Marlene Dietrich.

His novel about the hideousness of war would be the work that defined him as an author. Several other novels followed, including many whose themes also centered around war, but none would experience the success of his raw and honest account of a soldier's life, the life of Remarque and his friends, during World War I.

GONE WITH THE WIND,
Margaret Mitchell, 1936

❧

*But for all the modesty of her spreading skirts, the de-
mureness of hair netted smoothly into a chignon and the
quietness of small white hands folded in her lap, her true
self was poorly concealed. The green eyes in the carefully
sweet face were turbulent, willful, lusty with life, dis-
tinctly at variance with her decorous demeanor.*

When author Margaret Mitchell was interviewed by
the *New York Times* in 1938 it was the first formal interview the writer had given since the publication of her
blockbuster *Gone with the Wind* two years earlier. Asked
by the journalist if she intended to write anything else,
the thirty-eight-year-old replied that she was so busy an-
swering her fan mail and her telephone that she didn't
have the time. Likewise, five years later when the governor of Georgia asked the author to sit on the State Board
of Education, she politely declined the offer by saying,
"My time is not my own. It has not been my own since
Gone with the Wind was published."

Mitchell was an intensely private woman whose sudden fame was overwhelming to her. In many ways she
was an accidental author, as she began writing a novel as
an amusement to pass the time. When friends visited her
cramped Atlanta apartment and saw her tapping away
at an old Remington typewriter, they liked to joke that
she was writing one of the greatest novels the world had

ever seen. Nobody, especially Margaret Mitchell herself, expected that it just might be true.

Margaret Mitchell was born in Atlanta, Georgia, in 1900 to Eugene Mitchell and Mary Isabelle Stephens (known as Maybelle). Her father was a lawyer with a passion for history, and who was president of the Atlanta Historical Society. The family was proud of their Irish-Catholic roots and had a great love of the South, which was passed down to their children. Maybelle was an outspoken suffragette who campaigned for voting and economic rights for women.

Most prominent in the author's mind from her childhood (during which time she was nicknamed Peggy) were gatherings of her parents' circle of friends, many of them history buffs like her father, several of them Civil War veterans. The writer later recalled, "When we went calling, I was usually scooped up onto a lap, told that I didn't look like a soul on either side of the family, and then forgotten for the rest of the afternoon while the gathering spiritedly refought the Civil War. Cavalry knees had the tendency to trot and bounce and jog in the midst of reminiscences and this kept me from going to sleep . . ."

Maybelle instilled in her daughter the value of education and a love of reading. She would pay Margaret to read each of Shakespeare's plays, and by the time Margaret was eleven she had devoured the entire canon. She also enjoyed reading Charles Dickens and Sir Walter Scott. Despite a love of literature, her education was cut short in 1918 when her mother died in the Spanish influenza pandemic and the teenager was called home from college to take care of the household.

She made her society debut in 1920, but the headstrong twenty-year-old was not cut out for a debutante's life. She performed a racy dance at a debutante ball, which immediately made her the target of scandalmongers, and she regularly locked horns with other young women about the rightful recipients of charity funds. Outspoken and unafraid to speak her mind, Mitchell had indeed proved to be her mother's daughter. In 1922 she began work as a writer for the *Atlanta Journal Sunday Magazine* for a salary of $25 a week.

As one of the publication's first female columnists, over the next four years Mitchell produced hundreds of articles for the publication. Writing under the name Peggy Mitchell, the journalist penned celebrity profiles, book reviews, and feature articles and interviewed some of the era's most famous personalities, including Rudolph Valentino. She also began writing profiles of Civil War generals for the magazine. Her interest in the subject, and her careful research, made them extremely popular with readers.

In 1925 Mitchell married advertising executive John Marsh and the couple moved in to a cramped one-bedroom apartment in Atlanta that they lovingly called "The Dump." The following year, however, Mitchell had to resign from her job at the *Atlanta Journal Sunday Magazine* after a broken ankle left her bedridden.

Confined to her tiny apartment, Mitchell whiled away the days reading books her husband delivered to her bedside. Every few days he would stop by the Atlanta Public Library and borrow another stack of books, but one day he decided he'd simply had enough. Legend says he told her the library had run out of books and if she wanted another one she would have to write it herself. When she scoffed and asked what she would write about, he replied, "Write about what you know."

Taking her husband's advice, Mitchell drew upon the stories she had heard as a child, as well as the knowledge of the Civil War she'd gathered since. Using this information, she began an epic work about the Old South, the burning of Atlanta, and the days of postwar reconstruction.

There was no particular order to her writing. She actually began with the last chapter and wrote in fits and starts as she sat hunched over a portable typewriter at a table in a crowded alcove. As she finished each chapter, she would store it in a manila envelope. If she thought of an additional element for that chapter at a later date, she would scribble the idea on a scrap of paper and stuff it in the appropriate envelope. Nobody, apart from her husband and a few close friends, knew she was writing a novel, and no one, apart from Marsh, was allowed to read the manuscript.

In an effort to protect her secret, she would hide the ever-burgeoning document which, by its completion, stood taller than its petite, four-foot nine-and-a-half-inch author, under the bed, in drawers, under the sofa, and in closets around the apartment. On one occasion when the couple was having guests to dinner, she threw a rug over stacks of the pages that lay in the living room. Mitchell had no confidence in herself as a novelist and the thought of her book becoming public knowledge horrified the fledgling author.

By 1929 Mitchell's ankle had healed and the writer had lost interest in her novel despite the fact that, apart from an opening chapter and a few incomplete chapters, the book was almost complete. When Mitchell and her husband moved in to a larger apartment that year, she took with her the massive manuscript and found a home for it in a closet in the front room.

There it lay hidden until 1935, when Harold Latham, a Macmillan publisher, came to Atlanta on a talent scouting trip. He had heard of Mitchell and her mysterious novel from Lois Cole, an editor at Macmillan who was also a friend of the writer. Mitchell, at Cole's request, had agreed to show Latham around Atlanta. When Latham asked to see her manuscript, Mitchell denied any knowledge of it, telling him he'd simply heard a rumor that was not true. But when a friend who'd heard about the publisher's visit commented that she didn't have what it took to write a novel, her temper was fueled.

Spurred into action, Mitchell rushed home, collected the manuscript, and piled it into an old suitcase. Hotfooting it to Latham's hotel, she managed to catch the publisher on the way to the railway station, about to leave the city. Thrusting the case of pages at him, she told him to take it from her before she changed her mind.

When Mitchell arrived home, she immediately regretted her rash actions and telegrammed Latham in New York with the message "Have changed my mind. Send manuscript back." Fortunately, it was too late. Latham had begun reading the saga, tentatively titled *Tomorrow Is Another Day,* on the train to New York, and by the time he received Mitchell's message he'd read enough of it to know he had a bestseller on his hands.

After six months of revisions, which included writing a first chapter and changing the heroine's name from Pansy to Scarlett (it's thought that as the author came to know her lead character more intimately, she felt the name Scarlett would better suit her fiery temperament), *Gone with the Wind* was published in June 1936. Set in Georgia during the Civil War and Reconstruction, the sprawling story had at its center the willful southern belle Scarlett O'Hara, whose love for the gentlemanly Ashley Wilkes was unrequited but who developed a passionate and fiery relationship with the charming but scandalous Rhett Butler.

The novel won the Pulitzer Prize in 1937 and earned the author $1 million in four years. This included the sale of the film rights for $50,000 to Metro-Goldwyn-Mayer, the highest amount ever paid for movie rights at the time. The historical romance about the Old South, war, love, loss, gender, and class caused a worldwide sensation. But at its heart is something far more simple, according to the author. "If the novel has a theme it is that of survival. What makes some people able to come through catastrophes and others, apparently just as able, strong and brave, go under? It happens in every upheaval. Some people survive; others don't. What qualities are in those who fight their way through triumphantly that are lacking in those who go under . . . ? I only know that the survivors used to call that quality 'gumption.' So I wrote about the people who had gumption and the people who didn't."

THE HOBBIT,
J.R.R. Tolkien, 1937

*All alone it rose and looked across the marshes to the for-
est. The Lonely Mountain! Bilbo had come far and
through many adventures to see it, and now he did not
like the look of it in the least.*

For a young, fatherless boy growing up in a picturesque
English village outside the enormously polluted early
twentieth-century industrial city of Birmingham, it was
easy to develop strong beliefs about light and dark, good
and evil, power and corruption. When that boy also
turned out to have a stunning imagination and a great
love of words—to the point where he invented languages
of his own—there was little doubt that he would grow
up to become a renowned author. But for John Ronald
Reuel Tolkien, the road to fame and fortune would be
paved with rejections before his most famous children's
story, *The Hobbit,* would turn his life around.

Tolkien was born in Bloemfontein, South Africa, in
January 1892. His father, Arthur, was a manager with
the Bank of Africa. Even as a toddler Tolkien would
have experiences that set his imagination alight. While
exploring the family's garden in what was then known
as the Orange Free State, he was bitten by a large and
disturbingly named baboon spider (known in the rest of
the world as a tarantula). As a result, he needed much
bed rest, allowing the youngster plenty of time to reflect

on his run-in with one of nature's most frightening creations.

When Tolkien was three years old, his mother, Mabel, took him and his younger brother, Hilary, to England on an extended vacation to visit her family. As the boys met their maternal grandparents—shop owners in Birmingham—their father, who had stayed in South Africa, contracted rheumatic fever and died. Rather than returning to the family home in Bloemfontein, the widowed Mabel decided to stay close to her own family support network and moved to the English village of Sarehole, which, although just a few miles from the smokestacks and street urchins of Birmingham, retained a rural charm that would never be lost on young Tolkien.

In *The Hobbit* Tolkien writes about the Shire, a peaceful, rustic society that is home to the Hobbits, who are blissfully ignorant of the dangers and adventures that exist in the unknown world outside their borders. Blissful ignorance, one imagines, also would have been a valuable trait for a young boy who'd recently lost his father and who sought comfort and solace in his reduced family unit and their quaint and scenic surroundings. But Tolkien soon would receive another blow, just as cruel as the last.

For four years the children lived in Sarehole, tutored by their mother. Mabel introduced them to literature, science, botany, and languages, and to many great stories, legends, and writers. Outside of their mother's classes the brothers would keep themselves entertained by exploring local hills, mills, forests, bogs, and their aunt's farm, which was called Bag End. All that they explored held a magical attraction to boys with limitless imaginations.

But in 1904 their adventurous lives and carefree existences once again would be turned upside down when their mother, who had developed diabetes, died. A few years earlier Mabel had converted to Catholicism, which so offended her Baptist family that they cut her off, removing all financial assistance. Tolkien is said to have considered her a martyr for her faith, and he would grow to develop his own powerful Catholic belief system.

Before Mabel's death the family had moved in to the suburbs of Birmingham so that her sons could attend King Edward's School, where his already burning love of languages was further flamed by classes concentrating specifically on Old and Middle English. Rather than exploring neighborhoods as he had in the countryside, Tolkien dreamed of far-away lands as he watched trains roll by on the tracks that the family home backed onto.

Upon the passing of their mother, the brothers were moved to an orphanage run by Father Francis Xavier Morgan. Once again they were surrounded by powerful symbols and edifices, including Father Morgan's Birmingham Oratory, religious statues and ornaments, medieval paintings, and local landmarks, including the dark and imposing tower of the Edgbaston Waterworks. While in the orphanage sixteen-year-old Tolkien met the love of his life, Edith Mary Bratt, but Father Morgan prohibited them from even communicating with each other until Tolkien had turned twenty-one, an order they both obeyed. In the meantime, his schooling at King Edward's continued.

Over the following years, Tolkien's fascination with language would continue to build, to a stage where he began to invent his own languages loosely based on Old English and Gothic. In 1911 he moved to Oxford to study English, and the same year took a cycling vacation in

Switzerland, where he was captivated by the grand and magical mountain scenery.

Tolkien's love story would have a happy ending when, on his twenty-first birthday, he wrote to Edith and declared his feelings, which he had kept under wraps for the previous five years. She was engaged but had never forgotten the boy from the orphanage. She separated from her fiancé and threw herself into a relationship with Tolkien that would last until her death in 1971. The two were married in 1916 and would have four children (John Francis, Michael Hilary, Christopher John, and Priscilla Anne) between 1917 and 1929.

During World War I Tolkien had served at the front as a signaling officer with the Lancashire Fusiliers. Having seen several of his closest friends killed in action, Tolkien was sent back to England in October 1916, after suffering from trench fever. It was during this recovery period that he began writing stories in order to keep his mind active. The regular recurrence of the illness meant he would add more stories to his collection, which eventually became known as *The Book of Lost Tales*.

After the war Tolkien worked on another book that would develop its own iconic status, the *Oxford English Dictionary,* and in 1920 he was awarded the job of Reader in English Language at Leeds University. During this time he continued to add to his collection of stories, mainly fantasy tales of fantastical worlds, and in 1925 he became Rawlinson and Bosworth Professor of Anglo-Saxon, a role he would fill for the next two decades.

While marking exam papers during the 1920s, Tolkien came across a page a student had left blank. Without quite knowing why, on the page he wrote, "In a hole in the ground there lived a hobbit," smiled, and continued marking. He didn't consider this a beginning to any kind of story, but did decide to look into what exactly a hobbit was in order to perhaps one day include the creature in his fantasy writings.

As his children were growing up, Tolkien would read them bedtime stories from his own collection. He also used to write them long letters from Santa Claus at Christmastime. Around 1931, though, Tolkien began work on a bigger project in which he began to bring together several of the themes, characters, and storylines from his shorter pieces. His new tale, about an unassuming but courageous hobbit who goes on an adventure across Middle Earth with a group of dwarves, was also read to his children. The fantastical novel may never have been published were it not for the fact that Elaine Griffiths, a family friend who worked in publishing, was shown part of the unfinished manuscript. Griffiths worked for George Allen & Unwin and told Susan Dagnall, one of the publishers, about the book. Dagnall liked what she heard. After reading the unfinished work herself, she encouraged Tolkien to finish the story, which he finally did in 1936.

The completed novel contained elaborate and detailed descriptions of magical lands and memorable characters, many of whom spoke unique languages. The dark cities and mystical mountains, soaring towers and stunning rural scenes all seemed bigger and better versions of the scenery that had surrounded Tolkien as a boy.

Dagnall passed the final version on to company chairman Stanley Unwin, who reportedly gave it to his son to read. Unwin Jr. apparently was so thrilled by the book that his father agreed to publish it almost immediately. *The Hobbit*'s massive success led to Allen and Unwin's request for "more about Hobbits," leading to the *Lord of the Rings* trilogy.

The series of books, of course, eventually went on to be turned into one of the world's most successful film trilogies, directed by New Zealand's Peter Jackson and breaking several records. *The Lord of the Rings: The Return of the King* earned the most Oscars won by any film, with eleven (equal to *Ben Hur* and *Titanic*), and also grossed $1 billion at the box office faster than any movie in history, taking just nine weeks and four days after its 2003 release. The previous record was held by *Titanic*, which hit $1 billion at eleven weeks.

The Grapes of Wrath,
John Steinbeck, 1939

❧

And the women came out of the houses to stand beside
their men—to feel whether this time the men would
break. The women studied the men's faces secretly, for
the corn could go, as long as something else remained.

The day after Pulitzer and Nobel Prize–winning author
John Steinbeck died, Charles Poore, a reviewer from the
New York Times, wrote of the novelist, "His place in
literature is secure. And it lives on in the works of innu-
merable writers who learned from him how to present
the forgotten man unforgettably." John Steinbeck's legacy was profound. His extraordinary talent combined
with his unyielding desire to bring the plight of the
underdog to the fore was a powerful force in twentieth-
century literature.

Steinbeck was born in 1902 in Salinas, California.
His father, John, was an unsuccessful businessman and
the family was by no means well off, but his mother,
Olivia, was driven. The college-educated teacher was
ambitious for her only son and instilled in him a love
of literature. Among young Steinbeck's favorite books
were Dostoevsky's *Crime and Punishment* and Milton's
Paradise Lost and *Le Morte d'Arthur*.

The Steinbecks planted deep roots in the small, conservative community of Salinas and participated in many
local organizations and activities. Their son, although re-

membered by many as being shy and observant, was also rebellious and reacted against what he called "Salinas thinking." By the age of fourteen he had decided to become a writer and spent many solitary hours in his room composing stories and poems.

Steinbeck attended the local high school but was not an outstanding student. More interesting to him were school vacations, when he would work on nearby farms and ranches. Mixing with ranch hands and itinerant farm workers gave the teenager an insight into the life of the common man, and working on the land implanted in him a great appreciation of the environment around him.

Salinas's economy was based largely on agriculture. Located in one of the country's most fertile farming regions, the area known as "the salad bowl of the nation" produced abundant fruits and vegetables, making Salinas one of the wealthiest cities per capita in the United States. But the idealistic young writer was soon to learn that much of this prosperity was gained through untold human sacrifice.

To please his mother, Steinbeck began classes at Stanford University in 1919. Enrolling in literature and writing courses, along with the occasional science subject, the seventeen-year-old had no intention of taking university seriously. Steinbeck simply still was determined to become a full-time writer. A one-time president of the university's English club once said Steinbeck "had no other interests or talents that I could make out. He was a writer, but he was that and nothing else."

As a result of this myopia, Steinbeck's academic performance at Stanford was at best erratic and at worst dismal. At the same time, though, he developed a fascination with the farm workers and drifters he met during college vacations. Through these experiences the young man developed a great understanding of, and passion for, the homeless and the hopeless.

Without having gained a degree, Steinbeck finally left Stanford in 1925. The twenty-three-year-old's desire to write fiction still burned as strong as ever, and after a brief stint working on a ranch, then as a reporter for the *New York American,* Steinbeck moved to Tahoe, where he found employment as a caretaker on a lake estate. This new position gave him the time he needed to devote to writing. Over the next few years Steinbeck wrote several drafts of his first novel, *Cup of Gold* (1929), a historical tale of the pirate Sir Henry Morgan.

The following year he married Carol Henning, a woman who was to play a pivotal role in her husband's early novels. While working to support her husband, she also typed his handwritten manuscripts, edited his work, advised him on plot and structure, and suggested titles. Steinbeck often would work on a number of projects simultaneously, resulting in the publication of *Pastures of Heaven,* a short story collection, in 1932, and *To a God Unknown* in 1933.

Steinbeck's first three works received little critical attention and went unnoticed by the public. However, the mystical *To a God Unknown* did introduce concepts that were to become fundamental to the writer's later works. The novel chronicles the story of a farmer, Joseph Wayne, who, on receiving a blessing from his father, establishes a farm in a far-away valley. Encountering a drought, Wayne sacrifices himself to bring an end to the dearth.

While Steinbeck did not explain the conclusion and knew the book would not be a success with readers, the novel did highlight Steinbeck's philosophy of the powerful bond between man and his environment. In a journal he kept while working on the novel, Steinbeck wrote, "The trees and the muscled mountains are the world—but not the world apart from man—the world and man—the one inseparable unit man and his environment. Why they should ever have been understood as being separate I do not know." Set in California and written in an uncomplicated naturalistic style, the novel captured the hopes and agonies of the common people and their connection with the land they inhabit.

Steinbeck earned his first critical success with his 1935 novel, *Tortilla Flat*. Set in the Depression, *Tortilla Flat* told the tale of a group of poor but adventurous young men whose exploits resembled those of King Arthur's knights. For his efforts Steinbeck won the California Commonwealth Club's Gold Medal.

On the wave of this triumph, in 1936 Steinbeck and his wife moved to Los Gatos, California, and began a period of prolific and profound work. Also at this time Steinbeck attended a few meetings of the local chapter of the John Reed Club. Although Steinbeck disliked the fanaticism of the Communist organization, he was attracted to the group's sympathy for the working man. Steinbeck's empathy with the suffering farm workers of California inspired the author to write *In Dubious Battle* (1936). The novel depicts the struggle of nine hundred migratory workers in California apple country who rise up against the greedy landowners for whom they work.

At the height of his abilities as a writer, Steinbeck followed *In Dubious Battle* with another novel dealing with the plight of the common man, *Of Mice and Men* (1937).

Intended as both a novel and a script for a play, the tragic and moving story of two drifters who dream of a place of their own was an instant success with critics and with the public. Adapted into an acclaimed stage play, the universal tale of the human need to find a home won the New York Drama Critics' Circle Award for best play.

As he was making revisions to *Of Mice and Men,* Steinbeck already had begun planning his next work. His inspiration came from a journalistic assignment in 1936 for the *San Francisco News.* Sent to cover the migrant situation in California, Steinbeck interviewed nomadic workers, oppressed minorities, and government officials who were trying to solve the problem of the poverty these people faced.

Visiting camps established by the government to house the migrant communities, Steinbeck spoke with people who, forced from their homes and land by the Depression, traveled westward, where they hoped to make a new life. Upon reaching their destination, however, they were confronted with monopolies and farming conglomerates that exploited the plentiful and cheap labor supply without concern for the welfare of the individual. The author was appalled to discover poverty, disease, and starvation rife in the land where he was raised, and he became determined to expose the crimes of those responsible. After thoroughly researching the situation, Steinbeck wrote a series of columns for the *San Francisco News* that were published as "The Harvest Gypsies." But the author knew there was enough material in what he'd discovered for a work of far grander scale.

Even in its title, *The Grapes of Wrath* was a blatant indictment against the system. Taken from the Civil War anthem, the "Battle Hymn of the Republic," Steinbeck was suggesting a new Civil War was being staged between the rich and poor. The story followed the movement of one family from the drought-stricken Oklahoma Dust Bowl to the Promised Land of California.

The book combined biblical and mythical elements as tenant farmers, the Joads, set out on an exodus similar to the Jewish flight to Canaan from Egypt. Undertaking the challenging and treacherous journey west, along with thousands of others who shared the same dream, the Joads lose several of their family members along the way. When they arrive in California, there are hundreds of applicants for every position, and their hopes of earning a decent wage in an industry controlled by greedy corporate farmers dwindle. Although their dream is so simple—a home and a steady job—it seems an impossible goal.

After the book's publication, effigies of Steinbeck were burned by angry Californians who saw his work as a scandalous distortion of the migrant situation. Considered obscene by conservatives for its sexual innuendo and graphic detail, *The Grapes of Wrath* was banned in some public schools and libraries. Nevertheless, it was considered by critics to be Steinbeck's greatest masterpiece. *The Grapes of Wrath* won the author the Pulitzer Prize and played a significant role in earning Steinbeck the Nobel Prize for Literature in 1962.

For Whom the Bell Tolls,
Ernest Hemingway, 1940

. . . Lietenant Berrendo made the sign of the cross and then shot him in the back of the head, as quickly and as gently, if such an abrupt movement can be gentle, as Sordo had shot the wounded horse.

In 1937 American writer Max Eastman, frustrated by Ernest Hemingway's public displays of machismo, fired a well-aimed gibe at his peer. He said, "Come out from behind that false hair on your chest, Ernest. We all know you." Legend says that when the two met in the New York offices of the publisher they shared, they came to blows, with Hemingway finally ripping open his shirt to prove that his chest hair was, in fact, real.

It is often difficult to separate the writer from the myth. So many of the images we have of Hemingway are of a weathered and bearded man standing proudly on the deck of his boat with a freshly reeled-in marlin, or holding a rifle aloft over an animal recently killed on safari. Hemingway the deep-sea fisherman, the big-game hunter, the drinker, the rugged and gruff individualist who did things his way bears little similarity to the sensitive author who perfectly captured situation, character, and emotion with his minimalist and direct yet elegant prose. But the two personalities, it seems, managed to exist together in one body.

According to legend, when Grace Hemingway gave birth to her first son, Ernest, in 1899, so proud was her husband, Clarence, that he ran out to the front porch of their Oak Park home and blew a horn to inform the neighborhood of the new arrival. The couple was to have six children altogether, but nothing could match the intensity of emotion Clarence felt at eight o'clock that morning in July.

Oak Park, a middle-class suburb of Illinois, was later described by its most famous son as having "wide lawns and narrow minds." It was an intensely conservative area where the Protestant work ethic reigned supreme. Hemingway's physician father and music teacher mother instilled these values in their offspring—if one worked hard and believed in God, the children were told, success inevitably would follow.

Young Hemingway was a good scholar and an excellent sportsman at school, and at home he received a well-rounded education from his parents. From his father the boy learned rational scientific thinking and from his mother he inherited a love of the arts. Grace once had aspired to be an opera singer, and after marriage and children she partially satisfied her ambition by giving voice and music lessons. It was from Clarence that Hemingway learned a love of the outdoors and physical activity—each summer the Hemingways would retreat to their house by Walloon Lake in Michigan to take refuge from the heat, and there the children would go fishing, boating, and hunting, pastimes to which Ernest had a natural affinity.

From childhood Ernest loved writing, and he regularly contributed to his school's newspaper and literary magazine, but on completing high school the teenager had no desire to go to college. At the age of eighteen Hemingway began his writing career at the *Kansas City*

Star as a cub reporter, covering local fires, crimes, and strikes. He worked for the publication for only twenty months, but it was a pivotal period for the young journalist, for in that time his unique writing style was born.

Throughout his career, Hemingway was to use the *Star*'s style guide as his own manifesto on writing. The newspaper's policy promoted short sentences and paragraphs, active verbs, realism, compression, clarity, and immediacy, which Hemingway would adopt in his own fiction. The writer later said, "Those were the best rules I ever learned for the business of writing. I've never forgotten them."

In 1917 America had joined the World War I conflict, and Hemingway was eager to be an active participant. Failing the medical exam due to poor eyesight, the teenager was disappointed but immediately joined the Red Cross Ambulance Corps. He was keen to get as close as possible to the action, and on his first day on the job he received a shocking introduction to the horrors and brutalities of war. When a munitions factory was bombed in Milan, medics, including Hemingway, were sent to retrieve the body parts of the civilian women who had worked there. The memories of that day stayed with the young man forever and became a part of his later writing.

In the following year, as Hemingway was delivering chocolate and cigarettes to front line Italian troops, an Austrian mortar shell landed nearby and knocked the young medic unconscious. With more than two hundred pieces of shrapnel in his legs, Hemingway managed to carry a wounded Italian soldier back to the first aid station while under a hail of machine gun fire. Hemingway was awarded the Italian Silver Medal for Valour and was sent to recover in a Milan hospital. The war ended before Hemingway could return to the front.

Upon returning to the United States, Hemingway moved back to the family home in Oak Park. For the injuries he sustained he received $1,000 in compensation, which was enough for the young man to live on for a year. But after experiencing war firsthand, his middle-class existence seemed dull, and the twenty-year-old longed for new experiences. Although home, Hemingway felt lost in many ways. His parents had no notion of the psychological impact of war and the feelings of frustration he was experiencing. He later fictionalized this predicament in the short story "Soldier's Home" in 1925.

To please his parents, who wanted him to find employment, Hemingway often spoke to small civic organizations about his time in Europe. But he frequently exaggerated and glorified his experiences for the benefit of the middle-class audience that wanted to hear of battlefield heroics.

In 1921 Hemingway married Hadley Richardson and found employment as a foreign correspondent for the *Toronto Star Weekly*. Moving to Paris, the newlyweds immediately found their niche as part of a group of expat writers and artists that Gertrude Stein dubbed the "Lost Generation." Disillusioned with the state of post–World War I society, their feelings were conveyed through their art. In Paris Hemingway witnessed a major creative renaissance going on around him with expat Americans, including Stein, Ezra Pound, Ford Madox Ford, Max Eastman, and F. Scott Fitzgerald. The twenty-two-year-old was able to hone his style while being strongly influenced by these writers.

Hemingway the journalist covered world events such as the Geneva Conference, the Greco-Turkish War, and the Lausanne Conference. He also wrote lifestyle pieces, including articles about bullfighting, fishing, and skiing. More importantly, inspired and influenced by the artistic circle of which he was a part, he was able to write his own fiction. After his first book, *Three Stories and Ten Poems* (1923), was published in Paris, Hemingway resigned from the *Toronto Star* to dedicate himself to fiction.

The period between 1924 and 1929 was a time of significant creative output for the author that saw the publication of his first work in the United States, *In Our Time* (1925), a collection of short stories. Only 170 copies of this book were printed, but the work proved significant because it encapsulated Hemingway's artistic theory. Putting what he had learned at the *Kansas City Star* into practice, Hemingway believed that omitting information actually could strengthen a story. The author likened a piece of writing to an iceberg, where only one eighth of the object can be seen above water, but the remaining unseen portion below the water provided the iceberg with its shape and momentum. In the same way, what is not shared in a story is equally or more important as the words actually conveyed to the reader. By having *In Our Time* published in the United States, Hemingway proved his minimalist style was acceptable.

In the following year, Hemingway used the American ex-pat community in Europe as his inspiration for *The Sun Also Rises* (1926). Written in a mere six weeks, the novel was a semiautobiographical tale that followed a group of Americans as they traveled to Pamplona, Spain, for the annual running of the bulls. The novel met with immense critical success and was acclaimed internationally.

After his first marriage failed, Hemingway married Pauline Pfeiffer, and the couple returned to the United States in 1928. Moving to Key West, Florida, Hemingway penned his next great novel, *A Farewell to Arms,* considered by many to be the definitive World War I story. Heavily autobiographical, the novel deals with the relationship between an American soldier and a British nurse. It was inspired by an affair Hemingway had had with a nurse while recovering from his war wounds. The success of the novel earned Hemingway financial independence as well as a reputation as one of the most important writers of the twentieth century.

The years at Key West were productive for Hemingway. Although by this stage the writer had a reputation as a heavy drinker, he was also an extremely disciplined writer who worked five hours each day. In fact, Hemingway rarely would drink after dinner, as he knew this would interfere with his ability to rise at 5:30 a.m. to begin work.

Between 1929 and 1940 Hemingway lost favor with the critics, as his writing went through an experimental stage. *Death in the Afternoon* (1932), an essay on Spanish bullfighting, and *Green Hills of Africa* (1935), an account of a safari, were both nonfiction works in which Hemingway became not only the author but a character in the story. Literary critic Edmund Wilson said of the latter, ". . . he has produced what must be the only book ever written which makes Africa and its animals seem dull." But by portraying himself as the courageous protagonist, Hemingway had begun promoting his public image as the gritty masculine hero.

In 1937 Hemingway was sent to Spain by the American Newspaper Alliance to cover the Spanish Civil War, waged between the Nationalists led by General Franco and Republican troops. The fruits of his trip, apart from the news articles, were the script for the pro-Republic documentary film *The Spanish Earth,* a play called *The Fifth Column,* and a few short stories. These works reflected Hemingway's support of the Republican cause, a position he held early in the war. But as the war went on, Hemingway's stance changed. While still unsympathetic toward Franco and his army, who were supported by Benito Mussolini and Adolf Hitler, he realized that the Republicans were far from innocent. He believed that the materials and advice the Republicans received from Stalinist Russia tainted the purity of their democratic cause.

His 1940 novel *For Whom the Bell Tolls* was an even-handed look at the conflict through the eyes of an American volunteer, Robert Jordan, fighting in a Republican guerrilla unit in the mountains of Spain. Set over just four days, it is the story of the tragic love affair between Jordan and a young Spanish woman, Maria.

Jordan accepts the Communist support of the Republicans, despite its flaws, because he sees it as a necessary evil in the defeat of Fascism. He is also a firm believer in the notion of the greater good for the greater number and is aware that after each mission, when he retreats to the safety of Madrid, those who have helped him will face the vengeful fury of Fascist forces. He is a detached and cold man who justifies the deaths of individuals as part of the sacrifice that must be made for the greater Spain. But his love for Maria teaches him that no man can cut himself off from other human beings. These feelings are conveyed in the title of the novel, which was taken from a meditation by John Donne.

For Whom the Bell Tolls marked Ernest Hemingway's return to favor with the critics and was also a popular success, selling 200,000 copies in the first two months of publication. Immediately after publication the writer was offered $100,000 for the film rights. Considered by many to be Hemingway's finest full-length novel it earned him, after more than a decade of decline, the reputation as one of America's greatest writers.

The 1943 film, starring Gary Cooper and Ingrid Bergman, won one Oscar and was nominated for eight more, including Best Picture. Although the script was penned by Dudley Nichols, who removed much of the political commentary that was contained within the book, the film's success only served to further enhance the standing of Hemingway.

NINETEEN EIGHTY-FOUR,
George Orwell, 1949

~~~

*No emotion was pure, because everything was mixed up
with fear and hatred. Their embrace had been a battle,
the climax a victory. It was a blow struck against the
Party. It was a political act.*

In 1946 George Orwell published an essay called "Why I
Write." In this work he attempted to summarize the driv-
ing force behind his works, the most famous of which, so
far, was the novel *Animal Farm*. His most strongly held
beliefs, he said, were a direct result of the fact that he did
not live in a peaceful age. He had worked in Burma for
the Indian Imperial Police, where he'd witnessed the
destructive side of imperialism. World War II had just
ended, causing him to view the world in a political light.
Even before the war his political beliefs were being shaped
by world events, turning him into what he described as a
"pamphleteer" for specific political movements.

"First I spent five years in an unsuitable profession (the
Indian Imperial Police, in Burma), and then I underwent
poverty and the sense of failure," he wrote. "This increased
my natural hatred of authority and made me for the first
time fully aware of the existence of the working classes,
and the job in Burma had given me some understanding
of the nature of imperialism: but these experiences were
not enough to give me an accurate political orientation.
Then came Hitler, the Spanish Civil War, etc . . ."

The Spanish Civil War in particular had an enormous effect on the Englishman. His beliefs in the cause were so strong that he traveled to the troubled nation in 1936 to fight for the Loyalists, but was forced to withdraw when, after just ten days at the front, he was shot in the neck. Thereafter, he says, he knew exactly where he stood politically.

> Every line of serious work that I have written since 1936 has been written, directly or indirectly, against totalitarianism and for democratic socialism, as I understand it. It seems to me nonsense, in a period like our own, to think that one can avoid writing of such subjects. Everyone writes of them in one guise or another. It is simply a question of which side one takes and what approach one follows. And the more one is conscious of one's political bias, the more chance one has of acting politically without sacrificing one's aesthetic and intellectual integrity . . .
>
> *Animal Farm* was the first book in which I tried, with full consciousness of what I was doing, to fuse political purpose and artistic purpose into one whole. I have not written a novel for seven years, but I hope to write another fairly soon. It is bound to be a failure, every book is a failure, but I do know with some clarity what kind of book I want to write.

In just a few paragraphs Orwell summed up the beliefs he had derived from a lifetime of unique experience. It was this experience of poverty, of imperialism, of propaganda, of socialism, of autocracy and of bureaucratic hypocrisy that went into the writing of the next book. The book would be released in 1949 and Orwell would give it the title *The Last Man in Europe,* but his publisher Fredric Warburg would convince him to change the name in order to make the book more marketable. The new title would be *Nineteen Eighty-Four.*

George Orwell, real name Eric Arthur Blair, was born in Motihari, India, in 1903. His father, Richard Walmesley Blair, worked for the British Civil Service in India, but his mother, Ida Mabel, took him to live in England when he was still a baby. Eric also had two sisters, Marjorie (older) and Avril (younger).

As a young boy Blair impressed academically and was awarded scholarships to St. Cyprian's School in Sussex, one of the United Kingdom's elite preparatory schools, and to Wellington College (where he completed one term) and Eton College, where he was a King's Scholar from 1917 to 1921, writing and editing two college publications. At Eton College Blair was taught French by Aldous Huxley, another ex-King's Scholar, who would go on to write *Brave New World.*

After graduating from St. Cyprian's, which he'd only been able to attend on account of the scholarships, his family couldn't afford to send him to college, so as a nineteen-year-old Blair followed in his father's footsteps and moved to Burma to join the Indian Imperial Police. Rather than developing a respect for English imperialism, Blair began to relate to the Burmese and their struggle against the oppression of their country's foreign rulers. After five years in Burma, disgusted with the "unsuitable profession" that he refers to in his essay "Why I Write," he took a few weeks leave back in England and during that time resigned from the Imperial Police to become a full-time writer.

Moving to Paris in 1928, Blair hoped to make money by writing and publishing short stories, but the publishing world was not yet interested in his words. His strong belief system was further developed when he was forced to take menial, low-paying jobs in order to simply survive. He would write about these experiences in the 1933 novel *Down and Out in Paris and London.* Blair's life in Paris was so unhealthy that he developed a serious case of pneumonia and, after recovering his strength but having completely run out of money, was forced to move back to the United Kingdom in 1929. There he lived at his parents' house in Suffolk and in East London and began working on novels while writing feature articles for magazines. He also briefly worked as a schoolteacher in Middlesex. Prior to the publication of *Down and Out,* Blair adopted the pen name George Orwell—which some say was to avoid embarrassing his family with his admissions of the goings-on during his life as a pauper, detailed within the book.

Ill health continued to dog the writer and forced him out of his teaching job. Between 1934 and 1936 he wrote novels and worked in a bookshop, but it was his book *The Road to Wigan Pier,* released in 1937, that would reconfirm his political beliefs. His research for the book, an in-depth account of the struggles of working-class miners in northern England, brought home to him the enormous gap between social classes in the United Kingdom, and Orwell felt he could no longer stand by and allow such injustice and inequality to cause hardship to the lower classes.

In December 1936, once he'd finished *The Road to Wigan Pier,* and the same year he'd married Eileen O'Shaughnessy, Orwell and his new wife traveled to Spain to help fight against the Nationalist uprising of Francisco Franco. After ten days on the front line he was forced to withdraw from fighting after being shot in the throat by a sniper early one morning. "This ought to please my wife, I thought; she had always wanted me to be wounded, which would save me from being killed when the great battle came," he wrote in an essay in which he describes the experience of being shot.

During his recovery Orwell stayed in Barcelona, where he and Eileen joined the Workers' Party of Marxist Unification—which strongly believed the working class needed to revolt in order to overthrow capitalism and defeat Franco. This philosophy, however, went against what the Spanish Communist Party believed, and when the Communists began to gain power they set out to purge the Workers' Party, going so far as to murder some of its members. Fearing for their lives, Orwell and his wife escaped back to England just in time for the buildup to World War II.

During the war Orwell joined the home guard and, against his beliefs, worked with the BBC Eastern Service. His job was to create propaganda programs that would help gain and retain the support of people on the Indian subcontinent for the British war effort. Orwell was said to have enjoyed the challenge of the job, while also feeling very dirty about what he was doing. When he resigned from this role with some savings in the bank, he was finally ready to write full time. The result, in 1944, was *Animal Farm*.

The next year Eileen died during an operation and, having recently adopted a baby boy (Richard Horatio Blair), Orwell worked in journalism in order to guarantee a reliable income for himself and the boy. *Animal Farm* proved to be a critical success, and also provided handsome royalties, but it would be his next book,

Nineteen Eighty-Four, released in 1949, that would prove to be his tour de force. Indeed, the book would be a product and culmination of its author's personal philosophies, political beliefs, and life experiences.

The book describes a futuristic world ruled by the omnipresent Big Brother, where citizens have few rights and are constantly watched over, and terrorized, by the Thought Police. The plot revolves around the miserable, lonely life of Winston Smith. Like Orwell, Smith despises the totalitarian state but still works at the Ministry of Truth, creating propaganda and altering historical documents in order to produce a new version of the past. As Orwell did for so long, Smith lives a squalid, lower-class existence and, in another similarity to his author, the lead character of *Nineteen Eighty-Four* eventually meets a woman who shares his passions and beliefs, and the two begin an illicit affair. As a result of his experiences during the Spanish Civil War and during World War II, Orwell had developed a hatred for such regimes as Stalin's Soviet Union and Hitler's Nazi Germany, and the society he developed in *Nineteen Eighty-Four* was modeled on these states.

In the society portrayed in *Nineteen Eighty-Four* there exist gaping chasms between the rights and lifestyles of the inner party, the outer party, and the hoi polloi. This parallels the way Orwell viewed English society as he lived among the downtrodden miners of northern England in order to research and write *The Road to Wigan Pier.* Just as enemies of the state were killed by the Communists in the Spanish Civil War, the role of the Thought Police in the novel is to hunt down and kill, or torture, those who threaten Big Brother's totalitarian regime. And the novel's failed revolution that could have saved society from becoming a monstrous, corrupt beast was, of course, related to the democratic socialist revolution that Orwell had hoped to encourage in Spain, and that he also had hoped would take place in England during World War II.

Nineteen Eighty-Four, perhaps more than any other novel, has left a permanent mark on society. It has changed the way people speak, adding such words and sayings to our vocabulary as "big brother is watching you," "doublethink," "thoughtcrime," "room 101," and "thought police," and oppressive regimes are now described as "Orwellian." Along with *Animal Farm,* Orwell's *Nineteen Eighty-Four* took political writing out of the creatively barren fields of academia and newspaper reportage and into the realm of entertainment and art.

In 1949, the same year his major work was released, Orwell was admitted to the hospital with tuberculosis, a disease he had been suffering from for several years. He died from the illness in January 1950, having squeezed a stunning amount of experience into his forty-six years of life.

THE CATCHER IN THE RYE,
J. D. Salinger, 1951

❧

*"What I have to do, I have to catch everybody if they
start to go over the cliff—I mean if they're running and
they don't look where they're going I have to come out
from somewhere and catch them. That's all I'd do all
day. I'd just be the catcher in the rye and all."*

Since 1980 J. D. Salinger has led the life of a recluse.
For more than twenty-five years the author has refused
all interviews and has not made a public appearance. In
1992 a fire at his New Hampshire home was seen by re-
porters as a rare opportunity to interview the writer. But
despite the journalists' best efforts, Salinger fled the scene
without detection. In the mid-90s news leaked of Salinger's intention to publish a book version of one of his
old short stories. The literary world spun itself into a
frenzy of excitement, but at the eleventh hour Salinger
pulled out of the deal. A Jewish Catholic by birth, and at
various times a follower of Scientology, Hinduism and
Zen Buddhism, Salinger, who has not published any new
work since 1965, is perhaps literature's greatest enigma.

Such is the intense mystery surrounding the author
that his only published novel, *The Catcher in the Rye*,
has achieved a level of fame reserved only for a few cultural icons. Although Salinger retreated from public life
shortly after its publication, there are other reasons the
novel became a phenomenon. Published in 1951 and set

in the late 1940s, *The Catcher in the Rye* managed to capture the timelessness and universality of teenage angst in such a way that for each new generation of readers their concerns, problems, and yearnings are easily aligned with those of the book's protagonist, Holden Caulfield.

The fact that the sixteen-year-old narrator tells the story as if on intimate terms with the reader lends the book enormous emotional impact. He pulls the reader into his world in such a way that the author doesn't seem to exist. How did a thirty-two-year-old writer who had seen the horrors of war capture so brilliantly the voice of an alienated, oddball teenager? The answer lies in the life and times of J. D. Salinger.

Jerome David Salinger was born in 1919 to Solomon and Miriam Salinger. Jerome's father was an importer of European cheeses and meats and his Scottish mother had changed her religion and her name (she was born Marie) to marry the Jewish Solomon. The Salingers led an affluent life in an impressive apartment overlooking the streets of Manhattan. The view from the apartment on the corner of Park Avenue and East 91st Street was Salinger's world view until he was fifteen years old.

An unmotivated and unimpressive student, when the writer was in his mid-teens his father enrolled him in the Valley Forge Military Academy in Pennsylvania. Jerome was not a troublesome boy, but Solomon Salinger hoped a more disciplined environment would drum some drive into his shiftless son. At military school Salinger managed to achieve respectable grades, joined the dramatics society, and was literary editor of the school's yearbook.

However, on graduating in 1936 the seventeen-year-old reverted to old habits. He enrolled at New York University briefly, but in 1937 Solomon decided to take matters into his own hands once again and packed his son off to Europe to learn the family business. Living in Vienna for five months, Salinger perfected his French and German speaking skills but did not discover a passion for the importing business. When Salinger returned to the United States he lasted only one semester at Ursinus College in Pennsylvania.

In 1939 Salinger enrolled in Whit Burnett's writing class at Columbia University. Burnett was the founding editor of *Story* magazine, and Salinger found in the evening class what he had long been searching for—a calling. Finding his niche in the short story genre, the twenty-year-old writer impressed Burnett with his talent. In the following year in the March/April issue of *Story,* Salinger's first short story, "The Young Folks," was published.

For Salinger, the publication of "The Young Folks" began a period of intense writing in the 1940s for such titles as *The New Yorker, Collier's, Good Housekeeping, Cosmopolitan, Esquire,* the *Saturday Evening Post,* and *Story.* Such was his enthusiasm that not even a world war could bring a halt to the young writer's creative output. In 1942 Salinger entered the army and he was shipped to Europe in 1944. Following training in army intelligence, Salinger took part in the D-Day invasion of Europe, participated in a number of heavy combat battles, and entered Paris on the day the capital was liberated from the Nazis. It was in Paris that he struck up a friendship with Ernest Hemingway, who was acting as a war correspondent. Still the writing did not cease. In a letter that Staff Sergeant Salinger sent to Whit Burnett in 1944 the author wrote, "Am still writing whenever I can find the time and an unoccupied foxhole." According to legend, one soldier in his division could recall Salinger carrying a typewriter in his jeep and, on one occasion, typing under a table while the area was being bombed.

When the war ended Salinger returned to New York City and found a home in Greenwich Village among the area's bohemian crowd of writers and artists.

In total Salinger completed twenty-one short stories between 1941 and 1948. The themes of these tales ranged from social conventions and family relationships to the corruption of innocence and the psychological effects of war. Although they appeared in high profile publications at the time, the works remain uncollected to this day. One of the most popular stories ever published in *The New Yorker* was *A Perfect Day for Bananafish* (1948). Not only did it make Salinger one of the magazine's best-known authors, but it also introduced the world to the Glass family. The lives of this talented and troubled family are chronicled in the main body of Salinger's short stories, most of which were published by *The New Yorker*.

Salinger also wrote a second series of short stories featuring the members of another family—the Caulfields. Numbering eight in total, these preliminary sketches for the novel *The Catcher in the Rye* feature a character named Holden Caulfield. In "Last Day of the Last Furlough" (*Saturday Evening Post,* 1945) Holden is a soldier missing in action. In "Slight Rebellion Off Madison," (*The New Yorker,* 1946) teenager Holden is on vacation from Pencey Prep, and in "I'm Crazy" (*Collier's,* 1945) Holden narrates the story.

Other characters from the novel are also included in these stories but, like Holden, they are not always the exact same person presented in the novel. For instance, "This Sandwich Has No Mayonnaise" (*Esquire,* 1945) is narrated by Vincent Caulfield, whose character became Holden's brother D.B. in *The Catcher in the Rye*. And the unpublished "The Last and Best of the Peter Pans" (1942) features a reference to a child being caught while crawling off a cliff. The other three stories in the Caulfield collection are the unpublished "The Ocean Full of Bowling Balls" (1945), "A Boy in France" (*Saturday Evening Post,* 1945), and "The Stranger" (*Collier's,* 1945). The latter is the last chronologically in the Caulfield series and, by the end of this story, all three Caulfield brothers—Vincent, Kenneth (later Allie in *The Catcher in the Rye*), and Holden—are dead!

But Salinger wasn't about to let Holden Caulfield rest in peace. The author believed the character deserved a full-length novel of his own, and as a result *The Catcher in the Rye* was published in 1951. Narrated by sixteen-year-old Holden Caulfield, *The Catcher in the Rye* follows the teenager's encounters in Manhattan following his expulsion from Pencey Prep in Pennsylvania for not applying himself. The reader is given the impression that Holden's stream-of-consciousness monologue is being told while recovering in a mental hospital in California.

The cynical adolescent is haunted by his younger brother, Allie, who died three years earlier from leukemia. In Holden's mind Allie was the perfect child, and now everything he encounters in the adult world he views as hypocritical and phoney. He feels he must protect the children of the world from this corruption and be the "catcher in the rye," a title he adopts from a Robert Burns poem. Holden mistakenly thinks the line from the poem is "When a body *catch* a body, comin' through the rye" rather than "When a body *meet* a body, coming through the rye." Interpreting the line literally, Holden imagines children playing in a field of rye close to a precipice and sees himself as the person who must save them before they fall.

At every turn Holden encounters the ugliness of the adult world and, as his ten-year-old sister, Phoebe, explains, he just doesn't like anything that's happening. When he comes across four-letter curse words graffitied on the walls of his sister's school, for instance, he worries about the effect they will have on the children who see them. At the end of the novel he sits crying with joy as he watches a happy Phoebe riding on the Central Park carousel. It begins to rain torrentially but Holden refuses to move, as he is overcome with happiness. Although nothing is spelled out for the reader, one assumes the troubled boy has realized he cannot be the savior of all children, and this awareness is the first step in his recovery.

After its publication the novel quickly jumped to number four on the *New York Times* bestseller list and today is a staple on high school reading lists, selling approximately 250,000 copies each year. The success of the book most likely has to do with its timelessness, the sense that Holden could be any sixteen-year-old at any time in any city. As Salinger himself said, "There's no more to Holden Caulfield. Read the book again. It's all there. Holden Caulfield is only a frozen moment in time."

From Here to Eternity,
James Jones, 1951

❦

> *Men had come from the Dayrooms to the porches to lis-*
> *ten in the darkness, feeling the sudden choking kinship*
> *bred of fear that supersedes all personal tastes. They stood*
> *in the darkness of the porches, listening, feeling suddenly*
> *very near the man beside them, who also was a soldier,*
> *who also must die.*

The author of what is arguably the most definitive novel on the experience of going to war, James Jones once summed up what it is to be a soldier by saying, "I think that when all the nationalistic or ideological and patriotic slogans are put aside, all the straining to convince a soldier that he is dying for something, it is the individual soldier's final full acceptance of the fact that his name is already written down in the rolls of the already dead." Jones spoke from experience. He'd seen combat during World War II when he was enlisted in the U.S. Army from 1939 until 1944. This experience was to shape the rest of his life. Jones hoped to capture the essence of the soldier during three different stages of war, and the first novel in this trilogy would be named *From Here to Eternity.*

James Ramon Jones was born in Robinson, Illinois, in 1921 to a middle-class family. However, when the stock market crashed in 1929 his father, Ramon, a dentist, fell on hard times and the family suffered financially. Struggling throughout the 1930s to make ends meet and to support his ill wife and son, Ramon sought solace in alcohol. In order to escape his troubled home life and no longer be a financial burden, when James graduated from high school he turned his back on further education and joined the army.

He was stationed in New York, Puerto Rico, and California and then, on the eve of America's involvement in World War II, the teenage soldier was transferred to Schofield Barracks in Hawaii. Nicknamed the Boxing Company, the 19th Infantry was stationed near Honolulu and Jones, with his heavy build, became an integral part of the Golden Gloves boxing tournaments. It was while stationed at Schofield that Jones discovered his passion for writing after reading Thomas Wolfe's semi-autobiographical *Look Homeward, Angel*. Jones has since listed as his other literary influences William Faulkner, Ernest Hemingway, F. Scott Fitzgerald, John Steinbeck, Henry James, Nathaniel Hawthorne, James Joyce, and Fyodor Dostoevsky.

On the morning of December 7, 1941, the unimaginable happened. Sitting in the mess hall, Jones and others heard the sound of aircraft and bombing in the distance; at first they believed the noises were coming from Wheeler Airbase nearby. The men became alarmed when the explosions came closer. Rushing to the door of the mess tent, Jones ducked low as a Japanese bomber roared low above the barracks. Others who witnessed the scene claimed the enemy plane was so low that the gunner sitting in the rear of the aircraft gave a wave and a smile to the stunned soldiers. Jones, who'd recently turned twenty, realized history was being written.

Jones survived the Japanese attack, and with the United States now formally involved in the war he awaited deployment to a combat zone. During this time Jones enrolled in writing courses at the University of Hawaii, the first step in his newly discovered dream to become a writer. In 1942 Jones was shipped to the Solomon Islands and then, in the following year, saw combat during the Battle of Guadalcanal, a significant victory for the Allied forces. Injured in battle, Jones received the Bronze Star and the Purple Heart and was honorably discharged from the army in 1944.

Shortly after returning home to Robinson, Illinois, Jones moved to New York City and enrolled for a semester at New York University. This was as far as his formal education in writing went, explaining in an interview with the *Paris Review* in 1958 that education can injure a writer. He said, "Most of the desultory courses that I've taken in literature have had a peculiar snobbism about them. An adulation of certain writers is inculcated in the student by the instructor, who is probably a frustrated writer anyway, to the point where the student finds himself asking whether he has anything to say that Tolstoy or James haven't already said better."

Although Jones became disillusioned with the education system, his time in New York proved fruitful for another reason. It was there he met Maxwell Perkins, an editor at the publishing company Charles Scribner's Sons. Jones had been working on a novel called *They Shall Inherit the Laughter,* a story based on his experiences postwar returning to Robinson, Illinois. Jones submitted a first draft of this novel to Scribner's, but it was rejected. However, the editor recognized Jones's obvious talent and gave the twenty-four-year-old an advance of $500 to write something else—a novel based on his experiences at Schofield Army Barracks. After several rejections

They Shall Inherit the Laughter was eventually published as *Some Came Running,* in 1957.

Jones immediately returned to Illinois and began work on what was to become *From Here to Eternity*. It took the author five years to complete the 861-page epic about army life prior to and immediately following the Japanese attack on Pearl Harbor. Jones intended *Eternity* to be the first installment of a trilogy that examined the process of becoming a soldier. *The Thin Red Line* (1962) looked at jungle fighting in Guadalcanal and *Whistle* (1978), which was published posthumously, chronicled the life of wounded soldiers recovering in a Memphis hospital. Running throughout the three books are two personae; in *Eternity* they are named Robert E. Lee Prewitt and Milton Warden. Of the three novels Jones stated, "It will say just about everything I have ever had to say, or will ever have to say, on the human condition of war and what it means to us, as against what we claim it means to us."

The beautifully written narrative tells the tale of the experiences of the soldiers in G Company at Schofield Barracks in Hawaii in 1941. Prewitt, like his creator, joins the army to escape the Great Depression. An exceptional bugle player and boxer, he refuses to box for his company after blinding an opponent in the ring. His stand infuriates his superiors and, in order to break him, they carry out "the treatment"—a series of soul-destroying measures designed to physically and mentally cripple. Sergeant Milton Warden, also a soldier of integrity and principle, begins a passionate affair with the philandering wife of his corrupt commanding officer. Originally instigated as an act of rebellion against his superior, Warden falls in love with the woman and must deal with the consequences of their relationship.

Even though Jones's vision for *Eternity* was one part of a greater whole, the author allowed the lengthy story to evolve organically without keeping a tight rein on the narrative. He gave the characters their own life and never planned, for instance, that Warden would have an affair. But when a connection between the two characters developed three hundred pages into the work, the author revised what he already had written to accommodate the relationship.

The novel detailed the corruption of the officer class and the brutal violence that was often carried out on soldiers under their orders. This, teamed with the open sexuality displayed on its pages, proved a sensation with the buying public. With a title taken from the Rudyard Kipling poem "Gentlemen-Rankers," the power in the novel lies in the conflicts faced by Prewitt and Warden. Both are bound to an establishment that is brutal, corrupt, and uncivilized, yet their willingness to die for it goes far beyond duty.

Much editing had to be carried out before the novel was printed because of its explicit violence, sexuality, and use of obscenity, but within a month of its release *From Here to Eternity* had sold 90,000 copies and the film rights immediately were purchased by Columbia pictures for $87,000. With the profits from the novel Jones established a writers' colony in Illinois. Despite the book's length, critics praised it. The *New York Times Book Review* said, "When a book is as commanding in its narrative power as this one it bears comparison with the very best that is being done in American fiction today. *From Here to Eternity* is the work of a major new American novelist. To anyone who reads this immensely long and deeply convincing story of life in the peacetime army it will be apparent that in James Jones an original and utterly honest talent has restored American realism to a preeminent place in world literature."

The novel edged out *The Catcher in the Rye* to win the National Book Award in 1952 and was named one of the 100 Best Novels of the 20th Century by the Modern Library. There is no doubt Jones tapped deeply into his own military career and experience when writing *Eternity,* and when asked by the *Paris Review* why he wrote, the author responded, "Well, I suppose you could say that I want to impose my personality upon the world . . . You must really want to tell the truth about yourself, and no matter what any writer says, every character he creates is a part of himself, romanticized or unromanticized. But in order to do this you have to get down into yourself and try to find out what it is that makes us desire certain things and be afraid of other things."

CASINO ROYALE,
Ian Fleming, 1953

❧

As he tied his thin, double-ended, black satin tie, he paused for a moment and examined himself levelly in the mirror. His grey-blue eyes looked calmly back with a hint of ironical inquiry and the short lock of black hair which would never stay in place slowly subsided to form a thick comma above his right eyebrow.

While the exploits of superspy James Bond are fantasy and far from autobiographical, the creation of Her Majesty's most ruthless and suave secret agent only came about as a result of the many and varied life experiences of his author, Ian Fleming.

Ian Lancaster Fleming was born in London in May 1908, to Evelyn and Valentine Fleming. His grandfather Robert Fleming was a wealthy Scottish banker. His father, a land owner and Conservative MP, was a trusted friend of Winston Churchill. Being born into such an exceptional bloodline was both a blessing and a curse for the Flemings' second son—while his pedigree provided him with a privileged life, he soon discovered there was much to live up to.

As a boy Fleming attended the exclusive Durnford Boarding School in Dorset, where he excelled at sports and enjoyed reading the adventure novels of Robert Louis Stevenson and John Buchan. Leading an idyllic life, the nine-year-old's life was disrupted in 1917 when his father was killed in action during World War I. Post-humously awarded the Distinguished Service Order for meritorious actions in war, his lengthy obituary, which appeared in the *Times,* was written by Churchill. Suddenly the nine-year-old not only had to meet his family's exacting standards, but also faced the extra pressure of living up to the image of a larger-than-life war hero.

After Durnford, Fleming attended the elite private school Eton but found academic studies difficult. Although the adolescent excelled at athletics, winning the Victor Ludorum ("the winner of the games") two years running, his successes were always overshadowed by his older brother Peter, who was a gifted scholar and also a talented writer.

A daring and witty teenager, Fleming enjoyed testing the tempers of his teachers and pushing the limits of authority. Consequently, after graduation his mother thought the Royal Military Academy Sandhurst might provide some discipline for her reckless son, but the rigid atmosphere did not suit a young man with an independent streak. Fleming left the institution without taking an officer's commission after he was caught out after curfew. It was a frustrating time for Fleming, now in his early twenties, as he attempted to carve out an identity for himself separate from his father and brother.

After his ignoble departure from Sandhurst, he was sent abroad by his mother to study languages with the aim of taking the Foreign Office Entrance examination. Initially living in Austria, then Munich and Geneva, Fleming thrived. Away from the high expectations of his family and the unbending regulations of Eton and Sandhurst, Fleming found the freedom to forge his own path among people who knew nothing of his father the war hero and brother the well-known travel writer. Handsome, dashing, confident, and with a keen sense of humor, Fleming impressed all who he became acquainted with, particularly if they were female.

Fleming may have discovered himself in Europe, but he still didn't manage to discover what he wished to do with his life. Failing the Foreign Office entrance examinations, Fleming thought he would try his hand at writing. He'd never previously shown much interest in writing, but he was a true lover of books and took pride in the poetry and prose in which he'd dabbled while in Europe.

Gaining a position with Reuters in 1931, Fleming came into his own as a journalist. Honing his skills, the twenty-three-year-old learned to write quickly, concisely, and accurately. Furthermore, he impressed his bosses and colleagues with his coverage from Moscow of an infamous espionage trial involving a number of Royal Engineers in 1933.

Despite success as a journalist, the job did not pay enough to support Fleming's self-indulgent lifestyle. The young man-about-town hosted elegant dinner parties in his Belgravia flat and participated in high-stakes bridge games. Furthermore, with his crop of black hair, piercing blue eyes, and slim athletic body, Fleming developed a reputation as a notorious ladies' man.

He also indulged his love of books, acquiring an outstanding collection of first editions. Ranging from *The Origin of Species* to *Mein Kampf* and *Scouting for Boys*, Fleming eventually boasted six hundred books in his private library. He played golf religiously, loved fast cars, and treated himself to the highest quality food and alcohol.

But this lifestyle required funding and, due to a complicated inheritance, Fleming would receive no family money until his mother passed away. He decided, therefore, to enter the family business—banking. But he was easily tempted by risky investments and soon realized making money for other people was not his area of expertise, later describing himself as "the world's worst stockbroker."

Since his father's death Fleming had attempted to find his place in the world. From rebellious student to successful journalist to disastrous banker, he had yet to find his vocation. But in 1939, when Germany invaded Poland, the thirty-one-year-old finally found his true calling.

When World War II erupted Fleming joined the Royal Navy and was commissioned as a lieutenant in the Intelligence branch. An exceptional officer with a flair for subterfuge, Fleming soon was promoted to commander. Working as the assistant to the director of Naval Intelligence, Fleming coordinated Operation Goldeneye. A plan to maintain communication with Gibraltar should Spain join the Axis powers, Operation Goldeneye was crucial to Britain's defense of Europe.

He also worked as part of the team responsible for cracking the Nazi's Enigma code, and soon took charge of 30 Assault Unit, a team of specialized commandos that Fleming regularly sent on various top-secret intelligence missions.

Having finally found a niche in life, Fleming thrived. The navy opened up the world to the Englishman, who traveled to France, Spain, and North Africa. But it was a visit to Jamaica in 1945 that steered Fleming in a new direction. Visiting the Caribbean island for a conference, he was mesmerized by the tropical paradise, where there was no war rationing, no food shortages, where rum flowed like water and plentiful fruit literally was rotting on the trees. Fleming bought a small piece of land by a coral reef on which he built a bungalow. He called the house Goldeneye.

Unable to afford to live in Jamaica full time, Fleming returned to England after the war and was hired by the newspaper magnate Lord Kemsley to manage the foreign news sections in several of his newspapers. Audaciously, Fleming accepted the job on the proviso that he could take two months of vacation each year, and for the next six years Fleming traveled each winter to Jamaica.

During the war, Fleming had begun an affair with a married woman, Lady Anne Rothermere. In 1952, she became pregnant, and he realized he would have to settle down into a more reliable, predictable lifestyle. Waiting for Anne's divorce to be finalized, Fleming retreated to Goldeneye, called upon all of his life experiences thus far, and penned the first draft of a spy thriller called *Casino Royale*. The author later joked that he only began working on the book as a distraction from his upcoming marriage.

Completing the first draft in just two months, Fleming drew on various wartime experiences to fill the pages of *Casino Royale*. Likewise, the story's hero bore a remarkable resemblance to the author himself. A handsome and cultured Lothario, Bond had served as a Commander in the Royal Navy. A mass of contradictions, the secret agent with a double-O, license-to-kill prefix was a sophisticated womanizer who struggled with the role of merciless assassin.

The character's name was borrowed from the American ornithologist author of *The Ultimate Guide to Birds in the West Indies,* a book Fleming had in his eclectic collection. The author admitted he chose the name because it was "brief, unromantic, Anglo-Saxon, and yet very masculine—just what I needed."

Casino Royale was the launching pad for a cultural phenomenon, with readers introduced to the Russian spy agency SMERSH, a lethal, high-rolling villain known as Le Chiffre, and the very first Bond girl, Vesper Lynd. The narrative was fast paced, the writing concise, the descriptions sensuous, and the violence palpable.

With the novel complete, Fleming rewarded himself with a custom-made gold-plated typewriter and sent the manuscript to his friend William Plomer, a poet and reader for publisher Jonathan Cape. Plomer immediately saw the sales potential of the novel, even though it lacked literary merit, and recommended it to his employers. Published in 1953, Fleming admitted he targeted the novel ". . . somewhere between the solar plexus and, well, the upper thigh."

Casino Royale was derided by one critic as being filled with "sex, sadism and snobbery." Likewise, a critic for the *New York Times,* having enjoyed the first part of the story, wrote, "But then he decides to pad out the book . . . and leads the weary reader through a set of tough clichés to an ending which surprises no one, save operative 007."

Nevertheless the novel, launched at the height of the Cold War, captured the public's imagination and achieved moderate success. Each year subsequently, until his death in 1964, Fleming returned to Goldeneye and wrote another Bond thriller, resulting in eleven more novels and nine short stories. While popular, the stories didn't become the cultural phenomenon we know them as today until the author sold the film rights to producers Harry Saltzman and Albert R. "Cubby" Broccoli in 1962, but a film version of Fleming's very first Bond novel wouldn't be released until 2006.

LORD OF THE FLIES,
William Golding, 1954

❧

> *Piggy and Ralph, under the threat of the sky, found them-*
> *selves eager to take a place in this demented but partly secure*
> *society. They were glad to touch the brown backs of the*
> *fence that hemmed in the terror and made it governable.*
>
> "Kill the beast! Cut his throat! Spill his blood!"

One particular event from William Golding's child-hood in England was so memorable for its surprisingly high levels of fear and violence that he still recalled it clearly as he wrote his memoirs over half a century later. As he grew up Golding spent a great deal of time enter-taining himself and as a result was an accomplished reader from a very young age, but on this occasion he was on the local common playing cricket with his older brother Joseph, whom he called "Jose," and some other children. William swung the wooden bat and missed the ball, only to see the bat continue its trajectory and slam into the side of his brother's head.

Jose turned and ran in the direction of home without even muttering a sound. It was William who whimpered in anguish, then dropped the bat and ran after his brother. As he chased his older and faster brother across the com-mon, many thoughts and emotions ran through his mind, including how badly he might have hurt Jose, and how much trouble he'd be in at home. "I trundled back across the common and down the road to the green, my fears growing deeper. I can just remember them," he wrote in his memoirs, *Scenes from a Life*. "I ended at the house, terrified and now as silent as my brother. I remember no more. But years later my parents told me that Jose had described the whole scene to them. He wasn't really hurt they said. But I crept in to the house with my terror and hid from everyone else under the dining room table."

The joys and fears of childhood would come to fascinate Golding who, even as a young teenager, was mature and knowledgeable enough to know that the happy endings of the teamwork-based adventures described in R. M. Ballantyne's 1857 novel *The Coral Island,* about three boys stranded on an idyllic Polynesian island, were not what would really happen if boys were left to their own devices. *The Coral Island* was just one of the thousands of books that Golding devoured as a child growing up in a family that rarely spent time together, but it was one that would have a profound effect.

Golding was born in 1911 in Cornwall and grew up in Wiltshire in the southwest of England, returning to Cornwall for family vacations. Unlike children in the major cities of the United Kingdom, young Golding was able to enjoy adventures on beaches, in forests, and on coastal cliffs, but still his preferred form of escapism was in the pages of books. His father, Alec Golding, was a science master at Marlborough Grammar School in Wiltshire. Alec hoped his second son would grow up to be a scientist. William's mother, Mildred (née Curnoe), was an active supporter of the suffragette movement, unintentionally giving her sons a solid education in the sometimes grim realities of British politics.

Golding attended his father's school before earning a place at Brasenose College at Oxford University in 1930 where, to his father's delight, he studied natural sciences. But after two years his love of language proved greater than his interest in science and he transferred to English literature, graduating with a degree in 1934. That year he would publish his first book via Macmillan & Co. in London—not a novel but instead a collection of works of poetry titled *Poems*.

After college Golding took a job as a teacher of English at a school in South London's Streatham, where he worked for two years before returning to Oxford to study a Diploma of Education. In the meantime he worked as a teacher at Bishop Wordsworth's School in Salisbury. Once his diploma was complete in 1938, he moved on to Maidstone Grammar School. His experiences with the children at each of these schools would be a vital ingredient in his first and most famous novel, *Lord of the Flies*. The children confirmed his prior beliefs in the unpredictability of their own behavior and their unprincipled nature when it came to dealing with one another, and with life in general, outside the guidance of their elders.

Soon Golding also would have a child of his own. Having met chemist Ann Brookfield in 1938 and married in 1939, the two had a son, David, in 1940. But as war had broken out, Golding left his teaching job to join the navy, so he would not be around for large parts of his boy's early years.

Having experienced some of the anarchistic tendencies of young children during his time as a teacher, in the navy Golding witnessed firsthand the terror that adults were capable of wreaking upon one another. He served on battleships in the North Atlantic and had some involvement in the exhaustive and ultimately brutally successful pursuit and sinking of the German battleship

Bismarck. He also worked in Liverpool and Bucking-hamshire, served in New York helping bring ships built in New Jersey dockyards back to the United Kingdom, and commanded a rocket-equipped landing craft during the D-Day landings.

When the war ended, Golding returned to teaching and, with the adventure and experience of being at sea during the war still fresh in his mind, began to write his first novel. His experiences over the previous decade quite clearly had demonstrated to him the fragility of society, the lessened value of the life of an individual, the barbarism of war, the possibility of civilization being brought to its knees by the irresponsible use of power, and the danger posed by an unfit leader. All of these themes would shape the plot of his novel, which he tentatively titled *Strangers from Within*.

Like Ballantyne's *The Coral Island*, his book followed the lives of a group of boys stranded on an island, this time as a result of war. Ballantyne's main characters were Ralph, Jack, and Peterkin; Golding's lead characters were Ralph, Jack, and "Piggy." Both novels began with the boys enjoying their freedom on islands with plentiful resources for their survival. But where Ballantyne's characters faced challenges as a team and always overcame the odds, Golding's boys would create a society closer to the one that Golding himself had come to know—one where peace and security were never guaranteed, where power struggles and tyranny created savage behavior, where blind faith toward a person or a philosophy led a group to commit acts of barbarity. A very approachable and digestible piece of storytelling, Golding's novel nonetheless provided a vivid insight into the author's beliefs on moral and political philosophy. It vividly illustrated the rarely discussed fact that everybody has a duality of personality, a darkness in their heart, a form of evil that manifests itself in certain situations and that allows perfectly reasonable men to go to war and kill each other for no purpose other than the fact that their leader told them to.

Golding said his novel was inspired by the amoral nature of school boys, with whom he'd had plenty of experience during years of teaching, as well as his experience of war and the "vileness beyond words" of the fascist and totalitarian regimes. Memories of his own childhood, of course, helped shape the work, including the brutal fear and guilty excitement he felt the day he accidentally hit his brother with a cricket bat.

The book was rejected by about ten publishers but in 1953 was accepted by Faber and Faber in London and, the next year, was published as *Lord of the Flies.* The title was a literal translation of "Beelzebub" as well as the name the boys in the book gave to the severed pig's head on a stake. At first the book experienced unimpressive sales and was soon out of print, but within a few years demand picked up as education departments recognized the symbolic nature of the story. By 1960 it became required reading in many schools and colleges in the United Kingdom and the United States, as it remains to this day.

The success of *Lord of the Flies* meant Golding, whose wife, Ann, had given birth to a second child, Judith, in 1945, could give up teaching and write full time. He produced sixteen major works before his death in June 1993, by which time he had won the Booker Prize in 1980 with *Rites of Passage,* been awarded the Nobel Prize for Literature in 1983, and been knighted in 1988.

LOLITA,
Vladimir Nabokov, 1955

❧

Lolita, light of my life, fire of my loins. My sin, my soul.
Lo-lee-ta: the tip of the tongue taking a trip of three steps
down the palate to tap, at three, on the teeth. Lo. Lee. Ta.

The literary world, perhaps more than any other artistic field, is a fickle place. How else could a manuscript for what is now said to be one of the greatest novels of the twentieth century have been rejected by every publisher to which it was originally sent? Why else was its author, already a well-respected writer in several countries across many continents, forced to accept publication via a purveyor of pornographic titles? And why was that author made to live in permanent exile from his country of birth, even after he had become famous around the globe?

The story of Vladimir Vladimirovich Nabokov, unlike so many writers, is not one of intense suffering, crippling poverty, or constant struggle—the writer was born into aristocracy. By the time Vladimir was born in April 1899, the Nabokov dynasty had enjoyed a long and proud history as one of Russia's most noble families. While their home was in St. Petersburg, the family owned large properties in various cities as well as luxurious country estates. Taking care of the family and their many properties was a battalion of servants.

His father, Vladimir Dimitrievich Nabokov, was a lawyer as well as a sometime politician and journalist.

He and his wife, Elena Ivanovna, insisted on the finest education for their children. Hence from 1911 to 1917 young Vladimir was sent to the Tenishev School, known at the time as one of St. Petersburg's finest and most innovative educational establishments. When not at school, during extended vacations, he was tutored by experts. At home his parents spoke Russian, English, and French, so from a very young age Nabokov was trilingual. As a result of his privileged surrounds he often referred to his upbringing as an English one rather than a typical Russian childhood.

In 1917, however, during the Russian Revolution (also known as the February Revolution), the Nabokov family, along with many other aristocratic families, was forced to flee the country for what they assumed would be a temporary exile. For eighteen months they stayed on a friend's estate in the autonomous republic of Crimea, and when they realized the exile from their homeland would, in fact, be a permanent one, they emigrated to England. Having managed to leave Russia with a good amount of their wealth (trusted servants had helped smuggle jewelry and other valuable items out of the country), Nabokov's parents made sure his education would continue in England. In 1919 he was sent to Trinity College at Cambridge University, where he studied languages.

Upon graduation in 1923, Nabokov moved to Berlin, where his family had settled in 1920. One year earlier his father had been shot dead in Berlin by Russian monarchists as he attempted to protect exiled Democratic Party leader Pavel Miliukov during a political rally. Still reeling from the death of the man who gave him everything, Nabokov immersed himself in Berlin's rich literary world, which was heavily populated by exiled Russians. There he began writing, and in order to supplement the dwindling funds from his family trust he also became a private tutor of languages and a tennis coach. His original works were written under the name Vladimir Sirin, in order to avoid confusion with his late father, whose mistaken violent death would become a theme in several of his son's works.

Nabokov's first novels, including *Mary* (1926), *King, Queen, Knave* (1928), and *Glory* (1932), were written in Russian. He produced ten novels or novellas between 1926 and 1938, and those that were published received critical acclaim within the literary circles of Berlin and Paris. But their small sales figures within these regions meant becoming a full-time novelist was not a financially viable option. In his novel *The Gift* (1938), however, there was a hint as to the story that would one day make this writer one of the most successful in history. In the book a minor character discusses what he considers to be a great idea for a novel, suggesting that a story about a man who becomes so obsessed with a young girl that he courts and marries her widowed mother would make great tragic reading, thanks to its themes of temptation and eternal torment.

Nabokov was, in fact, expressing his own belief that this story would make a fascinating novel. The very next year, in 1939, he wrote *The Enchanter,* a novella that was unpublished (finally published in 1986, nine years after Nabokov's death), which told the story of a pedophile who works his way into the life of a twelve-year-old girl by marrying her mother, whose ill health means her life is soon to end. The protagonist's intentions are to make the girl his sex slave once her mother is out of the picture.

His plans, however, go awry when the girl refuses his advances in a hotel room. As she screams he panics, runs outside, and is run down by a passing truck.

The novella disappeared into Nabokov's enormous collection of unpublished written work, but the idea for another novel that further explored such a theme stayed with the author. In the meantime he had married Russian Jew Vera Slonim in 1925 and together they had a son, Dmitri, in 1934. To escape the ugliness being created in Berlin by the Nazi party, the family moved to Paris in 1937, where he wrote *The Real Life of Sebastian Knight,* his first novel in English. In 1939 Nabokov's mother died in Prague, and as German troops approached Paris in 1940, Nabokov took his wife and son to California, where he'd been offered a summer-school posting at Stanford University as a lecturer in Russian and European literature.

Over the next two decades he would hold several academic positions and also find time to pursue his love of lepidoptera, researching the order of butterflies and moths. He was responsible for much of the butterfly collection at Harvard University's Museum of Comparative Zoology, which still contains many of the specimens he collected during several field trips. Between 1949 and 1959, in fact, he is said to have traveled over 150,000 miles throughout the United States in order to research butterflies in the wild.

In between all of this, though, Nabokov still found time to write. During the 1940s he had begun to develop a reputation in the U.S. literary world as a fine writer, with some of his short works being published in *The New Yorker* and the *Atlantic.* In 1947 Nabokov produced *Bend Sinister,* a novel about a European nation ruled by a party that arrests and imprisons anybody who shows dissent. But it would be his next novel, a work that had been brewing in his mind for more than a decade, that would add his name to the list of the twentieth century's greatest writers.

Over six years, while lecturing at universities, traveling to collect butterfly specimens, and translating his previous works into English, Nabokov crafted what he considered to be his greatest work. It was the story of a pedophile, Humbert Humbert, also the narrator, who becomes transfixed by a young girl by the name of Dolores Haze—his Lolita. A beautifully balanced novel, it tells the story of the development of the physical and emotional relationship between the man and the girl, followed by the inevitable unraveling of that partnership and the destructive effects on everybody it touches.

Completed in 1954, *Lolita* proved a difficult sell to publishers. Nabokov simply was unable to find a U.S. publisher for the controversial work, and his search for publishers in Europe was equally fruitless until he received interest from the Olympia Press publishing house in Paris. While Olympia Press had published some books of literary value in the past, it was also well known for peddling smut, including a series of sex novels boasting titles such as *With Open Mouth* and *White Thighs*. Nabokov knew that his book's controversial content meant mainstream publishers would shy away, so in 1955 he signed up with Olympia Press, and the original print run, a tiny five thousand copies, sold out. Nabokov had only ever experienced mild success with his books, so he expected no more from his beautifully written story. "Writing has always been for me a blend of dejection and high spirits, a torture and a pastime—but I never expected it to be a source of income," he said during a 1964 interview for *Life* magazine. "On the other hand, I have often dreamt of a long and exciting career as an obscure curator of lepidoptera in a great museum."

But the book was not yet ready to disappear. During an interview with the London *Times* author Graham Greene mentioned that he'd read *Lolita* and that, in his opinion, it was one of the greatest books of the year. In response John Gordon, editor of a competing newspaper, the *Sunday Express,* wrote an editorial blasting the book for the fact that it was pornography posing as high literature. He claimed it was "the filthiest book I've ever read."

The resulting public uproar resulted in a ban on the book in the United Kingdom and France. Of course the ban, which lasted two years in France, only served to publicize the book around the globe, and it wasn't long before American publishers began to wonder what all the fuss was about. After U.S. officials gave up on a half-hearted attempt to ban the few copies of the book that were already in the country, publishers G.P. Putnam's Sons, who in 1955 had published Norman Mailer's controversially sexual *Deer Park,* bought the rights to *Lolita* and in 1958 it became the first book in the United States since *Gone with the Wind* to sell more than 100,000 copies in its first three weeks.

Rather than seeing it as a smutty work of pornography or pedophilia, critics praised the novel and its author for the skill with which it was written. Some went as far as calling it the ultimate love story of the twentieth century. Most importantly for Nabokov, it meant he had found the financial freedom to write full time. His days as a lecturer were over and finally he could experience a little of the luxurious life to which he'd grown accustomed over the first eighteen years of his life. Rather than purchasing a large estate, as his parents and grandparents had done several times, Nabokov and his family instead moved into the opulent Montreux Palace Hotel on the shores of Lake Geneva in Switzerland, which became their home for the rest of the writer's life.

While his later works also were successful in their own right, Nabokov forever would be remembered for his story of the nymphet Lolita, a fact that didn't concern him at all—in fact, he felt the same way.

"I would say that of all my books *Lolita* has left me with the most pleasurable afterglow," he said during the aforementioned interview for *Life* magazine. "Perhaps because it is the purest of all, the most abstract and carefully contrived. I am probably responsible for the odd fact that people don't seem to name their daughters Lolita any more. I have heard of young female poodles being given that name since 1956, but of no human beings."

THE CAT IN THE HAT,
Dr. Seuss, 1957

❧

Look at me! Look at me! Look at me now!
It is fun to have fun but you have to know how.

Released in 1957, *The Cat in the Hat* was no ordinary children's book. Its author was restricted to the use of just 250 words, and the puzzle of how to turn this miniature vocabulary into an entertaining, rhyming story took nine months to solve. The job fell to a brilliant man with the playful and sometimes naughty mind of a child, and the result changed the way kids learned to read.

The challenge for the book's production came from an article in *Life* magazine in the mid-1950s—the feature exposed the poor state of literacy among American children. The story's premise was that children's educational books were so boring that kids could not possibly want to learn to read. The books they were given at school, journalist John Hersey said, were filled with nicer-than-nice kids who never misbehaved and who universally enjoyed perfect lives. Several well-known writers, illustrators, and entertainers, said Hersey, could help solve the problem. Those he named included Howard Pyle, Walt Disney, and Dr. Seuss.

A German American by the name of Theodor Geisel happened to read this story and took it very seriously. Why? Because he was an illustrator and a writer. And because he was better known as Dr. Seuss, which, despite popular belief, was pronounced "zoice," like "voice," by Theodor and those who knew him well.

Geisel was born in March 1904 in Springfield, Massachusetts. His father was a brewmaster whose business was destroyed when Prohibition laws were introduced, but who found new work managing Springfield's public parks. His management region included the Zoo in Forest Park, meaning his son and daughter, Marnie, regularly were introduced to all kinds of animals. Theodor and Marnie's mother, Henrietta Geisel (née Seuss) worked in her father's bakery and often memorized the names of the pies by turning them into chants. At night she'd recite these to young Theodor to help him drift off to sleep, introducing him to rhythm and rhyme.

Although they grew up in the United States during World War I, amid increasing anti-German sentiment, the children had happy and comfortable childhoods. With his father, Geisel spent a great deal of time in the parks of Springfield, a citywide playground that provided endless forms of entertainment for the young boy, including zoo animals, open fields, tractors, trucks, motorbikes, and meandering streams. Many images from his childhood would appear in his books in years to come.

Geisel first wrote under a pen name at high school. He had left Springfield to attend Dartmouth College in Hanover, New Hampshire, where he was editor of the college magazine *Jack-O-Lantern,* but soon lost the job when his mischievous streak landed him in trouble with the school authorities. The son of a brewer was caught throwing an alcohol-fueled party, which was against school rules and against Prohibition laws, and as punishment he was banned from the school magazine. But he enjoyed contributing, so in order to continue having his illustrations published without the powers-that-be discovering his identity, he signed his works in his mother's maiden name—Seuss. "Dr." was not added to his nom de plume until years later—another sign of his wicked sense of humor. Geisel's father had always hoped one of his children would earn a doctorate, and when this failed to materialize Theodor decided to give himself the title of doctor, to keep his father happy.

Geisel did attend college, traveling to Lincoln College at Oxford University in England to study literature, but he failed to complete his degree, instead traveling Europe. College wasn't a complete loss, though, for it was there that he met Helen Palmer, who would become his wife.

In 1926 the two returned to the United States, where Geisel found great success as an editorial and advertising illustrator and copywriter, and in 1936 they took another ocean voyage to Europe. During the trip on the M. S. *Kungsholm* the intrusive rhythmic throb of the engine at first annoyed Geisel, but Helen suggested he use it to inspire his writing. He produced a poem that eventually became his first children's book—*And to Think That I Saw It on Mulberry Street*. Far from becoming an instant success, the book was rejected by twenty-seven publishers before being printed in 1937. He followed it up with another four illustrated children's books by 1940.

During World War II Geisel found a commission in the U.S. Army with Major Frank Capra's Signal Corps, where his skills as an illustrator and writer were utilized to make animated training movies. Some of the movies he helped produce, including *Gerald McBoing-Boing, Design for Death,* and *Hitler Lives,* were so impressive that they earned Academy Awards. But Geisel's future did not lie in film—it was a book he'd write more than a decade later that would earn him international fame.

After the *Life* magazine article Geisel's publishers, Houghton Mifflin and Random House, asked him to write a children's book. The catch was that he only would be allowed to use 250 words that had been chosen by literacy experts for their importance to a child's vocabulary. Geisel, who was now living in an old observation tower in La Jolla, California, struggled with the idea for nine months. Regularly locking himself into his studio in the tower for eight-hour stretches, he often would put on one of his large collection of hats, saying that this helped him organize his thoughts and avoid writer's block. Of course, he eventually produced *The Cat in the Hat* in 1957, using just 236 individual words throughout the 1,600-word story.

The book's simplified vocabulary and amusing images meant those new to reading could learn and be entertained. Parents and children fell in love with the book, and Dr. Seuss was catapulted into the limelight. The book would form the basis of Random House's Beginner Books division, headed by Geisel and his wife, the purpose of which was to promote literacy through creativity and editorial richness.

In 1960 Random House publisher Bennett Cerf, the mastermind behind much of the business success of Geisel's books, made a bet with the author that he could not write a book using a vocabulary of just fifty words. Geisel took the challenge, and the result was another one of his beloved children's books, *Green Eggs and Ham*.

Having suffered from ill health, including cancer, Helen passed away in 1967, and the following year Geisel married long-time friend Audrey Stone. Their hat parties at the La Jolla tower, where guests had to show up wearing a wacky hat or risk being forced to wear one from Geisel's collection, were legendary in their social circle. Even into old age Geisel's lighthearted view on life never waned.

"Ted's books came from his imagination and they seemed to sprout full-blown," Audrey said. "Of course once he came up with a character, such as The Cat in the Hat, he gave that Cat all of the child-like caprice he could not get away with as an adult . . . so some of the story ideas just came from a desire to have fun—to play. The Cat could be mischievous, but not mean-natured. He just caused chaos but then he took responsibility for it, too."

Geisel died in La Jolla on September 24, 1991, and in 2004 was posthumously awarded a star on the Hollywood Walk of Fame. But his most famous character, the Cat in the Hat, developed a life of its own and now lives on through popular culture, including books, films, CD-ROMs, and amusement parks.

DOCTOR ZHIVAGO,
Boris Pasternak, 1957

～⚬～

Lara was aware of touching the bedclothes with her left shoulder and the big toe of her right foot—these defined the space she took up in bed. Everything between her shoulder and her foot was vaguely herself—her soul or essence neatly fitting into the outline of her body and impatiently straining towards the future.

"Immensely thankful, touched, proud, astonished, abashed . . ." read the telegram Russian author Boris Pasternak sent to the Swedish Academy on receiving the news he had won the Nobel Prize for Literature. But four days later, the Academy received a second telegram from the writer. This telegram read, "Considering the meaning this award has been given in the society to which I belong, I must reject this undeserved prize which has been presented to me. Please do not receive my voluntary rejection with displeasure."

For the majority of the sixty-eight-year-old's career his values, beliefs, and creative force had been at odds with the Communist government of his homeland. When the writer was honored with the Nobel Prize in 1958, principally for his novel *Doctor Zhivago,* a torrent of criticism and abuse overwhelmed Pasternak who, for fear of losing his livelihood and freedom, was forced to refuse the award. Knowing the subject matter of his novel would enrage authorities, it had taken Pasternak close to ten years to complete the lyrical and poignant love story. Writing in secret the author, who previously had weathered hate campaigns and bans by the government, chose to tell a remarkable story about the Russia he remembered. Unfortunately for Pasternak, the truth that lay within the pages enraged the Soviet government and led to a thirty-year ban of the novel.

Boris Pasternak was born in 1890 into a secular Jewish family in Moscow. His father, Leonid, was a renowned artist who had illustrated Tolstoy's novel *Resurrection* and his mother, Rozalia Kaufman, was a famed concert pianist. Not surprisingly, the family's friends and acquaintances were a who's who of European intelligentsia. Composers Rachmaninoff and Alexander Scriabin and writers Leo Tolstoy, Rainer Maria Rilke, and Alexander Blok were frequent guests at the Pasternak home. As a result of these extraordinary influences, young Pasternak initially pursued a musical path and began his studies at the Moscow Conservatory. But despite being an exceptional musician, the teenager soon realized he did not have the technical skill needed to make music his career. Consequently he moved to Moscow University in 1909 to study law and then philosophy.

However, in 1912 Pasternak gave up his studies completely to begin writing poetry. In the years prior to World War I, artistic and intellectual life in Russia was at its most vibrant. Kandinsky, Chagall, Stravinsky, Scriabin, Blok, and Mandelstam were at the height of their creative powers and new movements in poetry, music, and art were flourishing. Spurred on by this atmosphere, twenty-two-year-old Pasternak burst on to the scene with poetry laced with original techniques. His early work garnered him recognition and praise in an environment already overflowing with talent.

Unable to enlist during the war because of a childhood accident that left him with a permanent injury, Pasternak instead worked as a clerk in a Ural's chemical factory, but still his output of poetry did not cease. In 1917, as a wave of revolutionary fever gripped the nation, Pasternak completed two experimental collections of poetry, *My Sister Life* and *Themes and Variations*. Although the publication of both works was delayed until 1922 and 1923 respectively because of the Bolshevik Revolution, they encapsulated the fervor of the time, had a huge impact on Russian poetry, and made Pasternak one of the nation's foremost writers.

The Bolshevik Revolution initially was welcomed by Pasternak. The potential for change and stimulation excited the writer, whose bold techniques were revolutionary in themselves. But soon the brutality of the regime came to appal the author, who grew more and more frustrated with the new government's ever-increasing control of the arts. The new leader, Lenin, believed art and political change were intertwined. Pasternak believed art should be shaped by universal truths such as love and faith—art was apolitical and should not be molded by social and political currents. In this climate artists who disagreed with the government credo lived in fear and insecurity.

When Joseph Stalin rose to power in 1928, further changes overtook every area of Russian life, including literature. In 1932 Stalin introduced the doctrine of Socialist Realism, a policy that stated that all art created should glorify Communism. The Union of Soviet Writers was established to impose observance of this policy. While many writers and artists became despondent, gave up their craft, and even committed suicide, Pasternak's artistic conscience told him to keep writing. In his autobiography, *Safe Conduct,* Pasternak summed up his thoughts on Socialist Realism by writing, "We cease to recognize reality. It manifests itself in some new category. And this category seems to be its own inherent condition and not our own. Apart from this condition everything in the world has a name. Only it is new and it is not yet named. We try to name it—and the result is art."

Pasternak was not oblivious to the political events occurring around him, but he firmly believed art needed to transcend these concerns. Like other artists at the time, Pasternak went on producing work, living in fear that he might be next on the government's list of dissidents secretly ushered away to a Gulag. So fearful was the composer Dmitri Shostakovich, for instance, that he kept his prison suitcase permanently packed. Pasternak himself wrote in a letter, "Of course I am prepared for anything. Why should it happen to everyone else and not to me?" Despite the dearth of meaningful cultural and artistic activity, Pasternak managed to produce a brilliant and stunning collection of poetry.

The Second Birth (1932) collection marked Pasternak's attempt to join the socialist endeavor on his own terms. Writing in a streamlined style, Pasternak altered his artistic values, and the collection signaled a stark change in his poetic vision. In his overly romantic work critics felt he was intentionally ignoring the negativity of what was going on around him in society, but his opinion was that politics and society should never affect the production of a work of art. Despite his soft line on politics, soon after the publication of *The Second Birth* the state banned him from publishing further works.

Stifled creatively and unable to earn a livelihood, Pasternak turned to translation. The translation of classic works by Shakespeare, Goethe, and Rilke into Russian ensured that Pasternak was well paid and, in 1936, the writer bought a house in a writers' village outside Moscow. Pasternak was an extremely gifted translator, and his versions of Shakespeare's tragedies are still the standard texts used in Russia today. Translation became Pasternak's chief employment throughout the late 1930s and World War II.

During the war the government's focus shifted to German invasion, and Pasternak managed to publish two collections of poetry. *On Early* (1942) and *The Terrestrial Expanse* (1945) marked his return to the literary scene. During this time Pasternak's focus began to shift. Although he had dabbled in prose throughout his career, most notably with his autobiography, *Safe Conduct,* in 1932, he was principally a poet. But after receiving many letters from front line troops praising him for the extraordinary influence his work had on their lives, Pasternak began to consider writing a novel—a candid tale that chronicled old Russia and the changes the country had undergone. Pasternak later said in an interview with the *Paris Review,* "When I wrote *Doctor Zhivago* I had the feeling of an immense debt toward my contemporaries. It was an attempt to repay it. This feeling of debt was overpowering as I slowly progressed with the novel. After so many years of just writing lyric poetry or translating, it seemed to me that it was my duty to make a statement about our epoch—about those years, remote and yet looming so closely over us . . . I wanted to record the past and to honor in *Doctor Zhivago* the beautiful and sensitive aspects of Russia in those years." The novel was begun in 1945 under the working title *Boys and Girls*.

Fully aware that writing a novel that sang the praises of the freedom Russians once enjoyed could have perilous consequences, Pasternak wrote the epic tale in secret. Following the war the Soviet regime carried out another clampdown on dissidents, and once again Pasternak was reviled in the press, but this only hardened the author's resolve to complete his secret novel. Also at this time Pasternak met Olga Ivinskaya, who not only became his long-term partner but also the living inspiration for the character of Lara.

Completed in 1955, the novel told the story of Yuri Zhivago, a physician and poet, and his love affair with Lara during the political unrest and upheavals of Russia in the twentieth century. Throughout the story, which begins in 1905 and continues through Russia's turbulent history to the late 1920s, Zhivago and Lara are continually separated by war and revolution, but their love remains transcendent of the chaos, brutality, and hatred that rages around them. The novel ends with a cycle of Zhivago's poetry. Seen as the voice of the author, Zhivago is a sensitive man living in a brutal age who, due to fate and the tragedy of his time, is helpless to control the events of his life.

Unable to have his work published in Russia, the manuscript was smuggled out of the country and first published in Italy in 1957. It was an instant success, and the first English translation appeared the following year. Since then the novel has been translated into eighteen languages, with the English version in constant print to this day. Although authorities initially took no action when Pasternak made the bold move of having *Doctor*

Zhivago published overseas, their retaliation was stinging the following year.

The Nobel Prize announcement provoked a storm of harassment and controversy for the author in Russia, and all publishing doors were closed to him. When the chief of the Communist Youth League, Vladimir Semichastny (later head of the KGB), stated that Pasternak was worse than a pig because "a pig never befouls where it eats or sleeps" and called for his expulsion from the country, Pasternak declined the award.

Pasternak passed away in 1960 and officially remained a national disgrace until President Gorbachev initiated the policy of glasnost in the 1980s. *Doctor Zhivago* finally was published in Russia in 1988.

TO KILL A MOCKINGBIRD,
Harper Lee, 1960

❧

I maintain that the Ewells started it all, but Jem, who was four years my senior, said it started long before that. He said it began the summer Dill came to us, when Dill first gave us the idea of making Boo Radley come out.

In 1931 nine black youths aged from thirteen to nineteen were arrested for raping two white females on a train bound for Paint Rock, Alabama. Taken to Scottsboro in the same state and incarcerated, a lynch mob soon gathered outside the jailhouse. So white hot were local tempers that the governor of Alabama was forced to call in the National Guard to protect the imprisoned teenagers.

Indicted by a grand jury, all were convicted and all, save the thirteen-year-old, received the death sentence. Later, on appeal, the two victims recanted their testimonies, but the jury still convicted. By the late 1930s all nine eventually were paroled, acquitted, or pardoned.

The media coverage the case attracted put the tiny Alabama town of Scottsboro on the map, and the nine youths became known across the nation as the Scottsboro Boys. The story laid bare the deeply rooted racial tensions in the United States, and one individual on whom it would have a profound effect was Nelle Harper Lee, at the time the five-year-old daughter of an Alabama lawyer.

Born in 1926 in Monroeville, Alabama, to Frances Finch Lee and Amasa Coleman Lee, Nelle Harper knew from an early age her calling was as a writer, revealing in a rare interview in 1964, "I think I've been writing as long as I've been able to form words." Nevertheless, she followed her father into the legal profession, studying at the University of Alabama following her education in Monroeville. But her dalliance with the law was short lived, as the hopeful writer withdrew from college only a few months before graduation to pursue her dream in New York.

Reading was a Lee family institution. The author recalls reading long before she began school. Her older siblings read to her, Frances read a story each day to her youngest child, and Amasa kept his daughter informed by reading the daily newspaper to her. In a town devoid of a cinema and parks, reading was one of the only forms of entertainment.

Depression-era Monroeville was a bleak place. There was little to do and even less money to do it with. Lee remembers spending many hours inventing games with her older siblings and her next-door neighbor, Truman Capote. Two years older than Lee, Capote had come to live with relatives in Monroeville when his parents divorced.

Lee says of her childhood, "We had to use our own devices in our play, for our entertainment. We didn't have much money . . . We didn't have toys, nothing was done for us, so the result was that we lived in our imagination most of the time. We devised things; we were readers and we would transfer everything we had seen on the printed page to the backyard in the form of high drama."

On moving to New York in her early twenties, Lee worked as an airline reservations clerk for Eastern Airlines. Renting a cold-water apartment, she lived a frugal lifestyle while commuting frequently between her new home and Monroeville to care for her ailing father. Between her job at the airline and her duties nursing an ill parent, Lee's writing was sporadic. But describing herself as someone who must write, over the next three years Lee drew from her childhood experiences and worked on a novel she fondly would nickname "The Bird."

Lee believed her compulsion to write was part of a long tradition in the South. "I think we are a region of natural storytellers, just from tribal instinct," she said. "We did not have the pleasure of the theatre, the dance, of motion pictures when they came along. We simply entertained each other by talking . . . I think that kind of life naturally produces more writers than, say, an environment like 82nd Street in New York."

Although unexciting in many ways, Lee saw a richness in southern life she believed utterly unique. "There is a very definite social pattern in these towns that fascinates me. I think it is a rich social pattern. I would simply like to put down all I know about this because I believe that there is something universal in this little world, something decent to be said for it, and something to lament in its passing. In other words all I want to be is the Jane Austen of south Alabama."

In 1957 Lee submitted a manuscript to J. B. Lippincott Company. However, the author might never have completed her novel if not for a generous gift of money from friends the year before. Witnessing her dedication to her craft, friends pooled their cash and gave Lee the best Christmas present of her life—a note attached to the envelope read, "You have one year off from your job to write whatever you please. Merry Christmas."

But the editors at J. B. Lippincott told the first-time author her story was too episodic—it read like a series of short stories. Nevertheless, they liked her ideas and encouraged her to continue. Under the guidance of editor Tay Hohoff, Lee's first and only novel, *To Kill a Mockingbird,* was published in 1960. Although Lee denies the novel is autobiographical, the author drew on her childhood in Monroeville, and the Scottsboro trial, to create the literary world of Maycomb.

At the heart of the novel is the trial of negro Tom Robinson. A black field worker, Tom is arrested for raping a local white girl. Assigned to defend him is Atticus Finch, an open-minded public defender who, despite public hostility and the knowledge the outcome would never go his way, proves his client's innocence. But in the intensely racist and intolerant environment of 1930s Alabama, the all-white jury still hands down a guilty verdict.

Told through the eyes of Atticus's six-year-old daughter, Scout, the novel is also a coming-of-age story for the young protagonist, her older brother, Jem, and their friend Dill Harris (a character said to be based on Truman Capote). The three learn the nature of prejudice through Atticus's involvement with the Robinson case and through their obsession with their phantomlike neighbor, Boo Radley.

Despite mixed critical reviews, *To Kill a Mockingbird* was an immediate success with the reading public. Lee was applauded for capturing the essence of a small southern town and its complex network of social class and racial tensions. Readers were spellbound by the characterization, the subtle balance of humor and tragedy, and the use of symbolism. Finally, readers were transported to the "tired old town" of Maycomb through the narrative of Scout. Although events are seen through the eyes of a child, Lee managed to convey a sense of hindsight with the voice of adult Scout simultaneously permeating the narrative.

Selling 2.5 million copies in the first year, *To Kill a Mockingbird* propelled Lee into the pantheon of great American writers, alongside Mark Twain and William Faulkner. The novel garnered its author a string of awards, including the Pulitzer Prize in 1961.

Becoming a staple of English lessons around the world, the book was voted Best Novel of the Century by *Library Journal* in 1999 and, in a survey of lifetime reading habits conducted by the Book-of-the-Month Club in 1991, it came in second as the book most often cited as making a difference to people's lives—beaten only by the Bible.

To Kill a Mockingbird's success came as a surprise to the modest author, who said, "I never expected any sort of success with *Mockingbird*. I was hoping for a quick and merciful death at the hands of the reviewers but, at the same time, I sort of hoped someone would like it enough to give me encouragement. Public encouragement. I hoped for a little, as I said, but I got rather a whole lot, and in some ways this was just about as frightening as the quick, merciful death I'd expected."

Perhaps this explains why Lee, despite the "encouragement," disappeared from public life in the mid-sixties and never published another novel, living a life of relative seclusion in Monroeville. A more likely explanation for her isolation is related in a story her cousin, Richard Williams, tells. When he asked the author when she was going to increase her literary output and add a second novel to her body of work, she apparently replied, "Richard, when you're at the top, there's only one way to go."

THE SPY WHO CAME IN FROM THE COLD,
John Le Carré, 1963

❧

> *It is said that men condemned to death are subject to sudden moments of elation; as if, like moths in the fire, their destruction were coincidental with attainment. Following directly upon his decision, Leamas was aware of a comparable sensation; relief, short-lived but consoling, sustained him for a time.*

Child prodigies have made their mark in many different fields of endeavor, often going on to enormous success and critical acclaim. In music Wolfgang Amadeus Mozart wrote his first compositions at the age of five. In art Pablo Picasso painted his first acclaimed oil painting at eight years old. And in golf, Tiger Woods shot 48 over nine holes when he was just three. For John Le Carré, born David John Moore Cornwell in 1931, the field of expertise was crime, and the valuable skill set taught to him as a youngster included lying, misleading, conning, and stealing, and in its own unique way it would carry him on to huge success and acclaim.

David's peculiar gifts came thanks to his conman father, Richard "Ronnie" Thomas Archibald Cornwell, an unscrupulous confidence trickster who sometimes utilized his sons in schemes to rip off unsuspecting wealthy victims. The children, David and older brother, Anthony, could have traveled a different road during childhood had their mother, Olive, stayed with the family, but when David was just five she left with another man, fed up with Ronnie's wicked ways. The boys, in the sole care of their father, became supporting actors in his elaborate and deceptive fabrications, which ranged from imaginary businesses to nonexistent products to massive investment scams.

The experience of creating false identities in order to intentionally deceive and mislead would lead David into the spy game, where such skills were prized tools of the trade. It was the knowledge gained in the dangerous world of espionage that ultimately would lead to his enormous success as one of the world's best respected spy novelists.

David was born in Poole in England's Dorset and educated at several boarding schools, including St. Andrews in Berkshire and Sherborne School in Dorset. His father was absent for long periods during his childhood, particularly during his time at boarding school, and it wasn't until David was eighteen that he discovered that Ronnie had, in fact, been imprisoned on several occasions when his scams had caught up with him. Previously David had justified the absences to himself by fantasizing that his father was a glamorous spy, a paid trickster fooling the unwary for the good of the nation.

School holidays were always a stressful time for David and Anthony, as they never were sure where their father's next "job" would take them, and what personas they would have to assume in order to carry out the next deception. David finally escaped his father's grasp when at sixteen he was sent to the University of Bern in Switzerland. There he learned German and proved to be an exceptional student of language. In Bern young David also ran errands for British diplomats, reveling in the knowledge that he possibly was assisting in missions for the British Secret Service. But his first real spying missions would begin soon enough, at Oxford University.

When he was eighteen David returned to the United Kingdom to continue his education at Lincoln College at Oxford University. There he voluntarily began collecting information and spying on fellow students on behalf of British intelligence.

"I think particularly the Oxford stuff was unpleasant and in retrospect, at a personal level, shaming," he confessed during an interview with Australia's ABC TV in 2001. "I still believe it was necessary. I still believe it was a perfectly reasonable argument that, as the Soviet Union recruited in the '30s from the Cambridge students, Burgess, MacLean, Philby, Blunt and so on, so we could assume they were doing the same things at the major universities among left-leaning middle class people who had not yet compromised themselves as Communists. Therefore, to do what I did and put myself in the way of the recruiters, and try to get into the stream, I think was a legitimate activity. What was unpleasant was masquerading as a neo-Communist and that stuff."

After graduating in 1956, David illustrated children's books for a short while before taking up a post as a teacher of German at England's exclusive private school Eton College. But a nine-to-five job was not what this self-confessed "espionage street kid" had been brought up to spend his life doing. After two years in the classrooms of Eton, he welcomed the approaches of the British Secret Service, who were keen to recruit him. David's fluent German, his experience in spying at university, and his ability to mislead and deceive, bred in him from a young age, all were highly regarded within the world of espionage, and he was happy to oblige.

"There was a kind of latent delinquency in me from childhood . . . because my dad had been this fantasy figure, this confidence trickster, and so on," he explained. "To put those larcenous instincts to the service of the country seemed to me to be a splendid thing."

For much of the next decade, during the heady years that included the building of the Berlin Wall, David was based in Germany as a member of the British Foreign Service. In reality his role was to make contacts and collect information, to spy. He has since revealed little detail of his role within Germany, but he has been openly critical of the bureaucracy within the spy game at both ends of the political spectrum.

"There are the desk men and there are the men who work in the field," he said in 2001. "The men who work in the field, they're the guys who do the hard work, if you like, and live the deception. The men who work at the desks are the manipulators, on the whole."

"I've always felt that secret services in some sense represent the subconscious of a nation," he continued. "That, what it's most afraid of, what its greatest appetites and fantasies are, these things are contained, enshrined in a secret service. So, if the Americans are secretly terrified of this or that situation, if they think they're being encircled, which seems to be their present amazing fantasy, that is where it will be expressed, within the secret corridors of the CIA. Inevitably, you'll get, therefore, a group of people who are sharing a fantasy."

The Cold War was one such "fantasy" in which David played a role, and the experience of spying taught him that there was little glamour, little reward, and little satisfaction. An author by the name of Ian Fleming, who also had spent time working with British Intelligence and who had served in the Royal Navy, recently had written a few successful novels concentrating on a British spy by the name of James Bond. Bond's life was all about beautiful women, fast cars, glamorous locations, and action-packed shoot-outs. During his time in Germany, David chose to tell it like it really was by writing a spy novel that accurately reflected the reality of the espionage game. At college he had dabbled in writing but had never been published—but that was all about to change.

Written under the pen name of John Le Carré, as the British Foreign Service had strict rules about their members publishing work under their real names, his first novel, *Call for the Dead,* was published in 1961. It was a spy/detective mystery story starring a central character named George Smiley. Smiley, like David, had been recruited into the secret service while studying at Lincoln College. Unlike James Bond, Smiley was in poor physical shape but instead relied on his scholar's intellect and endless research to solve cases. At the beginning of the novel Smiley's role in the secret service was a relatively lowly one and, in fact, the burnt-out agent looked forward to leaving the "Circus" and its top-heavy bureaucracy.

Call for the Dead did not even come close to knocking Fleming's Bond books from their bestseller perch. When Le Carré's second novel, *A Murder of Quality,* was published in 1962, it received a similarly lukewarm response from the reading public. Once again it starred George Smiley, this time having left the secret service for a job as a scholarly researcher at a small university—when a student is murdered at a local school he decides to investigate.

But it was a case of third-time luck for Le Carré, whose next novel would become an international bestseller. *The Spy Who Came in from the Cold* is a story deeply rooted in the world of espionage. Reflecting David's knowledge of, and increasing disrespect for, the spy game, the book's success gave its author financial freedom. It allowed him to escape the bonds of the secret service once and for all to become a full-time writer. Published in 1963, it sold over 250,000 copies in two years.

The Spy Who Came in from the Cold tells the story of Alec Leamas, a spy being manipulated by the director of the British Secret Service. A pawn in a bigger game, Leamas must convincingly defect to East Germany during the Cold War in order to infiltrate the enemy's spy network—the same spy network that Le Carré had worked against in Berlin for so many years.

The book went on to become a major film starring Richard Burton and won the 1964 Gold Dagger Award from the British Crime Writers' Association as well as the Edgar Award from Mystery Writers of America. More importantly, it gave a man who had spent much of his life pretending to be somebody else permission to finally be himself—even if it was under a different name!

VALLEY OF THE DOLLS,
Jacqueline Susann, 1966

❦

He stood up and pulled the string of her loose robe. It fell open, revealing her perfect body. The little man, who barely reached the young goddess's shoulder, ran his sun-tanned hand lightly over the arched breasts.

"Take a good look, Sam. But don't touch—this is mine."

Critics have accused *Valley of the Dolls* author, Jacqueline Susann, of typing on a cash register. Gore Vidal once famously said, "She doesn't write, she types," and Truman Capote called the glamorous and brash author "a truck driver in drag." When Susann threatened to sue Capote, he publicly apologized to all truck drivers. But despite the insults, criticisms, and ridicule, Jacqueline Susann was a hard-working writer and a tireless self-promoter. As a result of her efforts in the writing and marketing of her novels, she became the only writer ever to have three successive books hit number one on the *New York Times* bestseller list. In doing so she paved the way for other female authors such as Jackie Collins and Danielle Steel.

Susann was a failed actress, model, and playwright, but when it came to the craft of writing steamy fiction, she was an expert. Her sensational tales of Hollywood bed-hopping and pill-popping were based on her own personal experience as well as the lives of Hollywood stars whom she came to know. Her experiences of sex, secrets, and scandal, in fact, could have leaped from the pages of one of her very own stories.

Jacqueline Susann was born in Philadelphia in 1918 to unhappily married Jewish parents. Her father was an artist and philanderer who would take his young daughter to the cinema, only to leave her watching the film while he rendezvoused with his latest mistress. On the way home the dutiful daughter would outline the plot of the film in case his wife would interrogate him on his whereabouts. Although Susann is said to have been one of the laziest students in her school, she scored highly on an IQ test when she was in the fifth grade. And despite being unmotivated in most lessons, she was always praised for being a very talented writer.

Jacqueline's mother hoped her daughter would use these writing abilities when she finished school, but the pretty teenager had other ideas. After winning a local beauty pageant (it emerged later that the contest was rigged by her father), Susann set her sights on a career in acting and told her mother, "Acting is glamour but writing is hard work, so I'm going to be an actress."

Susann traveled to New York immediately following graduation in 1936. After twelve months of exhaustive auditions the nineteen-year-old finally secured a walk-on role in a play called *The Women,* for which she received a weekly salary of $25. By 1939, Susann realized drastic action was needed in order to boost her career. She married the influential press agent Irving Mansfield, who was known for his ability to put his clients in the spotlight. Susann's new husband was not able to work the magic that she had hoped he would, but by the late 1940s she was appearing as a regular on the *Morey*

Amsterdam Show on television and had secured a role in a Broadway musical titled *A Lady Says Yes* opposite Carole Landis and Jack Albertson. Landis and Susann struck up a friendship, but soon Landis's life began to unravel as her marriage failed. Susann watched helplessly as her friend entered into an ill-fated affair with married actor Rex Harrison. In 1948, when Harrison refused to leave his wife, Landis committed suicide by drug overdose.

Although she wasn't able to become famous for her acting, Susann did make a name for herself in New York for other reasons. She had a string of extramarital affairs with comedians such as Eddie Cantor, George Jessel, and Joe E. Brown. (She was also rumored to have had affairs with Ethel Merman, Carole Landis, and Coco Chanel.) She had a knack for making scenes in public, including throwing drinks in the faces of theater critics and openly fighting with her husband.

By the mid-1940s Susann was renowned in New York social circles for her raucous behavior. In 1943 she sent her husband an infamous "Dear John" letter while he was serving in the armed forces. It read, "When we were at the Essex House and I had room service and I could buy all my Florence Lustig dresses, I found that I loved you very much. But now that you're in the army and getting $56 a month, I feel that my love has waned." She is said to have read the letter aloud to the cast of the show in which she was appearing at the time.

The separation, however, was short-lived and, after the war, the couple reconciled. Previously Susann, with her acting career flagging, decided to try her hand as a playwright. The result, a performance called *Lovely Me,* bombed in every city it played. Susann had gotten pregnant, and on her play's opening night, in her hometown of Philadelphia, she went into labor. Her son, Guy, at the age of four, was diagnosed with autism, and as a result he spent his life in institutions. When friends asked about Guy's whereabouts, however, Susann often told them he was at boarding school.

In the mid-1950s Susann bought a poodle she named Josephine, and everywhere Susann went the dog would follow. Often dressing the canine in an outfit to match her own, Susann liked to call the pooch "the Elizabeth Taylor of poodles." By 1955 her acting career was dead, but as she was famous for her glamorous lifestyle, she won a contract as a fashion commentator for Schiffli Lace, often appearing on television with Josephine in matching lace ensembles. In 1962, Susann discovered she had breast cancer. Unbeknown to all but her husband, the forty-four-year-old had a mastectomy.

In the following year, while recovering from her surgery and at a loose end careerwise, Susann decided to write a book. The result was *Every Night, Josephine!*, a memoir based on her experiences with her poodle. The novelty book quickly sold almost 40,000 copies and hit number 10 on the *Time* magazine bestseller list. It was a decent debut, but had the publicity tour gone ahead sales would have been even more impressive. On the eve of her departure for the tour President Kennedy was assassinated. According to legend, on hearing the news Susann burst into tears. Told not to take the death so hard, she replied, "Don't take it so hard? My tour's been canceled!" Nevertheless, encouraged by sales, Susann decided to write another book.

Between 1964 and 1965 *Valley of the Dolls* was typed on Susann's hot-pink IBM Selectric typewriter. Using a blackboard and colored chalk to keep track of the plot, the writer worked eight hours a day planning the sordid details of her racy story. Of her writing process Susann said, "When I write I do five drafts. The first is on inexpensive white paper. I don't try for style. I just spill it all out. The second draft is on yellow paper, that's when I work on characterizations. The third is pink, I work on story motivations. Then blue, that's where I cut, cut, cut."

Dedicated to her husband, Irving Mansfield, and published in 1966, *Valley of the Dolls* tells the story of three women embarking on careers as actresses, each falling victim to prescription drugs (the "dolls" of the title), unsuccessful relationships, and the rigors of Hollywood. The novel deals with issues such as addiction, abortion, homosexuality, sex, and mental illness, all to an extent no other novel ever had. The book was an instant hit with the public, mainly due to the fact that the plot was a thin facade of fiction that barely masked the identities of real celebrities. Drawn from the author's own experiences, the characters in the novel were believed to have been loosely based on Judy Garland, Carole Landis, Ethel Merman, and Grace Kelly. Of her inspiration, Susann said, "I wanted to write it long before I wrote *Every Night, Josephine!* I'd been thinking about it a long time. I've been around show business for over twenty years. I've grown up with show business. I've seen people come starry-eyed and I've seen them hope to climb Mt. Everest, which as I call it is the top, and I've seen many of them go into the valley of the dolls."

The sexy brunette promoted her book extensively on the talk show circuit and even appeared on game shows to promote her work. Her risqué style of chat was previously unseen and unheard on television and radio, and the publicity had an enormous effect on the buying public. Susann often made a point of getting out of bed at dawn to deliver coffee and donuts to the truck drivers who delivered her books to stores. Likewise, she traveled the country and visited the stores selling *Valley of the Dolls,* charming the assistants to make sure they continued selling her book and gave it prime real estate on the shelves.

As a result of her tireless work, *Valley of the Dolls* is one of the greatest sellers of all time, with sales to date of more than thirty million copies. Nevertheless, her narrative was lambasted as trashy soap opera by critics who viewed Susann's style as loud, brash, and overly masculine. Much to the chagrin of her detractors, the novel stayed on the *New York Times* bestseller list for twenty-eight weeks, perhaps proving true the author's thoughts on writing. "I don't think any novelist should be concerned with literature," she said. "Literature should be left to the essayists."

THE GODFATHER,
Mario Puzo, 1969

❦

> *Carlo had the sense to realize that Sonny would kill him,*
> *that Sonny was a man who could, with the naturalness*
> *of an animal, kill another man, while he himself would*
> *have to call up all his courage, all his will, to commit*
> *murder.*

Although labeled a "lucky bestseller" by its author, *The Godfather*, with its memorable cover design of a puppet master's hand, sold more than 21 million copies and spent sixty-seven weeks on the *New York Times* bestseller list. Mario Puzo said his landmark novel was "the product of a writer who practiced his craft for nearly thirty years and finally got good at it."

Born in 1920 to illiterate Sicilian immigrants, Puzo was raised on the west side of Manhattan in the district known as Hell's Kitchen, an area associated with organized crime and gang wars. It seems an appropriate place for the author of literature's most definitive gangster novel to have grown up in, but when discussing his youth Puzo has said, "I had every desire to go wrong but I never had the chance." Responsible for keeping young Mario on the straight and narrow was a strong family structure. At its core was a formidable mother armed with a policeman's truncheon with which she kept her brood tamed.

His father worked as a railway trackman and Puzo lived with his six brothers and sisters above the railway yards. As a young boy he dreamed of being a cowboy, war hero, artist, even a great criminal, but his mother had more realistic goals in mind for her son. Hoping the teenager would become a railway clerk upon leaving school, the matriarch was disappointed when Mario, at the age of sixteen, announced his ambition to become a writer. According to Puzo, his mother took the news quite well, as she assumed this was simply a fantasy the boy soon would leave behind.

In the early 1940s, when the United States' involvement in World War II began, Puzo joined the U.S. Air Force and served in Asia and Germany. In 1945, when the war ended, the twenty-five-year-old stayed on in Germany and worked as a civilian public relations officer for the Air Force.

When he returned to the United States the following year, the young man had no idea what he wanted to do for a living. With little money and no career prospects, Puzo took advantage of the G.I. Bill, whereby returned servicemen received an entitlement of $120 per month if they enrolled in a full-time education course. Cash-strapped, Puzo signed up for literature and creative writing lessons at Columbia University.

That same year he married and, before long, had five children to support. Working as a clerk in a government office, Puzo's dreams of becoming a great writer were slow in being realized. It took him seven years to complete his first novel, *The Dark Arena*. Published in 1955, the book dealt with a disillusioned ex-serviceman and his German mistress. Drawing on his own experiences during and following World War II, *The Dark Arena* received excellent reviews for a first novel, with critics heralding Puzo as a writer to watch. But it was a failure on the sales front, with Puzo's heroic seven-year effort only netting the struggling family $3,500.

Unable to give up his administrative job, Puzo spent the snippets of free time available to him working on a second novel, which he began in 1956. Always searching for an outlet for his writing, he took a job in 1963 at a company called Magazine Management, a publishing house that circulated dozens of men's adventure titles. Puzo's position on staff required him to churn out 40,000 words of pulp fiction each month across the range of titles.

A lack of spare time, because of work and family demands, meant Puzo took nine years to complete his second novel, *The Fortunate Pilgrim.* Published in 1965, Puzo claimed the semiautobiographical story was his best work, referring to it as "art." Earning even better reviews than *The Dark Arena,* Puzo's story of an Italian immigrant family in the 1920s failed to attract readers. Although called a "small classic" by the *New York Times,* the novel sold only five thousand copies and netted Puzo a mere $3,000.

One editor mentioned to the disillusioned and frustrated author that he would have sold more copies if *The Fortunate Pilgrim* contained more Mafia content. It was not something the forty-five-year-old, who was $20,000 in debt, wanted to hear, but following an expensive gallbladder operation Puzo decided it was time to write a novel with wider appeal, one that would sell.

This decision was more difficult for Puzo to digest than expected. His favorite author was Fyodor Dostoevsky, and for years he had dreamed of writing a novel of the caliber of *Crime and Punishment.* The truth struck him hard—he was never going to be that kind of a writer. Instead of trying to be an artist of language, Puzo concentrated on simply being a great storyteller.

While working at Magazine Management, Puzo had heard many anecdotes about the Mafia, and the idea of a novel about the criminal organization began to appeal to him. After collecting material on the east coast branches of the Cosa Nostra, the author wrote a ten-page outline to present to book publishers.

Rejected by every publisher he approached, he was about to give up when a writer friend dropped by and Puzo unloaded onto him one of the many unsold copies of *The Fortunate Pilgrim*. After reading his book the friend took him to lunch, where Puzo mesmerized him with many of the Mafia anecdotes he had gathered. He showed his friend the plot outline and the friend, in turn, showed it to his publishers—G.P. Putnam's Sons. Putnam's loved the idea and gave Puzo a $5,000 advance. Puzo immediately set to work.

Chronicling a decade in the often violent existence of the Corleone family, *The Godfather* is a gripping read. At the family's head is Don Vito Corleone, whose olive oil importing business is a front for organized crime. The novel also charts the lives of his three sons: hot-tempered Sonny, reliable Fredo, and the youngest and most Americanized, Michael. An exploration of the emotional bonds of the family unit, *The Godfather* was often described by Puzo as more of a family saga than a crime novel. He later acknowledged that the heavy emphasis on family honor in his story actually romanticized the Mafia's illegal and immoral dealings.

Completing the novel in 1969, Puzo was unhappy with the finished product. Hoping to do one more rewrite, he went on vacation and left the manuscript with his publisher. When he returned, Putnam's had already sold the paperback rights for $450,000. Puzo never was able to do his rewrite and always felt *The Godfather* was not as good as it could have been, but he was comforted by the fact that his financial problems were permanently solved.

Approaching the age of fifty and having spent most of his adult life in debt, Puzo immediately took his six-figure check to his local bank and proudly handed it to the teller who, Puzo claims, regularly sneered at him when he asked for another overdraft.

Despite claiming that he'd never met a gangster and that the book was written entirely from research, the public automatically assumed *The Godfather* was based on firsthand experience. Looking at the subject matter of his previous two novels, critics and readers were convinced Puzo had mob connections. The baffled writer replied, "Where would I have time to be in the Mafia? I starved before the success of *The Godfather*. If I was in the Mafia I would have made enough money so I wouldn't have to write."

THE DAY OF THE JACKAL,
Frederick Forsyth, 1971

~~~~

"Will you assassinate De Gaulle?" asked Rodin at last.
The voice was quiet but the question filled the room.
The Englishman's glance came back to him and the eyes
were blank again.

"Yes, but it will cost a lot of money."

For several years Frederick Forsyth knew he was being followed by secret police representing various hard-line communist parties. In restaurants in East Berlin he'd raise his glass to the men observing him from a distant table, and they'd often smile and raise theirs in return. In Hungary they'd follow him, without bothering to disguise their intentions, from the moment he stepped off a plane or drove across the border until he left the country again. And one night in Prague a young, attractive woman enjoyed a drink with Forsyth in a bar, followed by dinner in a restaurant and a drive to the countryside for a nighttime swim in a lake, followed by a passionate outdoor lovemaking session on a rug. Only then did she reveal that she worked for the secret police and that her job was to keep a close eye on him.

Such was the life of a post–World War II journalist assigned by Reuters to cover the communist strongholds of East Germany, Czechoslovakia, and Hungary during the Cold War. In fact, for long periods between 1963 and 1965, while he lived in East Berlin, Forsyth was the only

Western journalist allowed into these territories. It was an exciting time for the twenty-five-year-old, and a major change from his first job in journalism, which had been at a local newspaper in quiet Norfolk, England. During his time in Eastern Europe the things he saw, the people he met, and the secrets he learned would set him up for a lifetime of literary success.

Forsyth was born in Ashford, Kent, England, on August 25, 1938. His father was a shopkeeper in Ashford, and from 1952 to 1955 his parents sent him to Tonbridge School, one of England's most highly respected schools for boys and the alma mater of several other writers, including E. M. Forster, Vikram Seth, and poet Sidney Keyes. During his childhood he spent several extended vacations in Germany and France, sometimes staying with local families on exchange. During these trips he became fluent in French and German, which would help to set him up for a career in continental Europe later in life.

But first he had to get the flying bug out of his system. During the Blitz in World War II, from his backyard in Ashford nightly he was able to watch the German bombers flying overhead on their way to drop their deadly loads on the city of London. By the morning's early light he'd often see bombers heading back to their bases in occupied France. Dogfights in the air were not an unusual sight, as RAF pilots bravely attempted to protect their homeland, and young Forsyth dreamed of one day flying through the sky.

Forsyth earned his pilot's license soon after he turned seventeen, and following school he studied for a short while at the University of Granada in Spain before moving into the Royal Air Force. At the age of nineteen he became one of the RAF's youngest pilots. His stay in the

Air Force would last just a few years, as the pull of writing proved to be stronger than that of flying, and in the late 1950s Forsyth found a job with a local newspaper.

His career took a giant leap forward when, as a twenty-three-year-old, Forsyth earned a position with Reuters. For two years he worked in the news agency's Paris bureau during a time when the French government, led by President Charles de Gaulle, was attempting to work out an end to the civil war in Algeria, finally giving the country its independence. But the French settlers and troops in Algeria were against the country's independence. In addition to being involved in two uprisings, the hard-line militants in this group set up an underground terrorist cell known as the "Organisation de l'Armée Secrète"—literally translating to the "secret army organization," aka the "OAS"—to cause trouble for, and attempt to assassinate, Charles de Gaulle. Several failed attempts were made on the president's life as he negotiated Algeria's independence, and Forsyth, of course, researched and reported on these incidents.

After working in Paris for two years, Forsyth was made an offer that no journalist could refuse—to take over the East German Reuters office. "Obviously I just jumped at it," Forsyth later recalled in an interview. "I had a one-man office and it was east of the iron curtain. The wall had gone up in '61 and I was there in '64, and because of the wall all east-western diplomatic contacts had been severed . . . because of this severing the only agency East Germany maintained was Reuters. And the reason was simple. They might propagandize the people but they, the hierarchs, the communist regime, they wanted to know what really was going on in the world without propaganda attached."

Living what was at times a lonely existence, Forsyth searched for the truth among the many false messages being fed to the people by the government. Part and parcel of the job, which also covered Czechoslovakia and Hungary, was being followed constantly by secret police, but while on sensitive fact-finding missions he learned to shake off the spies by simply passing through Checkpoint Charlie, where he was allowed passage but they were not. "Then I'd drive out into the East-German countryside and find out what was really going on . . . It was a fascinating experience, and it was only made possible because I could pass for a German.

"Covering France and Germany over that four-year period, I'd seen the France of de Gaulle, East Germany and West Germany, and it was very instructive," he said. "I later drew on this experience in writing my first books."

But his education regarding spies, mercenaries, assassins, international politics, and corrupt governments was not over yet. In 1965, twenty-seven-year-old Forsyth accepted a position back in England with the BBC as a radio and TV reporter. He soon became assistant diplomatic correspondent, which, in 1967, took him to Biafra—a newly created secessionist state in the south of Nigeria—to cover the civil war between Biafran and Nigerian troops. While they didn't publicly admit support, countries such as France and South Africa quietly provided Biafran troops with military assistance, while the United Kingdom and the Soviet Union supported the Nigerians.

One year later Forsyth left the BBC but returned to the Biafran state as a freelance journalist. In 1969 he wrote his first book, a nonfiction work about the brutal slaughter and humanitarian disaster that occurred on the way to Biafra's defeat, called *The Biafra Story*.

Once the journalist had the taste of writing a book, albeit a work of nonfiction, he began to concoct a plot for a fictional work, a novel that would be researched and written in a journalistic style and based as much in reality as possible. Of course, he'd had enough real-life experience to fill many books, but the topic he chose was an assassination attempt on President Charles de Gaulle funded by the OAS.

"It was based on reality," Forsyth said during an interview with talk show host Larry King in 2000. "The OAS did exist and they did make six attempts on his life. I mean, this was a genuine organization of terrorists in those days . . . They tried six times to kill the President of France. So all I did was create a seventh."

The story, written during 1970 and published in 1971, closely follows the movements of an extremely efficient assassin known as "the Jackal," who was commissioned by the OAS to kill the president. The detailed and riveting plot describes how the Jackal obtained false passports, how he researched the president's movements, and how he made trips into France from the United Kingdom to find the perfect position to make the kill. The book also outlines the efforts of a dedicated French detective who made it his life's work to stop the assassination. *The Day of the Jackal,* upon its release, became an instant bestseller and received rave reviews not only for its fast-moving, suspenseful story but for the sharp, journalistic, matter-of-fact style in which it was written.

His previous experience in Charles de Gaulle's France, the real attempts on the president's life, and his research into the operations of the OAS meant Forsyth was able to create a thriller that was not only entertaining but as accurate as a story could get without the event having actually occurred. His descriptions of criminal activities, such as obtaining a false passport, were so well researched that they caused headaches for many governments around the world, which had to change their policies in order to prevent copycat crimes.

When Israeli Prime Minister Yitzhak Rabin was assassinated in 1995, it was by Jewish law student Yigal Amir, who had hungrily devoured *The Day of the Jackal* as he researched past political assassinations, both from real life and from fiction. And, of course, real-life terrorist and hired killer Ilich Ramírez Sánchez was nicknamed Carlos the Jackal after evading capture for many years.

The Day of the Jackal went on to win several major prizes, including the 1972 Edgar Award from the Mystery Writers of America for Best Novel, and the international bestseller spawned a new career for Forsyth, who went on to become one of the world's best-read novelists.

CARRIE,
Stephen King, 1974

First had come the flow of blood and the filthy fantasies the Devil sent with it. Then this hellish Power the Devil had given to her. It came at the time of the blood and the time of hair on the body, of course. Oh, she knew the Devil's Power.

When looking into the past of the world's bestselling horror author it's easy to make the assumption that something singularly awful must have occurred, something so blinding in its terrible brilliance that it forever affected the thought patterns and imaginations of a once-healthy child. But while Stephen King certainly did have a challenging childhood, and while his upbringing and young adult years were far from perfect, it was actually a culmination of many experiences over several years that gave this prolific writer the combined gifts of a wonderfully healthy imagination and stunning storytelling skills.

In 1950, when Stephen was just two years old, his father went out to buy a pack of cigarettes and never returned. Donald Edwin King, who had served in the Merchant Marines in World War II and more recently sold vacuum cleaners door-to-door, left his wife, Nellie Ruth Pillsbury King, their four-year-old adopted son, David, and their natural son, Stephen, to fend for themselves. The shock of the loss of a parent as well as the resulting upheaval in Stephen's life would be a curse that the youngster eventually would turn into a blessing.

For the next few years Nellie and her children moved around the country to wherever she could find work, sometimes staying with her family, sometimes with Donald's family (although she'd never see Donald again), and often in various cheap rental properties. Often working two or three jobs to pay the bills, Nellie sometimes was so cash-strapped that she couldn't afford a babysitter for her sons. To entertain themselves while their mother was working late, the boys would read to each other—they particularly loved mystery stories and horror comics. As the immense tension of the Cold War seeped into every facet of American culture and lifestyle, many of the horror comics had begun to reflect the fears that people lived with every day, particularly those related to the undeniably diabolical effects of nuclear warfare. Like the rest of his generation (and many of his readers), Stephen would grow up with these fears as his reality, a child born into the Cold War.

All three members of the King family were avid readers, and after dinner they often would sit around the table in silence, each lost in his or her own paperback. In 1959, when David found an old mimeograph machine, he and Stephen created their own newspaper, called *Dave's Rag,* which they sold to locals for a nickel each. Stephen, just twelve years old at the time, contributed articles and short stories.

Much of young Stephen's inspiration for his stories came from horror comics as well as the horror films that he would treat himself to whenever he could afford a ticket. As an eleven-year-old he also collected newspaper articles about Charles Starkweather, who, with his girlfriend Caril Ann Fugate, had shocked Americans when they went on a killing spree across Nebraska and Wyoming. Several characters would be modeled around, and even named after, Starkweather in Stephen's published novels later in life.

In his teen years Stephen began writing stories whenever he had the chance, a compulsion that would characterize his behavior for the next several decades. He submitted many stories to horror magazines and pulp fiction titles but only would receive rejection slips. In 1960 Stephen experienced a fascinating moment of self-discovery when exploring his aunt's attic. He came across a box that had belonged to his father and in it found a large collection of rejection letters from magazines and publishers. The father he hardly even remembered, it seemed, also shared a great love of storytelling and the written word.

When Stephen was eleven the King family moved to Durham, Maine, where they settled for good. After attending the local primary school, Stephen followed his brother into Lisbon High School where, by all reports, he was an average student, standing out simply for the fact that he stood over six feet tall. Between 1965 and 1966 the eighteen-year-old wrote a 50,000-word novella called *The Aftermath,* about a nuclear apocalypse. At the same time he was still pumping out short stories, working on a novel, and writing articles for the school newspaper. At one point he was suspended from school for three days for printing a parody of the school newspaper, *The Village Voice*—his version was called *The Village Vomit.*

In between his schooling and his prolific extracurricular writing Stephen helped earn his keep by taking part-time work as a grave digger—a friend's father was the local undertaker and welcomed the assistance of the towering teenager. This job, which in retrospect seems so fitting, inspired the first story King ever had published in an official magazine, "I Was a Teenage Grave Robber." Published in 1965 by *Comics Review*, the story's title was changed to "In a Half-World of Terror," and although he was thrilled to finally be published, it was an unpaid commission. For his first paid story Stephen would have to wait another two years—in 1967 he sold the short story "The Glass Floor" to *Startling Mystery Stories* for $35.

Having entered the University of Maine in 1966 (he had won a partial scholarship to New Jersey's Drew University but couldn't afford the remaining fees), he studied English and wrote a regular column, called "King's Garbage Truck," for the university newspaper. While many of his fellow students regularly talked about becoming authors, Stephen did as he always had and wrote furiously. At college he wrote five novels, all of which remained unpublished. Extremely vocal in the anti–Vietnam War movement, the bearded, long-haired university student took a job in the university library, where he met Tabitha Spruce, with whom he had a daughter, Naomi, then married in 1971.

After graduating, he moved with Tabitha and Naomi into a trailer in Hermon, outside Bangor, Maine. To make ends meet, Stephen pumped gas at a gas station and worked in the local laundromat, and Tabitha worked nights at Dunkin' Donuts. Soon, depressed about the fact that his university education seemingly had gotten him nowhere, he began to drink, smoke, take drugs, and gamble, all addictions that would haunt him for the next decade. During this time he regularly was selling short stories to men's magazines, but a successful novel still eluded him.

The same year he and Tabitha were married Stephen found a job as a teacher of English at Hampden Academy, and nightly after work he'd return to the family trailer and clatter away at a typewriter balanced on his lap until the early hours of the morning. In the past he'd sent manuscripts, including *The Running Man,* to editor William Thompson at Doubleday. Thompson had been impressed with Stephen's storytelling but as yet had been unable to convince his colleagues to publish any of the novels. He encouraged Stephen to keep writing and to send more manuscripts as soon as he could.

In 1972 the King family was so poor that they regularly asked the phone company to cut off their telephone, as they couldn't afford the bills. During this time Stephen was experimenting with a story that mixed the subjects of high school embarrassment, something he witnessed in his students on a daily basis, and psychic powers. It was about Carrie White, a high school misfit with telekinetic powers, but partway through the novel he decided it was a bad idea and threw the manuscript in the trash can.

Fortunately for the King family, it was Tabitha who emptied the trash that evening. As she took the garbage outside, she noticed the manuscript, fished it out, read it from beginning to unfinished end and convinced her husband to continue, which he did. He finally sent the finished manuscript to William Thompson early in 1973, expecting a rejection letter in return, as usual.

A few weeks later when Stephen was in the staff room, he was paged over the school loudspeaker system and asked to come to the office. He raced through the corridors, thinking perhaps something had happened to one of his family members, and when he reached the phone Tabitha was on the other end. She had raced to a friend's house and rung him at school because a telegram from William Thompson had arrived. Thompson had tried to call, but the Kings' phone was, once again, cut off. The telegram read—"Carrie officially a Doubleday book, the future lies ahead. Love Bill Thompson. P.S. $2500 okay?"

A few months later the paperback rights were sold for $400,000, of which the author took half, meaning the days of poverty for the King family were finally over. Sadly, Stephen's mother, Nellie, who had worked so hard to provide a life for her sons, died after a battle with lung cancer in 1973. By this time *Carrie* had been accepted by Doubleday but was not yet published. Nellie would never realize the enormous success her son would achieve, although it was she who had provided the perfect environment for the development of his amazing appreciation for the power of words.

JAWS,
Peter Benchley, 1974

❦

*She reached down to touch her foot, treading water with
her left leg to keep her head up, feeling in the blackness
with her left hand. She could not find her foot. She
reached higher on her leg, and then she was overcome by
a rush of nausea and dizziness.*

Peter Benchley was a twenty-four-year-old university
graduate and junior journalist when in 1964 he read a
newspaper article about an enormous great white shark
that had been caught by a fisherman off Montauk Point
on Long Island, New York. This monstrous creature
weighed in at 4,550 pounds, and its proportions set the
writer's imagination into a spin. What would happen, he
wondered, if a shark of this size decided to stay, and feed,
in an area heavily populated by humans? What if the
area was a beach vacation haven, such as the seaside re-
sorts where he'd spent his childhood summers swim-
ming and snorkeling? What if it acquired a taste for
human flesh?

Young Benchley couldn't help but create stories and
scenes in his mind, just as he had little choice but to
become a writer. A healthy, creative imagination and a
talent for words were burned into his genes. Benchley's
father was Nathaniel Benchley, a well-known and respected author of books for children and a good friend of
Humphrey Bogart. Nathaniel wrote several novels, one

of which, *The Off-Islanders,* was made into an Academy Award–nominated film called *The Russians Are Coming, The Russians Are Coming.* It was about a Soviet submarine that accidentally ran aground off New England. Peter's grandfather was Robert Benchley, an extremely well-regarded humorist, writer of essays, newspaper columnist, actor, critic, and editor. Robert was famously one of the founders of the Algonquin Round Table, a group of writers that gathered every day for lunch at a round table at New York City's Algonquin Hotel from 1919 to 1929.

While his plethora of novels based by the seaside, or in the water, would lead one to believe that Peter Benchley grew up with sand between his toes, the truth is that he actually spent his childhood in New York City. For his secondary schooling he attended the elite Phillips Exeter Academy in Exeter, New Hampshire, as did his father and grandfather, before going on to major in English at Harvard University in 1961.

His impressive education included learning writing skills, but it was the summer vacations spent with his family that would shape the content of the work that would make him a household name. The family often would escape the stifling heat of summer in New York City by traveling to Nantucket Island, Massachusetts, where he and his father and his brother Nat regularly would go on unsuccessful expeditions to catch swordfish. "We couldn't find any swordfish," he once said in an interview, "but the ocean was littered with sharks, so we started catching them." He would never lose his fascination with sharks.

Benchley traveled around the world for a year after graduating from college, then, after spending six months in the Marine Corps reserve program in 1964, he worked for the next six months at the *Washington Post*. His next move was to *Newsweek* magazine, where he worked for three years as the television editor. In 1967 the writer took a step up in the world and accepted a job at the White House as President Lyndon Johnson's speech writer, a position he held until early 1969, when Johnson opted not to run for another presidency. Finally, he decided to work for himself and made a living from freelance journalism until a fateful meeting with a book publisher.

As a journalist Benchley had written several stories about sharks, but he was also keen to write nonfiction books. Of course, on top of all this he had been mulling over an idea for a novel, based on the killer shark that had entered his imagination five years earlier. A travel story he had recently written about the summer playground of Southampton, Long Island, had added a whole new angle to the story, as he told a journalist at the time. "My God," he remembered thinking, "if that kind of thing can happen around the beaches of Long Island, and I know Southampton, why not put the two together?"

In 1971, when Benchley still was working as a free-lancer, Tom Congdon, a literary editor from Doubleday who'd seen some of Benchley's articles, invited the journalist to lunch to discuss possible book projects. At the restaurant the two men brainstormed several ideas, and among the many proposals for nonfiction books Benchley let slip his idea for the novel. Congdon was hooked and immediately offered an advance of $1,000 for the manuscript.

"In those days I was working two or three days a week making a living doing television and newspaper stories," Benchley says. "That paid me enough so that I could have three or four days a week to work on the shark story. I sat in the back room of the Pennington Furnace Supply Company in Pennington, New Jersey, in the winters, and in a small, old turkey coop in Stonington, Connecticut, in the summers, and wrote what turned out to be *Jaws*."

In February 1974, after numerous rewrites requested by his publisher, the thirty-three-year-old author released *Jaws,* a book about a great white shark with a very healthy appetite for human flesh. The bloodthirsty killing machine terrorized the beaches around the South Shore of Long Island, feasting on swimmers, as the local population of a resort town at first denied, then faced up to the economic devastation it could cause. The fearsome thriller was an immediate success, taking just eight weeks to hit number two on the *New York Times* bestseller list—no mean feat for an author who was previously unheard of. *Jaws* stayed on the bestseller list for forty-four weeks. Within a few months of the book's release the film, starring Roy Scheider and Richard Dreyfuss, and directed by Steven Spielberg and coscripted by Peter Benchley, was being produced. The movie would break records by becoming the first to gross $100 million at the box office. It became Hollywood's first-ever summer blockbuster.

The book went on to sell over twenty million copies, and for a long time Benchley, who passed away in February 2006, at the age of sixty-five, had no idea why it was such a success. He finally put it down to one simple emotion—fear. "Completely inadvertently, it tapped into a very, very deep fear," he said. "If I had done it on purpose, it would be one thing. But I didn't know for years what was responsible for the enormous phenomenon of *Jaws*."

MIDNIGHT'S CHILDREN,
Salman Rushdie, 1981

❧

*Oh, spell it out, spell it out: at the precise instant of
India's arrival at independence, I tumbled forth into the
world. There were gasps. And, outside the window, fire-
works and crowds. A few seconds later, my father broke
his big toe . . .*

The publication of *The Satanic Verses* in 1988 caused an
immediate furor in the Islamic world, as it was perceived as a disrespectful depiction of Muhammad. The
novel's author, Salman Rushdie, suddenly made international headlines, not so much for his writing but for
the $1.5 million bounty placed on his head by Iran's
leader, Ayatollah Khomeini. Known as a "fatwa," this
edict sparked a crisis in diplomatic relations between the
United Kingdom (Rushdie's adopted home) and Iran,
and was to burden the writer for the best part of a
decade.

As a result of the controversy it provoked, Rushdie's
fifth book, *The Satanic Verses,* became his most famous
work. However, eight years earlier the Anglo-Indian author had published what many agree to be his most humorous, complex, lyrical, and magical work, *Midnight's
Children*. It was a novel that, according to the *New York
Times,* "redrew the literary map of India."

The comical allegory of Indian history revolves
around the life of its narrator, Saleem Sinai. Saleem is

born at the stroke of midnight, along with a thousand other children, on the day India gained independence from England—August 15, 1947. The title of the novel was inspired by the inaugural speech of the nation's new prime minister, Jawaharlal Nehru, who said, "Long years ago we made a tryst with destiny, and now the time comes when we shall redeem our pledge, not wholly or in full measure, but very substantially. At the stroke of the midnight hour, when the world sleeps, India will awake to life and freedom. A moment comes, which comes but rarely in history, when we step out from the old to the new, when an age ends, and when the soul of a nation, long suppressed, finds utterance. It is fitting that at this solemn moment we take the pledge of dedication to the service of India and her people and to the still larger cause of humanity."

Rushdie's masterpiece chronicles the narrator's life in Bombay from 1947 until 1977. It also charts the Republic of India's growth, from its conception in 1910 to its much anticipated birth in 1947, and to its forlorn adulthood under the leadership of Indira Ghandi.

Rushdie rejects the notion that the inspiration for *Midnight's Children* is his own childhood. "In every single book I've ever published people have assumed that I was the central character," he says. Saying similarities between himself and the narrator are coincidences, he admits, "There's the fact that it's my generation and also the circumstances of the book that [the main character] essentially grows up in my neighbourhood and goes to my school and those things, which is just the commonplace thing about writers. You set things in the world that you know, but beyond that the book goes off into very eccentric areas that have nothing to do with my family life."

Like Saleem Sinai, Rushdie was born in Bombay in 1947 to a wealthy middle-class Muslim family. His father was a Cambridge-educated businessman and the only writer in Rushdie's family was his paternal grandfather, an Urdu poet. At the age of fourteen Rushdie was sent to Rugby School in England. "Coming to Rugby was really quite brutal," he recalls. "I was not quite 14 and taken aback to be made to feel like a foreigner which, until that point, I had never thought of myself as. I did experience certain amounts of racial discrimination . . . and that was shocking and depressing." His education continued at King's College in Cambridge, where he studied history.

When his education was complete, Rushdie returned to his family's home in Pakistan, where they had moved in 1964. There he tried his hand at acting, which he'd been introduced to while at Cambridge. However, although he harbored a deep passion for the stage, he was to discover that acting was not his forte. Rushdie later reflected lightheartedly, "My problem as a university actor, which I can see in hindsight, was doing too much. One of the things that good actors will tell you is that you do less and less and less all the time. And, you know, I have a slight arm-waving tendency anyway and there was a little too much gesticulating and too much acting going on."

He decided to instead pursue his other deep-seated passion, writing. Rushdie had wanted to be a writer since the age of ten. An avid reader since childhood, he desperately had wanted to be a part of the literary world and to have something to do with creating what he saw as the magic that lay within books.

Returning to England in the early 1970s, Rushdie found employment as an advertising copywriter and at the same time continued to work on a novel. His first book, *Grimus*, a science fiction fantasy, was published in 1975, and it completely bombed. It was ignored by the buying public and lambasted by the critics. Advised by all around him to pursue another form of employment, Rushdie was angered by such reactions and soon came to a profound crossroads in his career.

"I remember thinking, well, you'd better either give up or do something much more conservative and middle-of-the-road and non-risky," he says. "Or take the biggest risk you can, so that if you're going to go down, at least go down in flames." Rushdie chose the latter path, and over the next five years he penned *Midnight's Children*.

The groundbreaking novel was an intricate tale of a country, the story of a boy's coming of age, and the history of a family. The narrator, a Hindu child, is switched at birth and raised by a wealthy Muslim family. His efforts to discover his own identity run parallel to India's struggles during the first years of the nation's independence.

A grand work on an epic scale, *Midnight's Children* deals with the complex themes of colonialism, history, and destiny, while blending supernatural elements with everyday settings. Exuberantly written, Rushdie's foundation for the novel was his beloved Bombay and the language with which he'd grown up. The writer remembers fondly, "When I was growing up, everyone around me was fond of fooling around with words. It was certainly common in my family, but I think it is typical of Bombay, and maybe of India, and there is a sense of play in the way people use language." Bombay's tumultuous and frenetic energy and Rushdie's affection for the city is reflected in the novel's themes, style, and structure.

When *Midnight's Children* was published in 1981, it took the literary world by storm, winning the Booker Prize that same year. The greatest accolade was heaped on the work in 1993 when it was awarded the "Booker of Bookers"—considered the greatest book to be given the honor in the prize's twenty-five-year history.

THE COLOR PURPLE,
Alice Walker, 1982

> *First he put his thing up gainst my hip and sort of wiggle*
> *it around. Then he grab hold my titties. Then he push his*
> *thing inside my pussy. When that hurt, I cry. He start to*
> *choke me, saying You better shut up and git used to it.*

Activist, essayist, poet, and author Alice Walker was born possessing a passionate spirit. The eighth and final child of humble sharecroppers was known throughout her birthplace of Eatonton, Georgia, as an outgoing and precocious youngster. This was to change in 1952, when she was eight years old. While playing a game of Cowboys and Indians with her siblings, young Alice was accidentally shot by her brother with a BB gun. As a result, she lost an eye and was left with an unsightly scar, but it was not the physical wound that had the greatest impact on her—it was the teasing and ridicule from other children that caused the greatest pain.

Suddenly overcome with shyness, Walker retreated into a private world of reading and poetry. Later describing the effect of the accident and its consequences on her artistic development, she said, ". . . It was from this period, from my solitary, lonely position, the position of an outcast, that I began to really see people and things, really to notice relationships and to learn to be patient enough to care about how they turned out . . . I retreated into solitude and read stories and began to write poetry."

By the age of fourteen, much of the scar tissue was removed and the passionate, gregarious, outspoken spirit once again began to bloom. As her outgoing character gradually reasserted itself, the studious teenager went on to become valedictorian and prom queen of her high school. Following graduation, Walker won a scholarship to Spelman College, a university for black women in Atlanta. While at college Walker became a vociferous supporter of the Civil Rights Movement, as she developed strong feelings and beliefs regarding the social injustices inflicted upon the black people of the United States.

After completing two years at Spelman, Walker transferred to Sarah Lawrence College in New York, where she completed her first book of poetry, *Once,* in 1965. It was published that same year. The poems dealt with a diverse range of topics from her experiences during a trip to Uganda as an exchange student in 1964, her suicidal feelings after having an abortion following an unwanted pregnancy in 1965, and her experience of the Civil Rights Movement. Walker was recognized at once by the literary establishment as a talented writer. *Negro Digest* noted her "precise wordings, the subtle, unexpected twists . . . [and] shifting of emotions." *The Dictionary of Literary Biography* highlighted Walker's "unwavering honesty in evoking the forbidden, either in political stances or in love."

Graduating from college in 1965 with a Bachelor of Arts, Walker stayed in New York and worked for the Department of Welfare, while continuing to write. The author's first short story, "To Hell with Dying," was included in the 1967 anthology *The Best Short Stories by Negro Writers,* and her essay "The Civil Rights Movement: What Good Was It?" won a prize from the *American Scholar.*

Walker, however, felt drawn to the South and soon moved to Mississippi. While exploring her heritage she continued to write poetry and fiction. It was during this period that the writer discovered the work of folklorist and author Zora Neale Hurston, the author of *Their Eyes Were Watching God,* and who by that time had faded into obscurity. Walker was drawn to Hurston's work, later explaining that it showed "a sense of black people as complete, complex, undiminished human beings, a sense that is lacking in so much black writing and literature." Hurston chose to represent the dialogue of her black characters using the speech patterns and idioms of the time and culture. The writer often was criticized for this, as it was seen to caricature black culture. But Walker praised Hurston's "racial health" and was responsible for a revival in her work after penning an article for *Ms. Magazine* in 1975 titled "In Search of Zora Neale Hurston."

In 1970 Walker's first novel, *The Third Life of Grange Copeland,* was published. Chronicling the oppression and hardships of a rural black family and the multigenerational cycle of violence that is born again with each new male, the novel was praised by critics for its honesty and simplicity.

Throughout the 1970s Walker continued to write a steady stream of short stories dealing with the sexism, racism, and violence facing black women. She explored the same territory in her second novel, *Meridian,* published in 1976. Using the Civil Rights Movement as a backdrop, the novel explores the development of a young black woman. The work was praised by the *New York Times Book Review* as "a fine, taut novel that accomplishes a remarkable amount." The publication also noted that Walker "writes with a sharp critical sense as she deals with the issues of tactics and strategy in the civil rights movement, with the nature of commitment, the possibility of interracial love and communication, the vital and lethal strands in American and black experience, with violence and non-violence."

As a writer and chronicler of the black experience, Walker was more concerned with the inner working of black culture rather than the relationships between blacks and whites. Concerned most of all with the black woman's experience, Walker's female characters showed strength, fortitude, and resourcefulness in the face of adversity—traits with which she personally had become very familiar during her early years. Recognizing the twin afflictions of the black woman—racism and sexism—all of the writer's thoughts and beliefs regarding these subjects came together in her 1982 novel, *The Color Purple*.

Told entirely in the black dialect of the day through a series of letters, *The Color Purple* tells the story of an impoverished black woman named Celie. Raped by her stepfather, her two children are taken from her and she is forced into a violent and ugly marriage to a man she does not love. Completely alone, Celie has nobody to talk to but God until she finds comfort, affection, and the eventual liberation of spirit through her relationships with the women of her community.

Winning the Pulitzer Prize in 1983, the novel remained on the *New York Times* bestseller list for more than a year. The film version of the book, released in 1985, directed by Steven Spielberg and starring Danny Glover, Whoopi Goldberg, Margaret Avery, and Oprah Winfrey, was nominated for eleven Oscars and won a slew of other major awards. Prior to *Schindler's List*, released eight years later, *The Color Purple* was the film that proved to Hollywood that Spielberg was capable of directing and producing serious cinema.

Most important, *The Color Purple* in film and book form served as positive inspiration to the downtrodden around the globe. The powerful story told its readers and viewers that no matter how abused and mistreated, people can survive, achieve freedom, and blossom through the strength, wisdom, and inspiration found within themselves and others.

HOLLYWOOD WIVES,
Jackie Collins, 1983

❧

Etta the Elephant, former secretary in New York City, was now slim and svelte. She was called Elaine Conti, and lived in a six-bedroomed, seven-bathroomed, goddam Beverly Hills palace.

It was very little surprise to anybody who knew them that the stunning Collins sisters, Joan and Jackie, of up-market Bayswater in London, both made the decision to move into the arena of showbusiness as soon as they possibly could. After all, their father was Joseph William Collins, a theatrical agent, and their mother was Elsa Bessant Collins, a dancer, and both encouraged their children into the world of theater. But while older sister Joan always showed a natural leaning toward performance, particularly toward acting, Jackie showed an altogether different type of skill during her time at school.

When she was just eleven years old, Jackie often would be seen with her head buried in books—a good sign for any child. But the books she was devouring were not intended for children so, during her reading time, Jackie actually was giving herself an entirely new type of education.

"I was reading Mickey Spillane and Harold Robbins, and they'd be absolutely filthy, and I'd think, 'This is so great!'" the writer recalled during an interview. "So I'd make up my own little sexual scenes. Of course, I didn't

215

know what the hell I was talking about until I was at least 13, and I'd tell my friends, 'I can let you have a peek at this if you pay me.' It was sort of like drugs."

From a very young age Jackie was learning the undeniable truth that sex sells, and it was a lesson that she would never forget. It wasn't just her reading habits, though, that were more advanced than the other pupils. Jackie regularly was truant from school, often snuck out to nightclubs, smoked cigarettes, and, bizarrely, sometimes openly poked fun at a local streaker, much to the embarrassment of her teachers.

"We'd be dressed in our little school uniforms and going through a park in England on our way to tennis lessons, and he'd be flashing away and I'd point and roar with laughter. 'Must be a cold day today, huh?' This absolutely infuriated the teachers," she said.

Eventually Jackie's behavior proved too much for the staff at her school, and in 1952, when she was just fifteen, she was expelled. Joan had already jetted off to Hollywood to chase her film career, and upon Jackie's expulsion her parents offered her a fairly simple choice— reform school or Hollywood. One seemed a punishment, the other a wonderful chance to escape into a world of glamour, so she headed to Los Angeles and moved in with her big sister.

In Hollywood Jackie made an attempt to break in to the film world, and thanks to her sister's profile she managed to earn a few roles in films, but unfortunately her movies met with little success. Most importantly, though, this precocious youngster was witnessing firsthand the strange goings-on in the world of showbusiness, including relationships between the powerful producers, the desperate starlets, the hangers-on, and the trophy wives.

Here was a world where all she'd learned about sexuality was lived out on a daily basis, a heady society where greed, money, power, and beauty controlled the lives, loves, enormous successes, and miserable failures of its population.

But Jackie would not find success in front of the camera, so, disappointed and disillusioned, she moved back to London, where in 1955 she married, had a daughter, divorced, and once again moved in with her parents. In 1966, eleven years after her first marriage, the twenty-nine-year-old once again tied the knot. Her second husband was the well-known nightclub owner Oscar Lerman, and this relationship would stay the course until his death from cancer in 1992.

Lerman could see that his new wife was keen to start a new career, and he encouraged the writing ambitions she'd had since she was eleven years old. For the first time in a long time Jackie put pen to paper, and in 1968 her first novel was published. It was called *The World Is Full of Married Men* and, true to her original experience as a student writer, it was filled with raunchy sex scenes— so much so that it was banned in some countries. The book was an instant bestseller. Jackie's learnings about the power of sex had paid off handsomely and her future novels, with titles such as *The Stud, Sinners, The Love Killers,* and *The Bitch,* would all share similar themes.

In 1980 Jackie and her family, which now included two more daughters, moved back to Los Angeles. Having already written eight novels, all of which were bestsellers, in 1983 she published a book centered around her experiences of living in Los Angeles as well as much that she had heard and experienced since. *Hollywood Wives* rocketed to number one on the *New York Times* bestseller list and would go on to sell fifteen million copies around the globe. The book also became a TV miniseries produced by Aaron Spelling and starring Anthony Hopkins, Candice Bergen, Angie Dickinson, and Rod Steiger. The series won massive ratings for ABC.

Several other books, including *The Stud* and *The Bitch,* also had been made into films. These two films, in fact, were credited with breathing new life into Jackie's sister's waning acting career, leading to Joan's most famous role as Alexis Colby in *Dynasty.* But none of the success of Jackie's past books came close to *Hollywood Wives,* which captured the imagination of readers at a time when the excesses of celebrity fascinated the general public.

Jackie Collins has now sold between 300 and 400 million books in about forty countries, and twenty-three of her novels have made it onto the *New York Times* bestseller list. As outrageous as her stories and characters are, she insists that they actually are watered-down versions of the real thing. "I write about real people in disguise," she says. "If anything, my characters are toned down—the truth is much more bizarre."

BRIDGET JONES'S DIARY,
Helen Fielding, 1996

⟨⁓⟩

> *Head is full of moony fantasies about living in flats with him and running along beaches together with tiny off-spring in manner of Calvin Klein advert, being trendy Smug Married instead of sheepish Singleton. Just off to meet Magda.*

When Helen Fielding was asked by her editor at the *Independent* newspaper to pen a daily chronicle of her life as a single woman in London, the journalist was aghast. The thought of documenting her own mishaps, triumphs, insecurities, and relationships horrified the thirty-seven-year-old, who knew it would be impossible to survive the embarrassment that such a column would generate. Fielding felt she could not write the piece under her own name. Moreover, she thought the whole idea was silly. But succumbing to pressure, Fielding decided the only way she could write the column would be under the safety of an alias. Her savior was a thirtysomething singleton named Bridget Jones.

Helen Fielding was born in Morley, West Yorkshire, England, in 1958. The daughter of a mill owner and a housewife, Fielding attended an all-girls' school then went on to study English at Oxford. After graduating in 1979, Fielding found employment in production at the BBC, where she worked on a broad range of the broadcaster's programs, from current affairs to children's television.

She even spent time in Africa, producing segments for Comic Relief. But after eight years as a producer, Fielding decided she wanted to try her hand at writing.

Displaying great bravado, every week for six weeks Fielding sent an article about car alarms to the *Guardian* in the hope that the publication would print it. She wasn't successful. She attempted penning a Mills & Boon romance, but that too was rejected. The letter from the publisher read, "Neither your characters nor your story are up to the high standards required by the Mills & Boon reader." Then, in 1987, Fielding collaborated with Oxford classmate Richard Curtis on a humor book about sex titled *Who's Had Who: In Association with Berk's Rogerage: An Historical Register Containing Official Lay Lines of History from the Beginning of Time to the Present Day*.

After a short freelance stint at the *Sunday Times* writing humorous observational pieces, Fielding decided to pen a satirical book based on her experiences with *Comic Relief* and on her knowledge of the media in London. The result was *Cause Celeb* (1994), a send-up of the relationship between African famine and London celebrity. Although not a success with buyers, the novel did receive excellent reviews. The *Independent* called the novel "sharp, gutsy and refreshing" and praised Fielding for her ability to exercise "her wit on those who deserve it without being flip about those who don't."

Encouraged by her critics, in 1995 Fielding set her sights on writing another book but, unable to support herself while doing this, she accepted a job offer from the *Independent*. The newspaper was impressed with the critical success of *Cause Celeb* and thought Fielding would be a perfect fit for a new column they wanted to introduce. The popularity of personal articles written by single women in their mid-thirties about their lives and loves had grown exponentially since the *New York Observer* began running Candace Bushnell's column *Sex and the City* in 1994. Hoping to jump on the bandwagon, the *Independent* gave Fielding the assignment of presenting the ups and downs of her life in a weekly column.

Cash-strapped Fielding accepted the job, but as she recalls, "The idea of writing about myself in that way seemed hopelessly embarrassing and revealing. I offered to write an anonymous column instead, using an exaggerated, comic, fictional character. I assumed no one would read it and it would be dropped after six weeks for being too silly." Drawing on an idea for a character in a sitcom she was planning to write, Fielding created the persona of Bridget Jones.

To gain further inspiration Fielding rediscovered the diary she'd written while at university. The writer was shocked to find that she had kept a list of calories eaten as well as pledges to be a better person. Although Fielding denies that she is Bridget Jones, she has confessed, "I tend to take a little bit from my life, a little bit from what people tell me, and a little bit from what I see around me."

Each week the humorous details of Bridget Jones's life were printed in the pages of the *Independent*. Plagued with insecurities, Bridget strove for both the physical and emotional perfection that was only ever found between the pages of women's magazines. While dealing with disastrous relationships, career mishaps, and embarrassing family dramas, Bridget had the support of a close-knit group of friends to guide her through her turbulent life.

Fielding said she also drew on Armistead Maupin's *Tales of the City* for ideas. "I was trying to create a generic urban family for Bridget, so that she's got her single friends, her gay friends, her smug married friends, which together form a very strong emotional setup," she explained. "It's almost like a tribe . . . That goes back to the question of single women, that they're not pitiable creatures with barren emotional lives, but quite the opposite.

"I didn't let anyone except the section editor know it was me. All the journalists at my desk were frightfully serious and writing about New Labour and global warming—I didn't want them to know that I was writing about why it takes three hours between waking up in the morning and leaving the house." Despite the author's misgivings, the column touched a nerve. At the time there was a growing proportion of women who had chosen to be single. Educated and career oriented, they were happy to wait for a man good enough to marry.

The popularity of the column led to a book offer, but turning her columns into a novel was not an easy task. The articles had to be linked by a traditional narrative. Fielding said of the problem, "I ended up with a year's worth of thousand-word bits that were very intensely written and chewed over. But then of course I wanted it to be a proper story." To solve her dilemma Fielding decided to use Jane Austen's *Pride and Prejudice* as a rough template for her story. She later joked, "I shamelessly stole the plot. I thought it had been very well market researched over a number of centuries."

The comedy novel *Bridget Jones's Diary* related a year in the life of Bridget Jones as told in a series of humorous diary entries. Working in the book publishing industry and then in television production, Bridget was single and lived alone in London. She liked the wrong man, the charming, handsome, and rakish Daniel Cleaver, and had a close network of trusted friends. Bridget's parents worried their thirtysomething daughter would never marry and attempted to set her up whenever possible, especially with a family friend, the uptight lawyer Mark Darcy. From January to December Bridget charted her weight, her alcohol and calorie consumption, and the number of cigarettes smoked, while also dealing with an unfaithful boyfriend, a new admirer, and her mother's midlife crisis.

Like many of Austen's heroines, such as Elizabeth Bennet and Emma Woodhouse, Bridget had a knack for creating for herself tremendously embarrassing situations and committing to unrealistic resolutions. But through her blunders and social faux pas she also constantly grew and became more aware of herself and others. As his name suggested, Mark Darcy was the contemporary equivalent to *Pride and Prejudice*'s Mr. Darcy. Arrogant and aloof, he secretly harbored a growing admiration for Bridget that eventually turned into love. Mistaking his coldness for superiority, Bridget developed a strong resentment for the lawyer and embarked on a relationship with Daniel Cleaver—modern literature's Mr. Wickham. Ultimately Daniel was exposed as a philanderer, Mark saved the Jones family from embarrassment by rescuing Bridget's mother from a Portuguese Lothario, and Bridget realized Mark was the man she had been searching for.

The novel became an instant hit and Bridget-Jonesisms such as "Singleton," "Smug Marrieds," and "fuckwittage" quickly found their way into popular usage. Fielding explained the book's abbreviated style by saying, "My column was supposed to be exactly a thousand words. It's like filling up the petrol in the car—you always try to get it to land at exactly 20 pounds. So I always try to make it exactly a thousand words, and the way I do that is, instead of taking out chunks, I just take out words. Unnecessary words."

Although Fielding claimed *Bridget Jones's Diary* had no literary merit whatsoever, reviewers loved it, one calling the book a "deftly executed urban comedy of manners." Readers similarly were enamored, and the book spent seventeen weeks on the *New York Times* bestseller list. A sequel was written in 1999, and successful film versions of both books followed. Suddenly Bridget Jones, who began life as a character invented to mask the identity of her creator, became a hero to single women the world over.

HARRY POTTER AND THE SORCERER'S STONE,

J. K. Rowling, 1997

❧

> *He wore round glasses held together by Sellotape because of all the times Dudley had punched him on the nose. The only thing Harry liked about his appearance was a very thin scar on his forehead which was shaped like a bolt of lightning.*

Muggles and mudbloods, animagi and Azkaban, Dumbledore and Dementors—today these characters, terms, and places are in common usage among Harry Potter enthusiasts young and old. But the magical world that is entered via Platform 9 ¾ at London's Kings Cross Station may have remained hidden forever if not for the imagination and determination of a single mother and her extraordinary on-again, off-again relationship with a bespectacled orphan.

Published in 1997 with an initial print run of just one thousand, *Harry Potter and the Sorcerer's Stone* surpassed all expectations as to what a children's book was capable of. The perfect blend of action, humor, terror, and danger had children, and their parents, completely enchanted.

Today, for the lucky few who own them, those first edition copies are valued at between $32,000 and $50,000. The author herself became the first person to earn a billion dollars by writing books—not a bad effort for an idea that the author claimed just strolled into her head, and for a two-hundred-page manuscript that initially was rejected by twelve publishers.

Rowling has always understated her monumental achievement, but *Harry Potter and the Sorcerer's Stone* was, in fact, five years in the writing and a culmination of a rich variety of life experiences.

Joanne K. Rowling was born in 1965 in South Gloucestershire, England. A bout of measles at the age of four gave the child her first real experience with books. Her father, the manager of a Rolls-Royce engine plant, would try to brighten his bedridden daughter's spirits by reading to her from *The Wind in the Willows*. It must have worked, because by the age of six she knew she wanted to be a writer and had already penned her first story, a work of fiction about an adventurous rabbit.

A voracious reader, Rowling has said of herself, "I was the epitome of a bookish child, short and squat, thick National Health glasses, living in a world of complete daydreams." Her favorite authors were E. Nesbitt, Paul Gallico, C. S. Lewis, and Elizabeth Goudge.

It was at the age of five or six that the first seeds of the Harry Potter franchise were planted in the fertile mind of young Joanne. With her younger sister, Dianne, and other neighborhood children, Rowling invented a game called "Let's Pretend," an improvised play performed in the Rowlings' front garden. Raiding her mother's closet, she cast herself and Dianne as witches, and a five-year-old friend who lived nearby won the coveted role of the wizard. His name was Ian Potter.

Her love of the written word continued into her teen years and perhaps became an escape from the blow that rocked the Rowling family in 1980. When Joanne was just fifteen her mother was diagnosed with multiple sclerosis.

Upon finishing school, Joanne had hoped to study English at college, but her parents had dreams of their oldest daughter working for the United Nations as an interpreter. Consequently, after crumbling under parental pressure, Rowling began a French degree at the University of Exeter.

Lacking motivation for her studies, Rowling relieved her boredom by trying her hand at writing novels. But as she was uninspired in her daily life, and with the specter of her mother's illness hanging over her, she failed to complete any of the numerous drafts that she had begun.

Graduating in 1987, Rowling took a series of jobs and drifted aimlessly through the next few years. Beginning two adult novels as well as a series of short stories, once again the budding author failed to finish what she'd started. But in the summer of 1990 an idea for a novel finally took hold, one that was to become Rowling's obsession for the next five years.

Having spent the weekend in Manchester visiting her boyfriend, who had recently relocated, Rowling was returning to London by train on a Sunday evening. Traveling alone during the four-hour trip, the twenty-five-year-old suddenly discovered welcome company in her imagination in the form of a boy-wizard named Harry Potter.

Rowling has said of the surprising incident, "All of a sudden the idea for Harry just appeared in my mind's eye. I can't tell you why or what triggered it. But I saw the idea of Harry and the wizard school very plainly. I suddenly had this basic idea of a boy who didn't know who he was, who didn't know he was a wizard until he got his invitation to the wizard school. I have never been so excited by an idea."

Rummaging frantically in her bag for a pen, pencil, even an eyeliner, anything with which she could jot down the ideas welling in her mind, Rowling became desperate to start writing. Too shy to ask another passenger for a pen, eventually she had to content herself by simply thinking about the story. As the train pulled into Kings Cross Station, Rowling had enough of Harry's life planned out to begin writing that very evening.

Although Rowling admits the original few pages written that night have little in common with the final version of *Harry Potter and the Sorcerer's Stone,* she already had conceived the stories behind all seven Potter books, which would take the lead character from boyhood to manhood. Tragically, six months later Rowling's relationship with Harry was halted abruptly when her mother passed away. Her world spiraled out of control, and within a few months Rowling left England for Portugal.

Living in the vibrant city of Porto and teaching English in the evening, Rowling's days were free to renew her acquaintance with the young wizard. As a result of her mother's death, Harry's motivations, fears, and insecurities became clearer in Rowling's mind. The death of James and Lily Potter became a central theme in the narrative.

Returning to England in 1994, Rowling brought with her a baby daughter—the product of an unsuccessful and short-lived marriage to a Portuguese journalist—and a rough and sketchy manuscript of *The Sorcerer's Stone*. Divorced and penniless, the single mother moved to Edinburgh to be near her sister, Dianne. With her life in shambles, the twenty-nine-year-old was forced to live in subsidized housing and to make ends meet on the meager $140 a week she received from welfare.

Depressed and desperate, Rowling contemplated giving up her writing to take a job teaching French at a local high school. But after her sister read the first three chapters and loved it, she decided to devote herself to finishing the novel. Heartened by Dianne's reaction, Rowling spent the next nine months writing.

Escaping her bleak surroundings by visiting local cafés, Rowling spent her days writing the script in longhand with her infant daughter by her side. On returning to her apartment each evening, she'd type her day's writing on a second-hand typewriter. Seventy-eight thousand words later, the manuscript was complete.

The book revolved around an eleven-year-old boy who seemingly was unexceptional except for a lightning-shaped scar on his forehead. An orphan living with his comically repugnant aunt and uncle, when Harry began receiving letters from the Hogwarts School of Witchcraft and Wizardry, he discovered his heritage and eventually embarked on a courageous and sometimes dangerous journey of self-discovery, friendship, and magic.

On completing the book in 1996, Rowling immediately made her way to the Edinburgh Central Library to find a literary agent in the Writers' and Artists' Year Book. She chose Christopher Little Literary Agents in Fulham, London, simply because she liked the name. After sending the first three chapters to Little, she received an encouraging letter a few days later asking for the remainder of the manuscript.

Little sent the manuscript to twelve publishers, without success. The market was flooded with children's books and no publisher had confidence in a book about a prepubescent wizard attending a school called Hogwarts. But eventually Bloomsbury took on the first-time author and sent Rowling an advance of $3,000. They also recommended she change her name.

Bloomsbury feared the target market of young boys might not buy a book written by a woman. After the publisher suggested Rowling use her initials, her pen name changed from Joanne Rowling to J. K. Rowling. Lacking a middle name of her own, Rowling borrowed her grandmother's name, Kathleen.

The following year, before the novel was published in the United Kingdom, an auction was held in the United States to secure the publishing rights on that side of the Atlantic. The editorial director of Scholastic Books had so much faith in Harry, Hermione, Ron, Dumbledore, and Hagrid, that he was determined to win. Having read the story on a flight from the United States to Italy, he had become completely enamored by the characters and the tale.

Three days after the novel's British publication, Rowling received a phone call from her agent informing her Scholastic Books had come through with the highest bid. The rights cost the publishing house a massive $100,000—unprecedented for a children's book.

Spawning six sequels, the Harry Potter chronicles have sold over 300 million copies and have been translated into sixty-one languages.

Following its tiny original print run of one thousand books (five hundred of which went straight to libraries) for the first novel in the series, the seventh and final title—*Harry Potter and the Deathly Hallows*—set a new world record with sales of 8.3 million copies in its first twenty-four hours.

TRUE HISTORY OF THE KELLY GANG,
Peter Carey, 2000

> *Ellen Quinn were 18 yr. old she were dark haired and slender the prettiest figure on a horse he ever saw but your grandma was like a snare laid out by God for Red Kelly. She were a Quinn and the police would never leave the Quinns alone.*

One of the most daring robberies in Australian history took place in 1879 in a small town called Jerilderie, in rural New South Wales, near the Victorian border. On the night of Saturday, February 8, 1879, the notorious Kelly Gang—led by Ned Kelly and also comprising his younger brother Dan, Steve Hart, and Joe Byrne—rode into town. Despite a £1,000 reward for their capture, they were able to sit down for dinner at the Woolshed Inn before bailing up the town's two policemen and imprisoning them in their own cells. The outlaws' previous exploits, as well as the fact that they only robbed banks and rich landowners, as well as the gang's stance against the oppressive British authorities, had made them heroes of the poor farmers in the harsh countryside of Victoria and New South Wales. At the time, as today, the Kelly Gang represented settler culture and therefore represented Australian culture. These outlaw bushrangers would live on in folklore and become an important influence over Australian national identity.

In Jerilderie their aims were twofold. The gang had come to rob the local bank, and Ned's secondary goal was to have a letter published, a manifesto of sorts, in order to help the public understand why he was forced to kill three policemen four months earlier at the infamous shoot-out at Stringybark Creek in the wild, woody Victorian highlands. He and his working-class Irish Catholic family had been targeted by British colonial police for as long as he could remember—Kelly's own father had died shortly after being released from prison.

Sunday in Jerilderie was spent at the police station planning their robbery. The only outings were a few quick trips through the town (wearing police uniform, the bushrangers explained that they were reinforcements sent from Sydney) to familiarize themselves with the location of the bank. On Monday the four emerged from the station (two still dressed as policemen) and forced about thirty people, at gunpoint, into the Royal Mail Hotel, which also contained the bank. The outlaws stole over £2,000 and, after a quick show of trick-riding to entertain the locals, many of whom were proud to have been held up by the Kelly gang, made their escape back into the bush.

During the holdup Ned had handed his lengthy letter to the bank's accountant and made him promise to have it published. It was an eight thousand-word manuscript that Ned had dictated to Joe Byrne prior to the Jerilderie raid, pleading for justice both for his own family and for other Irish settlers. His hatred of the British authorities was plain to see—after explaining why he had to kill the police at Stringybark Creek, he followed up by saying: ". . . Remember those men came into the bush with the intention of scattering pieces of me and my brother all over the bush . . . and is my brothers and sisters and my mother not to be pitied also who has no alternative only to put up with the brutal and cowardly conduct of a parcel of big ugly fat-necked wombat headed big bellied magpie legged narrow hipped splay-footed sons of Irish Bailiffs or English landlords which is better known as Officers of Justice or Victorian Police who some calls honest gentlemen but I would like to know what business an honest man would have in the Police . . ."

The missive, now known as the "Jerilderie Letter," was never published or distributed, but was instead handed to the bank's head office and later loaned to the police for use in Ned Kelly's eventual trial. It now belongs to the State Library of Victoria and represents a rare and valuable insight into the mind of a violent criminal who would become a folk hero.

Eighty-three years after the robbery, and eighty-two years after Ned Kelly had been hanged for his crimes, a twenty-year-old copywriter at a Melbourne advertising agency read a copy of this letter in 1962. The copywriter, who had also grown up in the Victorian countryside, was Peter Carey, and the Jerilderie Letter stuck in his mind. In fact, as a budding writer he often fantasized about using it in one of his works.

"This is not [a] fantastically well-educated man, but very smart and very angry and very funny," Carey said in an interview in 2000, describing Ned Kelly and the Jerilderie Letter. "I was very touched by this letter, quite apart from its anger. Reading it in 1962 I was so impressed by this letter, which was originally in his handwriting I think—about fifty-eight pages—that I sat down and typed it up so I would have it, thinking I would, such is the arrogance of young writers . . . do something with it one day."

In fact, Carey would, one day, do something with this letter, but almost four decades would stand between the moment of reading and the stunning result of his writing.

From 1962 until 1967 Carey worked in the advertising world, previously having dropped out of a science course at Melbourne's Monash University. His copywriting work brought him into contact with the works of various inspired and often experimental writers, including Franz Kafka, Saul Bellow, Alain Robbe-Grillet, James Joyce, Samuel Beckett, and William Faulkner. His first novel, *Contacts,* was written in 1964, but the young writer failed to find a publisher willing to put it into print. By 1968 he had written several other manuscripts, also unpublished, including *The Futility Machine* and *Wog.*

In order to escape the relatively conservative society of 1960s Australia, Carey traveled to Europe, settling in London in 1968 and once again working in advertising. There he discovered various counterculture movements, and when he returned to Melbourne in 1970, then moved to Sydney in 1974, it was with a very liberal attitude toward politics, writing, and the arts.

In 1977 Carey joined an alternative commune in the rain forest outside of Brisbane, and he regularly would commute between Sydney, where he still worked part time in advertising, and the commune, where he lived a hippie lifestyle, grew disdainful of corporate culture and capitalism in general, and, of course, developed a greater appreciation for the attitudes and beliefs of Ned Kelly. Although none of his previous novels had been published, Carey used his time at the commune to write yet another major work, convinced this time things would be different—and they were.

The novel he wrote at the commune was *Bliss* (1982), which would go on to win the Miles Franklin Award and various other major titles. Additional novels followed, including *The Illywhacker* (1985), the Booker Prize–winning *Oscar and Lucinda* (1988), and, after moving to New York City in 1988, *The Tax Inspector* (1991). Much of his work shared a theme of the uniqueness of Australian culture and the results and effects of its colonial heritage. The negative effects of capitalism also were regular themes within Carey's novels, and in 1995 *The Unusual Life of Tristan Smith* compared the culture of the country he had left to that of the country he was living in.

Around this time Carey found himself taking American friends in New York to see an exhibition of the works of Australian artist Sidney Nolan, which included Nolan's famous series of paintings of Ned Kelly's armor. "Where people in Ireland and people in Britain know a little bit about the Kelly story, people in New York know nothing," Carey recalled in an interview. "So I had to tell them the story and I'd take them and I'd tell them again and again and as I told the story I sort of rediscovered it for myself . . . I thought, god, I'd really just like to write this as a novel. And there was only one way that I really wanted to approach it—to write it in his voice."

And so Carey's original reading of the Jerilderie Letter in 1962, and his wishes to include it in his own writing somehow, had finally become a reality. Along the way Carey had, like the bushranger himself, developed a healthy disrespect for capitalism and for the methods of the British authorities who had colonized Australia. His next job, which would take years of research, would be to get to know Ned Kelly better than any other writer ever had.

Carey immersed himself in books about the Kelly Gang, spent countless weeks at state libraries in Australia reading original documents from Kelly's time, and, once again, absorbed not just the words, but the thoughts, emotions, and personal philosophies that had gone into the writing of the Jerilderie Letter. It was the Jerilderie Letter that gave the book's narrator, Ned Kelly, his voice. The rest of the research allowed Carey to create a sense of historical authenticity, all the while in a work of fiction.

True History of the Kelly Gang, first published in 2000, earned critical acclaim worldwide, winning for the author his second Booker Prize and the Commonwealth Writers' Prize, and making it to the short list for the Miles Franklin Award. More important, though, was the fact that the author somehow had breathed life into a long-dead legend whose name still captures the imagination of an entire nation.

The Da Vinci Code,
Dan Brown, 2003

❧

> *Thirty yards down the hall, a single spotlight on a porta-*
> *ble pole-stand shone down on the floor, creating a stark*
> *island of white light in the dark crimson gallery. In the*
> *center of the light, like an insect under a microscope, the*
> *corpse of the curator lay naked on the parquet floor.*

In March 2006, an unassuming author stood in the wit-
ness box of London's High Court. He'd been called in to
defend himself against claims of plagiarism, and at one
stage the well-dressed, polite American was approached
by the court clerk, who was brandishing a legal notepad.
Wondering what the young woman possibly could want,
the forty-two-year-old was surprised when she asked
him for his autograph—another sure sign that Dan
Brown pressed all the right populist buttons with his
novel *The Da Vinci Code.*

Selling forty million copies worldwide, Brown's
fourth novel went to the top of the *New York Times* bestseller list during the first week of its release and has earned
the author an estimated $76.5 million. Despite being posi-
tioned at number 12 on the *Forbes* magazine Celebrity
100 List in 2005, the reclusive writer leads an almost
monastic life. Rising at four in the morning each day to
begin work, Brown keeps an antique hourglass on his
desk to remind him to take breaks, which usually con-
sist of a brisk set of sit-ups and push-ups. The paradox

can be explained in part by Brown's extraordinary up-bringing.

Born and raised in Exeter, New Hampshire, Brown is the oldest of Richard and Connie Brown's three children. With his mother a professional musician and his father a mathematics teacher, Brown describes his childhood as an odd mix of science and religion. On the one hand his father, who authored several bestselling mathematics textbooks, would construct codes, puzzles, and cryptic clues for his children on birthdays and at Christmas as part of an elaborate treasure hunt. On the other, Richard's position on staff at the exclusive Phillips Exeter Academy meant the Brown family lived on campus and grew up in a very restrictive Christian environment.

Unlike most American families of the 1970s, the Browns didn't own a television. Instead of watching *Gilligan's Island* and *The Brady Bunch,* young Dan sang in the church choir, went to Sunday school, and, in the summer, attended church camp. When he reached the ninth grade the teenager was enrolled at Phillips Exeter Academy.

The author credits his interest in secret societies to his youth in New England, where he was "surrounded by clandestine clubs of Ivy League universities, the Masonic lodges of the Founding Fathers, and the hidden hallways of early government power."

After graduating, Brown attended Amherst College, where he completed a double major in English and Spanish. By the time he was twenty-two, Brown admits to two loves—one was writing fiction. Brown's list of favorite authors is an eclectic mix, from Jeffrey Archer to Shakespeare and from Robert Ludlum to John Steinbeck. But despite a natural affinity for literature and having been raised in a house jammed to the rafters with books, Brown decided instead to pursue his second interest when he graduated from college in 1986.

Brown loved to dabble in the music world and create effects with a synthesizer. One of his first efforts was a children's cassette called *SynthAnimals,* which included tracks with names like "Happy Frogs" and "Suzuki Elephants." Perhaps unsurprisingly, *SynthAnimals* did not make a big impression on the charts. Brown, however, was undaunted and soon moved to the West Coast to test his talents in Hollywood. It was in Los Angeles where he would meet the most commanding influence on his life and career.

Upon joining the National Academy of Songwriters in 1991, Brown met Blythe Newton, the Academy's director of artist development. Twelve years Brown's senior, she developed an instant respect for the fledgling musician and took him under her wing. Newton essentially became Brown's unofficial manager, writing press releases, setting up promotional events, and helping him network. It was not long before the pair became lovers, a fact kept secret from Academy bigwigs.

Over the following few years Brown, under Newton's guidance, released four CDs, without success. Finally realizing they should seek careers outside the music world, the couple left the United States for Europe. Spurred on by Newton's lifelong fascination with Leonardo da Vinci, the pair spent time in Seville, Spain, studying art history. Brown also became enthralled by the enigmatic Italian artist.

Upon their return to the United States in 1993, the couple took up residence in Brown's hometown and the twenty-nine-year-old began teaching English at his alma mater, Phillips Exeter Academy. Shortly after, lessons were interrupted when two United States Secret Service agents arrived at the school and detained a student, claiming the boy was a threat to national security.

Frustrated with government policies, the teenager had sent an e-mail to a friend the previous evening, comically suggesting he kill President Clinton. The agents finally left without incident, and the scandal died down as quickly as it had ignited, but Brown's fascination with government agencies, and their processes of evidence collection, was piqued. He believed the subject would be an excellent premise for a novel.

The following year Brown and Newton traveled to Tahiti for vacation. With little to do but lie in the sun, Brown devoured Sidney Sheldon's *The Doomsday Conspiracy*. Sheldon's 1991 thriller had made it to number one on the *New York Times* bestseller list, but after reading the tale about a brilliantly orchestrated international cover-up involving the National Security Agency, Brown was confident he could do better.

With his interest in conspiracy theories fueled and his batteries recharged, Brown began work on his first novel, *Digital Fortress*. At the same time he cowrote a book with Newton called *187 Men to Avoid: A Guide for the Romantically Frustrated Woman*, under the pseudonym Danielle Brown. The satirical self-help book sold only a few thousand copies and soon went out of print.

In 1996 Brown resigned from his position at Phillips Exeter Academy to concentrate on writing full time. That same year his first novel was published. A frantic-paced thriller about the National Security Agency and an unbreakable code that could alter the world's power balance, *Digital Fortress* failed to make an impact on the sales front, despite Newton's best efforts.

Having taken on the burden of the book's promotion, Newton booked Brown onto talk shows, lined up press interviews, and even sold books from her car trunk. Brown followed *Digital Fortress* with two further suspense thrillers, *Angels and Demons* in 2000 and *Deception Point* in 2001. Neither achieved major success.

While researching *Angels and Demons*—a story involving an ancient, secret brotherhood called the Illuminati and their war against the Catholic Church—Brown and Newton once again found themselves drawn toward the work of Leonardo da Vinci. They had become engrossed by the many puzzles and mysteries in and around da Vinci's works, and as a result a fourth novel was beginning to take shape in Brown's imagination.

As there were obvious links between the subject matter of *Angels and Demons* and his new endeavor, Brown decided to resurrect the hero from his previous work, Harvard symbologist Robert Langdon, about whom Brown once lamented, "Langdon is the man I wish I were. Langdon is cooler than I am. One of the luxuries of being a writer is that you can live vicariously through your characters."

Brown and Newton, who had married five years earlier, in 1997, spent a year researching the story line, including several days at the Louvre in Paris analyzing da Vinci's works with an art historian. While abroad they also researched other elements of the plot. Newton had her own very strong views of what should go into the book. "She became passionate about the history of the church's suppression of women," Brown explained, "and she lobbied hard to make it a primary theme in the novel."

Back in Exeter, writing commenced in earnest, with Brown spending entire days in the loft of the couple's

New Hampshire home, piecing together the narrative. In another part of the house his wife painstakingly scoured hundreds of books and Web sites for additional facts and theories, which she would summarize and e-mail to her husband.

Brown has called his wife his inspiration, and he happily admits she was the chief researcher on the theological whodunit. Contributing her insights and theories to her husband during the writing process proved invaluable to Brown who, once finished, penned the dedication— "For Blythe . . . again. More than ever."

Published in 2003, *The Da Vinci Code* easily eclipsed Brown's past works. A mass of symbols, riddles, and cliff-hangers, the plot follows academic Robert Langdon, who is called in to investigate the bizarre murder of the Louvre's curator. In a fusion of fact and fiction, Langdon discovers a series of clues buried in the works of Leonardo da Vinci.

In a book interlaced with conspiracies and the machinations of secret societies, a number of startling revelations emerge. Chiefly, Jesus married Mary Magdalene and had a child with her, his bloodline survived in France, and the Holy Grail was not a chalice but a woman.

Described by publisher Random House as a "thriller for people who don't like thrillers," its success was despite mixed critical reviews. One newspaper critic wrote, "It is terribly written, its characters are cardboard cut-outs, the dialogue is excruciating in places and, a bit like a computer manual, everything is overstated and repeated—but it is impossible to put the bloody thing down." Brown's masterpiece had a similar effect on a British reviewer, who called it "irritatingly gripping tosh."

On publication the novel not only raised the ire of critics but also of church leaders, who have branded the book sacrilegious. Meanwhile, other writers have claimed aspects of the bestseller were lifted from previously published works, but the 2006 trial in London saw Brown and his publishers acquitted of all wrongdoing.

The controversy, however, has only helped boost sales of *The Da Vinci Code* and of Brown's previous unsuccessful novels, which have all since spent time on bestseller lists.

Nonfiction

THE ENGLISH DICTIONARY

❧

Two names from history stand out as the fathers of the modern dictionary—Samuel Johnson in the United Kingdom and Noah Webster in the United States. But their all-encompassing texts, so large and bold in their vision that they required decades of painstaking research, actually were new and improved versions of old manuscripts.

Historians believe that one of the first dictionaries was written by teacher and grammarian Verrius Flaccus, who lived between 55 BC and AD 20. His skills as a teacher were renowned across the Roman Empire, resulting in his being employed to educate Gaius and Lucius, the grandsons of emperor Augustus. His life project, though, was an encyclopedic text called *De verborum significatu* (*On the Meaning of Words*), in which the letter *A* on its own took up four books.

Prior to this a famous Roman scholar by the name of Marcus Terentius Varro, who lived from 116 BC to 27 BC, had written a book on the Latin language called *De lingua Latina,* which, although based on language, has never been defined as a dictionary.

The work by Flaccus, though, was well used by thinkers such as Pliny the Elder, and in the late second century

BC it was updated by Sextus Pompeius Festus, who filled twenty volumes with explanations of the meanings of words as well as their origins. As a dictionary editor does today, Festus stripped obsolete words from the Flaccus text and added new ones, changing definitions wherever necessary. The only surviving partial manuscript from the work of Festus over 1,800 years ago, the *Codex Farnesianus* containing entries M to V, currently is being analyzed and translated at University College in London, providing stunning insight into history.

In the late eighth century Paul the Deacon, an Italian author and historian born into a noble family, chose a monastic life and entered the abbey of Monte Cassino. A poem that he had written caught the attention of Charlemagne, king of the Franks, who brought Paul to his court as a writer of poetry and a teacher. As well as being the great conqueror of Lombardy, Charlemagne is remembered for the arts renaissance that took place under his rule, and one of the commissions for which he personally was responsible was for Paul to update and summarize *De verborum significatu,* written almost eight hundred years earlier by Flaccus and last updated six hundred years earlier by Festus. Returning to Monte Cassino, he completed his task in the monastery before dying around AD 799.

But of course these dictionaries recorded the Latin language. One of the first English-language dictionaries was written in 1604 by teacher and deacon Robert Cawdrey. Known as *Table Alphabeticall,* it only contained three thousand words. A more thorough version, *Glossographia,* was penned by lawyer and lexicographer Thomas Blount around 1656—this volume contained about 11,000 difficult words and unusual terms.

Several other dictionaries appeared over the next century, but none were thorough in their coverage of the English language and one, *A New World in Words* (1658), by Edward Phillips, was thought to have had much of its text lifted directly from Blount's *Glossographia,* causing a long-lasting public dispute between the two men.

Then, on September 18, 1709, a poor bookseller by the name of Michael Johnson, and his wife, Sarah, had a son they named Samuel. As a youngster in the English cathedral town of Lichfield, Samuel suffered from scrofula—tuberculosis of the lymph glands. As a result, the youngster's hearing in his left ear was permanently damaged, as was the sight in his left eye. His face would be forever scarred by blisters and boils caused by the disease and from a case of smallpox. Before the age of ten Samuel also developed involuntary tics, which historians suspect was caused by Tourette's syndrome.

Although his family was forever in debt, at the age of nineteen Johnson attended Pembroke College in Oxford after a friend of the family offered to fund his education. But when the promised money never materialized, he was forced to leave college after little more than a year. Johnson took a job as a teacher, and when he was twenty-five married forty-six-year-old widow Elizabeth Porter. Two years later, in 1736, he opened his own private school, taking in just three students. A financial disaster, he closed the school twelve months later and moved to London, hoping to sell a play called *Irene* he'd written.

Ten years later, having had no luck with his script, Johnson still was living in poverty. Around 1747, having worked as a writer and after a planned project to publish an edition of Shakespeare's works fell through, he began work on *A Dictionary of the English Language,* the book that would earn him a place in history. For the next eight years he struggled in poverty, working mostly on his own. He often was forced to make requests for financial help from patrons, and to make ends meet he self-published a semiregular collection of his writings, called *The Rambler.*

In 1755 Johnson's dictionary was released in two enormous volumes. It was the first dictionary to use each word in a quotation in order to illustrate its usage. For the next 150 years Johnson's tome would be the standard English dictionary, but despite its influence it didn't make a great deal of money for its author, who went on to publish several other books, essays, and collections of poetry before his death in London on December 13, 1784.

As the *Dictionary of the English Language* represented the way the English liked to speak and spell, its symbolism was not lost on the Americans as they struggled, and bled, for independence from Britain. This irked Noah Webster who, like Johnson, had spent time as a schoolteacher.

Webster was born on October 16, 1758, in West Hartford, Connecticut, and grew up during the American Revolution. He spent his childhood helping out on his father's farm and, like Johnson, went to college as soon as he could, attending Yale. In another similarity to Johnson, Webster desperately wanted to continue his studies and go on to earn a law degree, but his family could not afford the fees so instead he became a schoolteacher.

When he began teaching, Webster didn't like what he saw at American schools. Classrooms were overcrowded with students of all ages, few teachers had any qualifications, and, worst of all, the textbooks came from England. Not one to sit back and do nothing, Webster decided to write his own textbooks. In 1783 he produced

A Grammatical Institute of the English Language, which, because of its cover, came to be known as the "blue-backed speller" and was the most popular textbook in U.S. schools for the next one hundred years—by 1861 annual sales had reached one million.

Concerned that the English language had been hijacked by the Brits, in his early forties Webster decided to take on a project that was almost unthinkable in its scope—he would rewrite Johnson's dictionary, this time for Americans. He chose to simplify spelling, and to spell many words phonetically, so *musick* became *music, waggon* became *wagon, centre* became *center,* and *honour* became *honor,* and he added uniquely American words, like *skunk* and *squash.* The dictionary took a massive twenty-seven years to complete, the final touch being added during 1825, a year he spent living in Paris. When *An American Dictionary of the English Language* was published in 1828, it contained over 70,000 words, 12,000 of which were unique to this dictionary. As his English counterpart, Johnson, also had experienced, Webster's dictionary, although enormously influential and well regarded, did not sell enough copies to make its author wealthy. After remortgaging his house to work on the second edition (published in 1840), he passed away on May 28, 1843, an American legend.

But there is one more chapter in the story of the dictionary, one that begins in 1857 and ends in 1928—the writing of the *Oxford English Dictionary.* The saga began when the Philological Society of London decided that Johnson's version of the English dictionary, like all others in existence, simply didn't do the job. They were all incomplete, and it was time to create a dictionary that accounted for every word in the English language.

That was in 1857, and at the time Society members were blissfully unaware of the amount of work involved. It wasn't until 1879, in fact, that they came to an agreement with Oxford University Press and work on a new English dictionary, headed up by Scottish lexicographer James A. H. Murray, began.

The team working on the dictionary estimated their job would take a decade, but they were in for a rude shock. Five years into the project they'd only reached the word *ant,* so they brought more editors on board and continued to chip away at the mountain. Of course the longer they took, the more words they'd have to review and change before the book was published.

Amazingly, the final volume of the dictionary wasn't published until 1928, thirteen years after Murray's death and forty-nine years after work had begun! Originally titled *A New English Dictionary on Historical Principles,* it filled ten volumes and contained over 400,000 words. In 1933 it was revised, renamed the *Oxford English Dictionary,* and reprinted in twelve volumes. Dictionaries finally had become a far bigger project than any one man could ever hope to handle.

ENCYCLOPAEDIA BRITANNICA,
1768

To those who balk at the effort involved in putting together a dictionary, the compilation, research, and writing of an encyclopedia must be unimaginable. But fortunately throughout history a few brave souls have decided to take on the enormous task of defining, informing, analyzing, and reporting the history as well as the current significance of everything everybody would ever want to know.

One such visionary was Emperor Zhu Di, the third emperor of the Ming dynasty of China, who is regarded as one of China's greatest leaders. Also known as the Yongle Emperor, Zhu Di was in power from 1402 to 1424, and during that time he commissioned the building of the Forbidden City. He also implemented the research and writing of what would become the world's biggest single publishing project, a record that stands to this day.

Zhu Di's publishing vision was to collect the entire library of Chinese literature and knowledge into one set of encyclopedias, one enormous collection of books that would define everything from the arts and sciences, from history and philosophy, from topic areas such as drama, geology, astronomy, technology, medicine, and religion. For four years, from 1403 to 1407, between two thousand and three thousand academics and officials worked on the project. All of their research and knowledge was directed toward one single set of encyclopedias, hand written with a brush dipped in ink, that eventually comprised 22,877 volumes of text as well as sixty volumes of catalogs used to navigate the main texts.

The work, stunning in its breadth, is known by historians as the *Yongle Encyclopedia.* In 1557, when fire ripped through the Forbidden City, the volumes narrowly were saved, and as a result the emperor at the time, Jiajing, ordered a duplicate set to be made—another Herculean task. Sadly, today only several hundred volumes from the original 22,877 of the copied version of the encyclopedia exist. Whether the original set is still hidden somewhere, or has been destroyed, is a mystery. Some believe it may be buried in a tomb with one of the emperors—possibly Jiajing.

Other collections of books that could be defined as encyclopedia had been completed in the past, including a thirty-seven-volume work about the natural world penned by Pliny the Elder, called *Naturalis Historia,* during the first century AD. But nothing ever had come close in its vision or its blanket coverage of all possible subject areas. Another major effort would take place in France in the mid-1700s.

A few decades earlier, in London in 1728, writer Ephraim Chambers had published *Cyclopaedia,* a two-volume encyclopedia in the English language that was also known as *A Universal Dictionary of Arts and Sciences.* Popular enough to be reprinted several times, it caught the attention of French publishers.

Paris-based publisher André Le Breton commissioned a translation of *Cyclopaedia* in 1743, but two years later discovered he'd been swindled by the translator, John Mills, an Englishman living in France who could hardly read or write a word of French. After reportedly giving Mills a whipping with his cane, Le Breton employed an editor, Jean Paul de Gua de Malves, to take care of the project. Malves hired several assistant editors, including writer/philosopher Denis Diderot and mathematician/physicist/philosopher Jean le Rond d'Alembert. One year later, Diderot took over.

Diderot's constant enthusiastic suggestions to Le Breton that his team, rather than simply translating Chambers's work, instead create their very own encyclopedia, eventually paid off. For the next quarter of a century Diderot and his team produced the work known as *Encyclopédie*—thirty-five volumes containing more than 78,000 articles and more than 3,000 illustrations. The work had enormous political and social influence, so much so that it was banned for several years because of its views undermining the teachings of the Catholic Church. It is also said to have played a major part in encouraging the French Revolution, having brought together and given voice to so many scholars and thinkers.

In the mid to late eighteenth century the city of Edinburgh was experiencing a golden age known as the Scottish Enlightenment—a renaissance of sorts. Scottish economist Adam Smith was publishing his most influential works and Robert Burns was writing verses that would see him recognized as the nation's, and indeed one of the world's, greatest poets. But it was a big idea between a printer and an engraver that would create the age's most all-encompassing work of publishing, the *Encyclopaedia Britannica*.

The printer/bookseller was Colin Macfarquhar, and the engraver Andrew Bell. Recognizing the current era of learning and academia, the pair decided to create an all-new encyclopedia, one that was a great deal more thorough than Chambers's two-volume *Cyclopaedia*. In 1768 they employed as the editor twenty-eight-year-old academic William Smellie, a naturalist, Fellow of the Royal Society, and friend of Robert Burns.

Smellie was commissioned to write the encyclopedia in one hundred sections so it could be released and sold weekly but eventually would be bound together into three volumes. The first section hit the stands on December 6, 1768, and sold for sixpence. Three years and 2,391 pages (most written by Smellie) later, and the first edition was complete. Bell, the engraver, was responsible for many of the illustrations.

Smellie was able to complete the work so quickly, as he borrowed heavily from works by other academics and experts. Some sections of his work in this first edition of the encyclopedia have been accused of being shoddily researched and of questionable factual value, but errors were corrected in later editions.

The three-volume set of *Encyclopaedia Britannica* was an immediate commercial success, quickly selling out. A second edition, published over ten volumes, was released between 1777 and 1784. By 1826 four more editions had been released, the sixth containing twenty volumes.

A pirated edition of *Encyclopaedia Brittannica* was printed in Philadelphia in 1790, introducing the product to the enormous American market. Although he lacked permission from the brand owners to do so, the master printer who published America's first copies, Thomas Dobson (originally from Scotland), actually did the brand an enormous favor, helping it gain a strong foothold in the country. The pirated version was even said to have been owned by Presidents George Washington and Thomas Jefferson.

Today printed encyclopedias are being fast replaced by Internet-based versions, some open to be edited by anybody, and digital versions. With the breadth of coverage offered on the Internet by such brands as Wikipedia, we finally may yet see a work as wide-ranging in its subject areas as Emperor Zhu Di's *Yongle Encyclopedia*, written six hundred years ago.

THE ORIGIN OF SPECIES,
Charles Darwin, 1859

❧

It is interesting to contemplate a tangled bank, clothed with many plants of many kinds, with birds singing on the bushes, with various insects flitting about, and with worms crawling through the damp earth, and to reflect that these elaborately constructed forms, so different from each other, and dependent upon each other in so complex a manner, have all been produced by laws acting around us.

When Robert Darwin took his son Charles out of school in 1825 for being lazy and inattentive in class, he supposedly cried with exasperation that the sixteen-year-old cared for nothing but shooting, dogs, and rat-catching, and that he'd be a disgrace to himself and his family.

It is true that as a youth Charles Darwin cared very little for anything but nature, and this was reflected in his blasé attitude toward his studies. But having been born into a distinguished lineage of renowned Englishmen, it wasn't long before young Charles developed a passion and obsession that was to see him develop into the single most important naturalist and one of the most significant thinkers of the nineteenth century.

When Charles Robert Darwin was born in Shrewsbury, Shropshire, England, in 1809 he already had a great deal to live up to. Placed on the baby's tiny shoulders was the burden of a father who was a reputed doctor and grandfathers who had amassed achievements of equal greatness. Charles's maternal grandfather was pottery tycoon Josiah Wedgwood, and his fraternal grandfather was Erasmus Darwin, famed naturalist, physician, poet and inventor. The fifth of six children, Charles, who was known as "Charley" or "Bobby" to his family, began his formal education at Mr. Case's Grammar School in Shrewsbury and, by all accounts, young Charley was not a good student.

When Charles was nine years old his mother, Susannah, died. But she was not without her influence on her son's later development. It was she who showed Charles how to change the color of flowers by mixing food coloring into their water. The naturalist later credited this as being the initial impetus for his future career.

In the following year Charles joined his brother Erasmus at Shrewsbury Grammar School, but much to his father's chagrin his ability as a scholar did not improve. Bored by his lessons, Charles was a slow learner and was not inspired by his studies. Outside of school, though, the boy's love of nature was ever increasing. Spending each summer vacation in Northern Wales, Charles would go on long hikes in the countryside and by the seashore, collecting vast quantities of seashells, insects, and rocks. Likewise, when his brother Erasmus built a science lab in the garden shed, Charles took to spending many hours concocting gases and potions instead of studying. Charles's friends gave him the nickname Gas Darwin, and he also earned the ire of the Reverend Samuel Butler, the proprietor of his school, for wasting his time on scientific nonsense.

In 1825, Robert Darwin enrolled his son at Edinburgh University to study medicine. Edinburgh possessed one of the most distinguished medical schools in the country, and Robert believed encouraging Charles to go into medicine would give the teenager the direction he needed in life. But Charles hated the sight of blood and found his lessons tedious. While his studies languished, Charles pursued outside interests and furthered his knowledge of the natural sciences. The taxidermy teacher at the university was John Edmonstone, a freed black slave originally from Guyana. Charles struck up a friendship with Edmonstone, who mesmerized the student with tales of the wilds of South America and taught Darwin the art of taxidermy. As his mind continually was being broadened by his growing circle of friends, in his second year at Edinburgh the teenager joined the Plinian Society, a club that examined the natural world from a scientific perspective. And importantly, at the same time, Charles began a friendship with zoology professor Robert Grant. Grant was a proponent of evolutionary theory, and the pair would analyze and discuss marine specimens collected during trips to the Firth of Forth. Grant taught Darwin much about observing nature and classifying specimens. He also introduced Darwin to the work of French naturalist Jean-Baptiste Lamarck, an early believer that evolution occurred in harmony with natural laws.

Angered that his son was wasting too much time on distractions, in 1827 Robert advised Charles to quit medical school. At the urging of his father, Charles enrolled at Christ's College at Cambridge University to study theology, with the view of becoming an Anglican minister. This new plan suited the eighteen-year-old well enough, as he believed working as a parson would give him ample time to spend with nature. Although Darwin eventually did very well in his final exams in 1831—placing tenth out of 178 students—by this stage he had no intention whatsoever of becoming a parson.

During his four years at Cambridge, Darwin's knowledge of the natural sciences increased dramatically. With his cousin William Fox, who possessed a passion for entomology, Darwin became a devout beetle collector. In the process he learned a great deal about insect classification and identification and how to work in the field, and his cousin introduced Darwin to Professor Reverend John Henslow, one of England's most respected naturalists. Henslow saw potential in his new protégé, and Darwin became a regular at Henslow's Friday night dinner parties, where the group would discuss all things science. Darwin accompanied Henslow on field trips, and they were often seen together on the streets of Cambridge deep in scientific discussion—Darwin became known around campus as "The man who walks with Henslow." Having found a great mentor in Henslow, it was at this point that the twenty-two-year-old decided to pursue a career as a naturalist.

Although he'd been enrolled in college for six years, Darwin never had taken his subjects seriously and had no formal instruction in the natural sciences. All he possessed was an avid love for, and interest in, the natural world. Consequently, the young man was thrilled when he was recommended by Henslow to Robert FitzRoy, captain of the HMS *Beagle*. As he was about to embark on a two-year expedition to chart the coast of South America, FitzRoy employed Darwin as the ship's naturalist. Robert Darwin, who saw the *Beagle* expedition as another of his son's flights of fancy, forbade his son to leave. But at the urging of a much-respected uncle, Darwin senior acquiesced, and the *Beagle* sailed in December 1831, with Charles Darwin on board.

Traveling to South America, the Galápagos Archipélago, and the Pacific Oceanic islands, Darwin recorded his field work and observations in a series of notebooks that later would become the basis for *Journal of researches* (1839), known today as *The Voyage of the* Beagle. An exciting travel log, as well as a detailed account of Darwin's scientific observations, the book garnered the naturalist considerable respect among the scientific community. The letters and specimens (many of them new to scientific circles in London) he sent back to England while abroad secured, on his arrival home in 1836, a celebrity's welcome. Most significantly, Darwin had earned his father's respect, with Robert readily agreeing to support his son financially in his scientific endeavors.

The *Beagle* trip marked a crucial point in Darwin's career. When he departed England in 1831, the twenty-two-year-old was an inexperienced naturalist with no formal qualifications. On his return in 1836 (the journey lasted three years longer than expected), Darwin's powers of observation had been honed and his scientific method was faultless. During his five years at sea, Charles Darwin had become a naturalist of the highest order. He later said the voyage was "by far the most important event in my life and . . . determined my whole career." Even more important was the fact that Darwin visited numerous locations in the Southern Hemisphere and observed many living creatures that possessed marked differences but also obvious similarities depending on their slightly different habitats. This planted the seed in

Darwin's mind of the mutability, or transmutation, of species.

The standard view among scientists at the time was that life was created where it was found, depending upon the environment. After consulting with ornithologist John Gould on the specimens of Galápagos mockingbirds, and zoologist Thomas Bell, who had examined Darwin's Galápagos tortoises, Darwin became convinced that the creatures had changed according to the environment of their particular island. Darwin began to contemplate why and how living forms changed over time and, in July 1837, began his first notebook on the transmutation of the species.

Keeping these initial ideas secret from the rest of the scientific fraternity because of their controversial nature, Darwin set about interviewing farmers on their animal husbandry techniques and pigeon owners on their breeding practices in order to understand how they produced different variations of the same breed of animal. After carrying out this preliminary research, Darwin came to believe that life evolves and that all living creatures are infinitely changeable. He wrote that selection was "the keystone of man's success in making useful races of animals and plants." Darwin was by no means the originator of the concept of evolution. His own grandfather, Erasmus, was an advocate of the principle, and Darwin had spent many hours with Robert Grant discussing Lamarck's ideas on the subject. But Darwin's theorizing took new and novel directions, and the concept of natural selection was the linchpin to his entire argument for evolution. As Darwin speculated, natural selection occurs when the positive characteristics of an organism become inherited, while those that are less favorable die out over successive generations. This flew in the face of traditional belief and church teachings that each organism was carefully planned by a higher power.

This idea was further strengthened after his reading of Thomas Malthus's *An Essay on the Principle of Population* (1798). In his autobiography Darwin wrote, "In October 1838, that is, fifteen months after I had begun my systematic enquiry, I happened to read for amusement Malthus on Population, and being well prepared to appreciate the struggle for existence which everywhere goes on from long-continued observation of the habits of animals and plants, it at once struck me that under these circumstances favourable variations would tend to be preserved, and unfavourable ones to be destroyed. The result of this would be the formation of new species. Here, then, I had at last got a theory by which to work." However, fearing damage to his reputation, Darwin decided not to publish any of his notes on transmutation until more research had been carried out. By the 1840s Darwin was confident enough in his findings to share his ideas with his close colleagues.

In 1846 Darwin shelved his work on transmutation to complete the final part of the *Beagle* project involving barnacles. He'd originally thought it would be a short task, but Darwin's work on the sea creatures took him eight years, and he later regretted all the time he devoted to this work. It wasn't until 1854, following several bouts of illness and his daughter's death, that he resumed work on transmutation. Still not ready to announce his findings publicly, Darwin worked rigorously into the 1850s to shore up his theory against the barrage of criticism and questions to which it surely would be subjected.

By 1858 the naturalist had written ten chapters of his

book on the subject when, in June that year, he received a copy of *On the Tendency of Varieties to Depart Indefinitely from the Original Type* by the English naturalist Alfred Russel Wallace. Concerned with exactly the same theory as Darwin's, the manuscript prompted Darwin to finish work on his book and publish as soon as possible.

Published in 1859, *The Origin of Species by Means of Natural Selection; or, The Preservation of Favoured Races in the Struggle for Life* proved enormously popular with the reading public. Selling for 15 shillings, the initial print run of 1,250 copies sold out on the first day. While Darwin's theory was not unique, his research and findings were much more accurate than previous scientists' work and his writing was also far more accessible to the general public.

Although Darwin went to great lengths to avoid any mention of human beings in his ideas of the evolutionary chain, and did not offer any explanation for the beginnings of life on Earth, it immediately was assumed that he was displacing God as the Creator. Ironically, Darwin, the former theology student, suffered no inner conflict regarding the battle between science and religion. Darwin regarded science as completely separate from religion—God was outside the scope of scientific inquiry.

The Origin of Species changed the scientific and cultural landscape of Victorian England and, as the book gained prominence in the rest of the world, the parameters for scientific study grew exponentially. In 1860 the term "Darwinism" was coined by naturalist Thomas Huxley, and in 1864, when philosopher Herbert Spencer talked of the "survival of the fittest," he was applying Darwin's ideas of evolution and natural selection to the economic makeup of society.

SCOUTING FOR BOYS,
Robert Baden-Powell, 1908

During the second Boer War the town of Mafeking in South Africa became the setting of a tense and deadly drama. This event would not only change the course of the war but would also produce a British national hero who would go on to change the world by writing a book.

Throughout 1899 tension had been building between the British Empire and the Boer republics of the Orange Free State and South Africa. As a result, Colonel Robert Baden-Powell of the British Army, who had been tasked with organizing a force in South Africa to assist the regular army, had begun building defenses around the perimeter of the strategically located town of Mafeking. But less than one month after work began, war was declared, and the town, containing Baden-Powell and about five hundred troops, was surrounded by the Boer army, which at times exceeded eight thousand men.

Utilizing his previous military and outdoors experience, Baden-Powell created a brilliant defense system. It included tunnels, trenches, and a certain amount of smoke and mirrors, including the planting of fake minefields (as he actually had no mines) and the building of fake gun turrets. When on the outskirts of the town and possibly in the enemy's sight, the British and allied soldiers were instructed to move as though they were avoiding barbed wire, although there was none.

Boys in the town aged twelve to fifteen were recruited to assist the soldiers by standing guard, running messages, and carrying out several other duties, allowing the heavily outnumbered troops in the town to concentrate on fighting. "My chief staff officer, Lord Edward Cecil, got together boys in the place and made them into a cadet corps for carrying orders and messages and acting as orderlies and so on, in place of the soldiers, who were thus released to go and strengthen the firing line," Baden-Powell explained in a magazine interview in 1937. "We then made the discovery that boys, when trusted and relied on, were just as capable and reliable as men."

British newspapers reported daily on Baden-Powell's exploits, and when, in 1900, the 217-day siege finally was broken and the Boers defeated, he returned to England a national hero.

Born on February 22, 1857, in London, Robert Stephenson Smyth Powell was the son of vicar and natural science professor H. G. Baden Powell and Henrietta Smyth, the professor's third wife. Robert was the fifth of seven children from this marriage, and the prolific vicar also had three children from a previous relationship. But when Robert was just three years old, his father died and Henrietta changed the family name to Baden-Powell, in the vicar's honor. From then on it was her job to bring up her many children, and she was determined to make sure the male influence was not lost on her boys.

Henrietta encouraged her children to read their father's many books about the natural world and supplemented their learning with great amounts of time in the outdoors, playing games with each other and enjoying long walks in wild areas while learning about flora and fauna.

Robert earned a scholarship to London's exclusive Charterhouse School, which was surrounded by forest. There he continued his own form of outdoorsman education, particularly when he had to hide from schoolmasters as they patrolled the forest, which was off limits to students. "When I was a boy at Charterhouse I got a lot of fun out of trapping rabbits in woods that were out of bounds," Baden-Powell said. "If and when I caught one, which was not often, I skinned him and cooked him and ate him—and lived. In doing this I learned to creep silently, to know my way by landmarks, to note tracks and read their meaning, to use dry dead wood off trees and not off the ground for my fire, to make a tiny, nonsmoky fire such as would not give me away to prying masters, and if these came along I had my sod ready to extinguish the fire and hide the spot while I shinned up some ivy-clad tree where I could nestle unobserved above the line of sight of the average searcher."

Baden-Powell was a talented musician, playing the violin and piano, and also enjoyed painting, drawing, and acting when not on canoeing expeditions or camping trips with his brothers. But his many talents did not extend to classroom studies—he was an average rather than an excellent student. While two of his brothers made it into college at Oxford University, Robert was not admitted, so instead he took an exam to enter the British Army. On this exam his results were excellent, so in 1876 he joined the 13th Hussars in India as a Lieutenant.

The officer was disturbed, though, when he discovered how ill-prepared the young soldiers in the army were for real-life outdoors situations. "They were nice lads and made very good parade soldiers, obeyed orders, kept themselves clean and smart and all that, but they had never been taught to be men and how to look after themselves," he said. "In action they carried out orders, but if their officer was shot they were as helpless as a flock of sheep . . . I wanted to make them feel that they were a match for any enemy, able to find their way by the stars or map, accustomed to notice all tracks and signs and to read their meaning, and able to fend for themselves away from regimental cooks and barracks."

So Baden-Powell took it upon himself to teach the young recruits about survival in the outdoors. To assist the learning process, he wrote a book called *Aids to Scouting*. Now the soldiers had a manual to which they could refer.

A natural leader, Baden-Powell quickly gained great respect in the armed forces. Several promotions followed, and between 1884 and 1887 he worked for the British Secret Services as a spy in Germany, Austria, and Russia. It's said he sometimes posed as a butterfly collector and kept detailed plans of military bases camouflaged in his drawings of butterfly wings.

In the following years he served in South Africa, where he learned more outdoor skills from the Zulu troops during several missions, and also in Malta, Rhodesia, and India. But it was his amazing success and survival, against all odds, in the besieged South African town of Mafeking that made this war hero a household name. Prior to the victory, the British public was not behind the war effort, but the heroism and ingenuity shown by Baden-Powell and his men during the seven-month siege gave them a reason to celebrate.

When he returned to England a hero, Baden-Powell's notoriety meant *Aids to Scouting,* the small instruction manual he'd written in the 1890s for the purpose of training members of the military, suddenly was a hit among English boys. Inspired by the invaluable teamwork shown by the young boys in the town during the siege, Baden-Powell decided to write a nonmilitary manual for English lads—a guide to many different outdoor activities.

Baden-Powell never intended his book to launch a worldwide movement—he simply felt that boys in current clubs such as the Boys' Brigade and the Church Lads' Brigade would find the book useful and interesting during their outdoor activities. By 1907 he'd completed a first draft, tentatively titled *Boy Patrols,* and in August of that year, in order to test the book's content, he took a group of about twenty boys on a camp on Brownsea Island off the Dorset coast. This camp has come to be known as the first-ever Scout gathering.

"We set up camp for a fortnight . . . we taught the boys camping, cooking, observation, deduction, woodcraft, chivalry, boatmanship, lifesaving, health, patriotism and such things," he recalled. "The results upon the boys in that short space of time taught me the possibilities which Scout training held for boys."

When *Scouting for Boys* was published in 1908 (first as a six-part series, then as a book), it became an instant bestseller. Scout troops immediately began to appear not only across the United Kingdom, but that same year they also formed in Australia, New Zealand, and India. These days the movement, which many critics said would be a flash in the pan, is still alive and well in 155 countries and boasts an international membership of over 28 million boys and girls—and it all started from just one book.

ETIQUETTE IN BUSINESS, IN SOCIETY, IN POLITICS, AND AT HOME,
Emily Post, 1922

❧

There is a simple rule, by which if one is a voluble chatterer (to be a good talker necessitates a good mind) one can at least refrain from being a pest or a bore. And the rule is merely, to stop and think.

Midway through the dessert course of a memorable gathering of the Gourmet Society in New York in 1938, a sudden and shocking silence came over the ninety-two members of the elite club. The polite hub-bub of conversation ceased, and all eyes turned to Mrs. Emily Post, the undisputed doyenne of good manners and taste, who had just dropped a spoonful of berries onto her lap. A few moments later conversation resumed and the diners continued as if nothing had happened, but the faux pas made it into the following morning's newspapers, which only confirmed Post's standing as a celebrity and an icon. She is said to have laughed the incident off with characteristic refinement and good humor, meaning the accident quickly was forgotten and, despite the stain on her evening gown, her reputation remained unsullied.

Post grew up at a time when manners were endlessly complicated. While she agreed with the need for propriety and decorum in all areas of life, she believed there should be simple rules that those in need of guidance could follow. As a consequence, in 1922 she put in print her commandments regarding etiquette. To Post, etiquette meant "the science of living. It embraces everything. It is the code of sportsmanship and of honor. It is ethics." Post's position was simple—by using a little common sense and thought, everyone from the president to a street sweeper can behave graciously. Americans, lost in a sea of elaborate manners and confusing social conventions, raced to bookstores and the guide became an instant bestseller.

Emily Price was born in October 1872 in Baltimore, Maryland, to a wealthy society family. Her father, Bruce Price, was a well-known and distinguished architect and, as the only child, Emily traveled widely with him in Canada and Europe to inspect the progress of his designs. Initially educated at home by a governess, Emily later was enrolled in private schools in Baltimore and New York. Her education was completed after graduating from Miss Graham's Finishing School in New York.

Beautiful and popular, Emily met Edwin Post at a ball in New York. The dashing banker stole Emily's heart, and the couple were married in grand style at Tuxedo Park in 1892. After an extended honeymoon vacation in Europe, the newlyweds settled in New York's Washington Square and Emily gave birth to two sons.

Emily enjoyed the life of a wealthy financier's wife until the early 1900s. Her relationship with Edwin gradually fell apart and, after discovering his infidelity with a showgirl, she separated from Edwin, even though good society frowned upon marital breakdown. She obtained a divorce in 1905, but because of a minor stock market crash that left Edwin in an unstable financial situation, Emily did not seek alimony payments. With her customary style and rationality, she sought other means to support herself and her sons.

Utilizing knowledge inherited from her father, Emily began writing articles on architecture and interior design for magazines such as *Harper's* and *Scribner's*. She also penned short works of fiction for titles such as *Ainslie's* and *Everybody's*. With a stable of contacts in the publishing world, book writing was a logical progression for the thirty-two-year-old mother, especially once her boys had moved to boarding school. Her first novel, *Flight of the Moth,* was published in 1904. This was followed by a series of novels, the highlight being *The Title Market* in 1909—her first bestseller. She also became a traveling correspondent for magazines such as *Vanity Fair, Collier's,* and *McCall's,* submitting articles on her journey by car across America on the eve of World War I. Post had developed into a highly successful writer, and her talent attracted the attention of publisher Funk & Wagnalls.

Post had gained a reputation as a highly versatile writer (she even wrote a comical travel book), and because of her standing in New York society the publisher approached her to write a book about etiquette. With a huge breadth of knowledge on manners, Post readily accepted the commission. Moreover, she had come to believe etiquette had gone too far, and it was no wonder the layperson was making mistakes. Post often used the example of cutlery at a dining table—if one picked up the wrong fork, she reasoned, there was a chance there were too many forks on the table.

Published in 1922, *Etiquette in Business, in Society, in Politics, and at Home* by Mrs. Emily Post stemmed from one basic credo—good manners began with consideration for others. Post believed the basis of proper deportment was that "no one should do anything that can either annoy or offend the sensibilities of others." By applying a little common sense in all social situations, from the correct mourning attire for a country funeral, to greeting the president, to eating corn on the cob at the dinner table, everyone could boast charming manners, she believed.

The book was an immediate bestseller, and within months of its release Post became a household name and a leading arbiter on social form and propriety. Within months the writer was bombarded with letters from desperate readers with questions on elements that she hadn't included in the book. The answers to these questions became the basis for later editions of the work.

Her extraordinary influence was proven once and for all one day in 1925 when she ventured into Tiffany & Co. on New York's Fifth Avenue. Seeking advice from the manager of the stationery department on the correct wording and style for an engraved invitation, the gentleman bent down and retrieved something from a drawer. Placing a book on the counter, he proceeded to tell the author he would be only too happy to look up the information she requested in *Etiquette* by Mrs. Emily Post.

By the time Post passed away in 1960, at the age of eighty-six, *Etiquette* was in its eighty-ninth printing and the author had become a national icon. Her book had influenced the behavior of an entire nation by teaching its people the value of simple manners.

GUINNESS WORLD RECORDS,
1955

❦

This book is a collection of facts—finite facts expressed in quantitative terms, predominantly those which by measurement are superlative or are records in their respective fields. The world's greatest man is, for this book, the man with the greatest girth rather than the man with the greatest intellect.

It is, of course, somehow fitting that a collection of brilliant and bizarre world records has gone on to become the world's bestselling copyrighted book, creating its very own record (sales surpassed 100 million in 2003). What's most surprising, though, is the fact that the *Guinness Book of Records,* now known as the *Guinness World Records* book, originally was not intended to go to retail at all. The fact-filled tome was written as a promotional item for Guinness beer, to be handed out to publicans in the United Kingdom to help settle arguments that commonly arose over several pints. It was in this exact type of situation, in fact, that the idea for the book first arose.

The year was 1951, and Sir Hugh Beaver, the managing director of the Guinness Brewery in Britain, was on an annual shooting party in County Wexford in the south of Ireland. One night, after a day in the wilderness hunting game birds, the group had settled at the bar and were enjoying several pints of their company's stout when an argument erupted over whether the golden plover or the grouse was the world's fastest-flying game bird.

Good-natured arguments such as this one regularly occurred among the hunters, but as this particular debate raged it became obvious that nobody in the group was 100 percent sure of the facts, and there were no books on hand to help. Beaver decided it was time to do something about this argument as well as other disagreements that surely took place at more than 80,000 pubs across the United Kingdom. He would commission a book, he decided, that publicans could keep behind the bar, a book that contained the answers to everything—the biggest, the longest, the smallest, the tallest, the slowest, and, of course, the fastest.

Back at the brewery one of the Guinness executives, Olympic distance runner and sports celebrity Christopher Chataway, recommended his old university pals, twins Norris and Ross McWhirter, to take on the job of collecting superlative facts to fill the book's pages. The McWhirters, sons of a newspaper editor, were sports journalists who ran a fact-finding agency on London's Fleet Street. Their business provided information to newspapers and other media.

In 1954, the same year that Norris famously stadium-announced Roger Bannister's sub–four minute mile, the McWhirters produced a thin promotional copy of the *Guinness Book of Records*. Only one thousand were printed, and these were given away to publicans and others in the industry. Feedback was positive, so the McWhirters continued collecting facts and one year later, on August 27, 1955, the first official edition of the *Guinness Book of Records* was bound.

"Wherever people congregate to talk, they will argue,

and sometimes the joy lies in the arguing and would be lost if there were any definite answer," wrote Rupert Guinness, chairman of Arthur Guinness & Co. from 1927 until 1962. "But more often the argument takes place on a dispute of fact, and it can be very exasperating if there is no immediate means of settling the argument. Who was the first to swim the Channel? Where is England's deepest well, or Scotland's highest tree, or Ireland's oldest church? How many died in history's worst rail crash? Who gained the biggest majority in parliament? What is the highest point in our country? What is the greatest weight a man has ever lifted? And so on. How much heat these innocent questions can raise! Guinness in producing this book hopes that it may assist in resolving many such disputes, and may, we hope, turn heat into light."

Sent out to pubs across the United Kingdom, the book was intended to be held behind the bar to help solve arguments and, of course, to help promote the Guinness brand. But this book would prove to have a life of its own, a life that included a much larger readership. In its year of release it hit the top of British bestseller lists as tens of thousands of copies were reprinted. Two extra print runs had to be organized to cope with household demand. The next year the *Guinness Book of Records* was released in the United States, where it immediately sold 70,000 copies—an enormous amount, particularly for a book that had, at the time, a very Europe-centric view of the world.

The original version of the book was earnest and encyclopedic in its tone, outlining records such as the highest rainfall in twenty-four hours (46 inches during a typhoon in the Philippines in 1911), the most powerful car (Ferrari 375 Mille Miglia, at 340 bhp) and, of course, the fastest game bird in Europe (the grouse, at 44 miles per hour).

As the McWhirters' stars rose, fueled by the success of the book and of the British TV series *Record Breakers,* so did their political activism. They both held strong right-wing viewpoints, opposed trade unions, and supported the rise of Margaret Thatcher. When the Provisional IRA set off several bombs in London in the early 1970s, the twins offered a $100,000 reward for information leading to the conviction of those responsible, but this action would have tragic consequences.

In November 1975, two gunmen hid outside Ross's London home as he prepared to attend the theater. When his wife, Rosemary, pulled into the driveway, she was accosted by the armed men and forced inside the house. When Ross appeared he was shot in the head and chest, and he died a short time later in the hospital.

The very next week Norris launched the National Association for Freedom (later to be known as the Freedom Association), which challenged ideas such as all-powerful government and the trade union movement. He also continued on with the *Guinness Book of Records,* which was, by then, a household name around the world, and remained a regular on *Record Breakers* and other TV programs. Norris was made a Commander of the British Empire (CBE) in 1980 and died after suffering a heart attack in April 2004. His involvement with the brand, now known as *Guinness World Records,* had waned in the decade before his death.

Since the book's inception people have taken on quirkier challenges in the name of *Guinness World Records.* Entries in the book are now a mix of serious and peculiar, including most body piercings in one session (1,015), longest ear hair (5.2 inches), and fastest jet-powered fire truck (407 miles per hour).

The book now sells over three million copies annually (the bulk in the United States and United Kingdom) in about one hundred countries and is translated into thirty-seven languages. As well as being the world's best-selling copyrighted book, it also holds the record for being the most stolen book from public libraries!

IN COLD BLOOD,
Truman Capote, 1966

❧

But then, in the earliest hours of that morning in November, a Sunday morning, certain foreign sounds impinged on the normal nightly Holcomb noises—on the keening hysteria of coyotes, the dry scrape of scuttling tumbleweed, the racing, receding wail of locomotive whistles. At the time not a soul in sleeping Holcomb heard them—four shotgun blasts that, all told, ended six human lives.

On November 16, 1959, Truman Capote was reading the back pages of the *New York Times* when he came across a small article that caught his attention. It read:

Wealthy Farmer, 3 of Family Slain

A wealthy wheat farmer, his wife and their two young children were found shot to death today in their home. They had been killed by shotgun blasts at close range after being bound and gagged.

The father, 48-year-old Herbert W. Clutter, was found in the basement with his son, Kenyon, 15. His wife Bonnie, 45, and a daughter, Nancy, 16, were in their beds.

There were no signs of a struggle and nothing had been stolen. The telephone lines had been cut.

"This is apparently the case of a psychopathic killer," Sheriff Earl Robinson said.

Mr. Clutter was founder of The Kansas Wheat Growers Association. In 1954 President Eisenhower appointed him to the Federal Farm Credit Board, but he never lived in Washington.

The board represents the twelve farm credit districts in the country. Mr. Clutter served from December, 1953 until April, 1957. He declined a reappointment.

He was also a local member of the Agriculture Department's Price Stabilization Board and was active with the Great Plains Wheat Growers Association.

The Clutter farm and ranch cover almost 1,000 acres in one of the richest wheat areas.

Mr. Clutter, his wife and daughter were clad in pajamas. The boy was wearing blue jeans and a T-shirt.

The bodies were discovered by two of Nancy's classmates, Susan Kidwell and Nancy Ewalt.

Sheriff Robinson said the last reported communication with Mr. Clutter took place last night about 9:30 PM, when the victim called Gerald Van Vleet, his business partner, who lives near by. Mr. Van Vleet said the conversation had concerned the farm and ranch.

Two daughters were away. They are Beverly, a student at Kansas University, and Mrs. Donald G. Jarchow of Mount Carroll, Ill.

A journalist's three-hundred-word afterthought, an item not considered significant enough to warrant a prime piece of newspaper real estate, fired the writer's imagination and catapulted him on a six-year journey that would challenge him personally, extend his creative talents, and culminate in his most controversial novel, *In Cold Blood: A True Account of a Multiple Murder and Its Consequences.*

Capote was born Truman Streckfus Persons in New Orleans in 1924. By the time he was four his parents' marriage had ended and his twenty-one-year-old mother, Lillie Mae, was left alone to raise a toddler. Like many small-town girls, Lillie Mae had always dreamed of a grander life and hoped her salesman husband Arch Persons would provide a way out. Incapable of shouldering the responsibilities of sole parenting and still seeking more than Louisiana could offer, Lillie sent her son to live with her aunts and female cousins in Monroeville, Alabama. Arch, despite promising to spend summers with his son, was too busy traveling the country searching for his next get-rich-quick scheme to take a part in the raising of Truman. Although forever tainted by this early rejection, especially by his mother, Truman was doted on by his female relatives.

Like his neighbor and friend Harper Lee, Truman taught himself to read before he entered the first grade, and by the age of ten he had written a short story called "Old Mr. Busybody," which won first place in a children's writing competition. At about this time the youngster developed a fascination and passion for writing, putting pen to paper every day. Capote later recalled, "I began writing really sort of seriously when I was about eleven. I say seriously in the sense that like other kids go home and practice the violin or piano or whatever, I used to go home from school every day and I would write for about three hours. I was obsessed by it."

During his years in Monroeville, Truman recalls feeling like a "spiritual orphan." Although his mother remarried and started again in New York with her new husband, Joseph Capote, Lillie Mae's new life did not include her son, which left the boy feeling alone in the world. He recalled later, "I was so different from everyone, so much more intellectual and sensitive and perceptive. I was having fifty perceptions a minute to everyone else's five. I always felt that nobody was going to understand me, going to understand what I felt about things. I guess that's why I started writing. At least on paper I could put down what I thought."

The adolescent's dream of a reunion with his mother finally came true when he went to live in New York. Capote adopted the boy and Truman Streckfus Persons became Truman García Capote. Although acquiring a flamboyant new name and a big city address, Truman simply craved the love and attention of a mother who constantly chastised him for his feminine appearance and poor performance at school.

In the late 1930s the teenager enrolled in a prestigious private school in Manhattan, but Capote disliked school and did not excel in any subject, not even English. Having been told by numerous teachers that Truman was mentally backward, Lillie Mae took her son to a psychiatrist, who told the anxious mother her son was a genius.

After many years of failure at the hands of the education system, Capote had no intention of attending college. With his passion for writing still burning strong, the seventeen-year-old found a job at *The New Yorker* magazine, which he described as, "Not a very grand job, for all it really involved was sorting cartoons and newspaper clippings. Still, I was fortunate to have it, since I was determined never to set a studious foot inside a college classroom. I felt that either one was or wasn't a writer, and no combination of professors could influence the outcome."

Capote never regretted his decision to abandon formal education and in the following years produced a constant stream of short stories, which were published in various magazines. In 1946 his potential brilliance was officially recognized when the twenty-one-year-old's short story "Miriam" attracted the attention of a publisher. Having won the O. Henry Award for Best First Published Story, Capote scored a contract with Random House and with it an advance of $1,500 to write a novel.

Capote returned to the solitude of Monroeville and wrote *Other Voices, Other Rooms,* a semiautobiographical story drawn partly from his childhood. Published in 1948, *Other Voices, Other Rooms* stayed on the *New York Times* bestseller list for nine weeks and skyrocketed the young author into New York's literary stratosphere.

Following this success, Capote traveled and lived abroad, all the while producing short stories, and nonfiction for *Vogue, Mademoiselle, Esquire,* and *The New Yorker*. He also completed the novella *Breakfast at Tiffany's: A Short Novel and Three Stories* in 1958, which he believed marked a turning point in his writing—he observed that a "more subdued, clearer prose" was evident.

However, it was the book *The Muses Are Heard* that sent the author in a new creative direction. Chronicling a tour of the Soviet Union by a black American theater company, *Muses* signified Capote's increasing interest in nonfiction. The author described the revelation by saying later, "The book was an important event for me. While writing it, I realized I just might have found a solution to what had always been my greatest creative quandary. I wanted to produce a journalistic novel, something on a large scale that would have the credibility of fact, the immediacy of film, the depth and freedom of prose, and the precision of poetry." Capote believed a novel's emotional impact could be built on the foundations of a factual account and that the result could be as gripping as fiction. Reading the tiny article about the Kansas murders in the back pages of the *New York Times* spurred the author into action.

Sponsored by *The New Yorker,* Capote and his old friend Harper Lee, a writer who in 1960 would publish the novel *To Kill a Mockingbird,* traveled to the scene of the crime—Holcomb, Kansas—and began their research. Initially hoping to record the impact the murder had on the town, Capote's assignment soon changed when, while he was in Kansas, the killers were caught. For the next five years the author became immersed in the lives of the townspeople and the backstories of the murderers.

Said to have taken over six thousand pages of notes from interviews with locals and with the accused, Capote also buried himself in correspondence, court records, newspaper and magazine articles, diary entries, and even weather reports.

So committed was Capote that he spoke of the assignment as a "full-24-hour-a-day job." From the opening of the trial to the moment the jury delivered its verdict, Capote furiously scribbled. Outside of the courtroom the author carried out more than two hundred interviews with the two killers while they were on death row. Capote later explained, "It's extraordinarily difficult and consuming, but for the writer who tries, doing it all the way down the line, the result can be a unique and exciting form of writing."

The result of Capote's exhaustive undertaking was *In Cold Blood: A True Account of a Multiple Murder and Its*

Consequences. First published in serial form in *The New Yorker* in 1965, *In Cold Blood* reconstructed the brutal 1959 murder of the Kansas farming family and examined the subsequent investigation. Its most fascinating content was an intimate look into the lives of two men who had committed an unforgivable crime but who were also shown to be completely human.

Published in hardcover in 1966 by Random House, the novel became an immediate bestseller. Some critics questioned its factual merit, but others, such as the *New York Review of Books,* called it "the best documentary account of an American crime ever written."

Hailed a masterpiece, Capote's brilliant fusion of journalism and narrative not only earned him a position among the literary greats, it also gave rise to a new genre—the nonfiction novel.

All the President's Men,
Bob Woodward and Carl Bernstein, 1974

❧

Woodward fumbled for the receiver and snapped awake. The city editor of the Washington Post *was on the line. Five men had been arrested earlier that morning in a burglary at Democratic headquarters, carrying photographic equipment and electronic gear. Could he come in?*

Although they were of similar ages and both ambitious journalists, no two men could have been as different as Carl Bernstein and Bob Woodward. Both in their late twenties when they were thrown together in 1972 to investigate a break-in at the Democratic National Committee's headquarters, the pair butted heads. But as they became more deeply entwined in what eventually became the greatest journalistic exposé of the modern era, they discovered their differences in personality, style, and talent complemented each other's weaknesses and, as a united force, their investigative skill and writing prowess had the power to bring down a government.

Bob Woodward was born in Geneva, Illinois, in 1943. He was raised in the conservative, middle-class family of Alfred E. Woodward, a judge and lawyer with Republican sympathies. Bob was the oldest of six children. While not an outstanding student at school, he was heavily involved in extracurricula activities such as sports and student radio and was named at graduation as the one most likely to succeed. Bob enjoyed a stable, middle-of-the-road, midwestern upbringing.

Carl Bernstein's upbringing was anything but stable. He was born in Washington, D.C., in 1944, the son of political activists Al and Sylvia Bernstein, communists who were devoted to civil rights issues. The couple once took their nine-year-old son to a protest march in support of convicted spies Ethel and Julius Rosenberg. Likewise, when the Rosenbergs were executed in 1953 young Carl accompanied his parents to a demonstration at the White House. So radical in their beliefs and actions were the Bernsteins that they were under surveillance by the FBI and, according to Carl Jensen in his book *Stories That Changed America: Muckrakers of the 20th Century,* the FBI even monitored those invited to Carl's bar mitzvah.

Where Woodward towed the line at school, Bernstein rebelled. Bernstein did poorly in his studies and was suspended in the eighth grade. As a teenager he lost his driver's license for speeding and failed to graduate from high school. He later said, "I was a terrible student. The only thing I could do in school was write. I'd pass the essay exams and flunk the true and false." One subject that did grab the surly adolescent's attention was his tenth grade journalism course, so he learned to type and discovered a vocation.

Meanwhile, on graduating high school Woodward enrolled at Yale University on an ROTC (Reserve Officers' Training Corps) scholarship. Earning a B.A. degree in History and English in 1965, Woodward was required to join the U.S. Navy for four years. He served as communications officer on an aircraft carrier, then acted as a communications liaison officer between the White House and the Pentagon.

When he left the Navy in 1970, the twenty-seven-year-old contemplated attending law school but decided instead to pursue a career in journalism. One month after leaving the service Woodward applied for a job at the *Washington Post*. As he had no experience in the field, he offered to work free of charge on a two-week trial. During that time the novice wrote seventeen articles, none of which were printed. His editors suggested he would be better served gaining further experience at a smaller publication, so Woodward got a job at a suburban weekly, the *Montgomery County Sentinel*.

Writing everything from state news to movie reviews, Woodward's work was noteworthy for its thorough research and for his knowledge of Washington's politics. His uncovering of a bankrupt savings and loan association was picked up by the *Washington Post,* and in 1971 he was offered a job with the esteemed metropolitan daily. Initially working on the overnight police beat, the twenty-eight-year-old soon began writing articles of greater personal interest. Using his insider's knowledge of politics and his contacts in Washington, he began scouring government offices and questioning bureaucrats in the hope of uncovering some sort of story. Within a year Bob Woodward's byline was appearing on the front page.

On leaving school at sixteen, Bernstein found employment as a copyboy at the *Washington Evening Star*. He rose quickly through the ranks at the *Star* and in 1965 took a reporting job at the *Elizabeth Daily Journal* in New Jersey. While at the journal he proved to be a gifted writer with a flair for investigative journalism. Before long Bernstein approached the *Washington Post* for a job, and in 1966, when he was twenty-two, they took him on board. Bernstein quickly grabbed the editor's attention with his no-holds-barred style of investigative journalism.

On June 17, 1972, five men were apprehended breaking in to and wire tapping the headquarters of the Democratic National Committee at the Watergate office complex. Woodward received a call from his editor early that morning and was assigned to cover the incident. Most other newspapers dismissed the story, but Woodward discovered one of the burglars was a former CIA employee who was working in security for President Nixon's reelection campaign. He also came across White House consultant Howard Hunt's phone number in one of the five's address books.

Bernstein initially was assigned to work on the story separately from Woodward. But while scouring Hunt's telephone records as well as the criminals' bank accounts, he found suspicious correlations, *Post* editors decided to pursue the story, and Woodward and Bernstein combined their talents. In a series of front-page articles the journalists showed connections between Watergate and the Committee for the Reelection of President Nixon (CRP). For months the pair attempted to directly connect the burglars with anyone close to Nixon, or to Nixon himself, but all of their leads terminated at dead ends. Most media outlets dropped the story and the president was reelected in a landslide victory in 1972. But finally, with the aid of an anonymous source known as "Deep Throat," with whom Woodward secretly rendezvoused in a parking garage, the journalists' suspicions were confirmed.

In an October 10, 1972, article Woodward and Bernstein proved that the Watergate break-in was an attempt to scuttle the Democratic Party's election efforts. Furthermore, the pair showed that the incident was funded by the CRP with the go-ahead of the President's senior staff. In the following year the *Washington Post* received the Pulitzer Prize for the Watergate coverage and publishers Simon and Schuster made the journalists a book offer.

While still covering the aftermath and political fall-out from the event for the *Washington Post,* Woodward and Bernstein worked nights and weekends on the book. Originally intending to tell the story from the burglars' perspective, the authors instead decided to make the book the story of their investigation of the break-in, the cover-up that followed, the obstruction of justice, and the massive misuse of presidential power. Based on their revelations, in February 1974, the House Judiciary Committee began impeachment proceedings. In May, seven of the president's closest aides were indicted for their role in the Watergate scandal.

Published in June 1974, *All the President's Men* was an instant bestseller and, as a result of the political climate in which the book was released, it received massive media attention and excellent reviews. On August 9, 1974, President Nixon resigned. Despite their differences, Woodward and Bernstein had proved to be a formidable duo. The tenacity with which they attacked the story, the tedious legwork they endured, and the ethics they maintained through the two-year episode (Bernstein was even subpoenaed to expose his sources) have become legend in the world of journalism.

ROOTS,
Alex Haley, 1976

As the explosion of pain bolted through him, Kunta's upper body spasmed forward and his hands went flailing downward as if to save the front half of his foot, which was falling forward, as bright red blood jetted from the stump as he plunged into blackness.

Every summer, at the home of his maternal grandmother in Henning, Tennessee, the elder women of Alex Haley's family would converge. Around dusk the ladies, aged in their forties and fifties, would gather on the porch and tell tales of the family's past. Aunts and cousins would assemble on wicker chairs and creaky rockers as the sun sank and the heat of the day gave way to the relief of night. Then the stories would begin, each woman's memory contributing different pieces to the family's long history, which had been passed down through many generations. At their feet, sometimes snuggled against his grandmother's legs, sat a boy, silent and still, who would not realize the significance of what he was listening to until some thirty years later. Nor would he discover the profound effect this oral narrative would have on his life when it came time for him to write it down.

Alex Murray Palmer Haley was born in Ithaca, New York, in 1921. His father, Simon, at the time was a graduate student at Cornell University studying agriculture. In order for Simon to finish his Master's degree, his wife and child moved to Henning, Tennessee, to live with her parents. This situation became permanent when Alex's grandfather died in 1926 and Simon took over the running of the family lumber mill.

As a student Haley did not excel at school. After spending two years at a teachers' college in North Carolina, the seventeen-year-old enlisted in the U.S. Coast Guard in 1939 as a mess boy. Following U.S. involvement in World War II, he was sent to the Pacific, where he discovered the most difficult battle he was fighting was the war against boredom. Haley became a voracious reader and soon devoured everything in the ship's library three times over. He'd learned to type in high school, so he then began writing letters to everyone he knew and even wrote letters for friends on board. When the list of acquaintances was exhausted, he decided to try his hand at writing fiction.

The idea of writing something that someone else wanted to read appealed to the now first class petty officer, and he set about penning short stories, mostly based on maritime adventures. The author later said, "The idea that one could roll a blank sheet of paper into a typewriter and write something on it that other people would care to read challenged, intrigued, exhilarated me—and does to this day." Writing during every spare moment, Haley began a process, one that continued over the next eight years, of sending everything he produced to magazines and newspapers in the hope it might be printed. He received hundreds of rejection slips, but the labors that Haley was inflicting upon himself taught him the art of writing. So impressed were Haley's commanders with his diligence, especially when he began to be published, that Coast Guard hierarchy created a new rating especially for the aspiring writer. In 1949 he became first class petty officer in journalism and began handling matters dealing with public relations.

After each literary effort, Haley's writing improved, and in 1959, after twenty years in the Coast Guard, the thirty-eight-year-old retired from the service to become a full-time writer. Beginning his new career writing adventure stories and historical maritime dramas for men's magazines, Haley soon found himself penning biographical stories on interesting people for *Reader's Digest*. Then in 1962 an opportunity arose that was to shape the next period of his career.

Haley once interviewed legendary jazz trumpeter Miles Davis. So insightful was the article that it was sold to *Playboy* and became the first of the publication's "Playboy Interviews." In the ensuing years Haley interviewed for the magazine, among others, Dr. Martin Luther King, Cassius Clay, Johnny Carson, Quincy Jones, Jack Ruby's defense attorneys, and, most notably, Nation of Islam spokesperson Malcolm X in 1963. A publisher reading the Malcolm X piece was impressed with Haley's work and asked the author to ghostwrite an autobiography on the controversial figure.

Haley spent one year interviewing Malcolm X and then an additional year writing the manuscript. When *The Autobiography of Malcolm X* was published in 1965 (Malcolm X was assassinated two weeks after the manuscript was completed), the book was a massive critical and popular success, and by 1977 it had sold more than six million copies. It was later named by *Time* magazine as one of the ten most important nonfiction novels of the twentieth century. Fame and financial security as a writer finally had become a reality for Alex Haley.

Following the publication of the autobiography, Haley was sent to London on assignment. Being an avid history buff, the writer took time to visit the capital's many museums and sights of interest. On an excursion to the British Museum, Haley viewed the Rosetta Stone, written in three different texts—hieroglyphic, demotic, and classical Greek. After learning about the stone, Haley became fascinated with the work of scholar Jean-François Champollion, who translated the script. Using comparative techniques, Champollion worked with what he knew of Greek and hieroglyphics and gradually translated the meaning of all three texts, deciphering an ancient code by matching what was known with the unknown. Haley called Champollion's work "The key that had unlocked a door into the past."

Haley began to consider his own past and the mystery concerning his family history and was transported back to the feet of his grandmother on the Henning front porch. He began to remember snippets of what they discussed and the odd words they'd been told, words brought to the United States by "the African" and passed down through successive generations.

The writer later explained, "'Kin-tay,' he had said, was his name. 'Ko' he had called a guitar. 'Kamby Bolongo' he had called a river in Virginia. They were mostly sharp, angular sounds, with k predominating. These sounds probably had undergone some changes across the generations as they were being passed down, yet unquestionably they represented phonetic snatches of whatever was the specific tongue spoken by my African ancestor who was a family legend." It struck Haley that, like the Rosetta Stone, his own family's past was waiting to be deciphered and the only clues available to him were fragments of boyhood memories. So began an eleven-year quest that took Haley around the world in an attempt to fill in the gaps in the oral history he had heard as a child.

After first confirming his memories with the sole survivor from those evenings on the front porch, his cousin Georgia Anderson in Kansas City, Haley scoured the National Archives in Washington, D.C., tracing his immediate family tree as far as possible. This was followed by extensive research into Africa and its history as well as a visit to the United Nations building in New York on the off chance that one of the African delegates might recognize the few African words he had at his disposal.

After tracking down a Belgian expert in African linguistics at the University of Wisconsin, Haley discovered the language he was speaking was Mandinka, from the Mandingo people, then set about finding the meaning of the words. He later wrote to the professor and informed him that, "One of them probably meant cow or cattle; another probably meant the baobab tree, generic to West Africa. The word *Ko* . . . could refer to the *kora,* one of the Mandingo people's oldest stringed instruments . . . An enslaved Mandingo might relate the kora visually to some among the types of stringed instruments that U.S. slaves had." The professor had no doubt that "Kamby Bolongo" was a reference to the Gambia River.

Haley flew to West Africa, only to be told he would need to speak with a griot, a man Haley calls "a living, walking archive of oral history." It was not until his second visit to Gambia, after borrowing money for the trip, that the author pinpointed a griot who had the relevant knowledge, but first he had to reach the griot's isolated village. He took with him three interpreters, four musicians (he'd heard griots liked music to be played while they spoke), and a crew of helpers, and three days later walked into the village of Juffure. Haley soon was rewarded for his efforts.

Haley later wrote, "There is an expression called 'the peak experience'—that which emotionally, nothing in your life ever transcends." For the writer, that moment came when the griot began to recite to him the ancestral history of the Kinte clan, as it had been passed orally through the centuries. It wasn't until the flight out of Gambia that Haley realized the information he possessed could be the basis of a book.

With pieces of the puzzle still missing, Haley traveled to London and searched maritime records for the ship that brought "the African," or Kunte Kinte, to America. Armed only with the knowledge that the ship landed in "Naplis," according to the ladies of the front porch, Haley assumed the landing spot was Annapolis, Maryland. After six weeks, Haley found the logs of a ship called *Lord Ligonier,* which sailed from the Gambia River to Annapolis in 1767 with an inventory of, among other African treasures such as elephant tusks and gold, ninety-eight "Negroes."

Haley had managed to successfully piece together scraps of information from three countries and with his book painted a picture of the last seven generations of his family. Published in 1976, more than a decade after Haley began his extraordinary pursuit, *Roots: The Saga of an American Family* begins in the village of Juffure in West Africa in 1750 and details the subsequent abduction of seventeen-year-old Kunte Kinte from his family and home by white slave traders. Reaching America, the defiant and proud slave endures mistreatment and torture at the hands of his owners but marries and begins his own family in America. The book chronicles the lives of each succeeding generation and draws to a close with the birth of the author.

Although genealogists have since concluded much of Haley's writing was untrue and have discovered incongruities in the author's research, *Roots* sold more than 1.6 million copies in the first six months of publication and nearly five million copies by 1978. The novel won a special Pulitzer Prize for its author in 1976, the National Book Award in the same year, and the Spingarn Medal from the National Association for the Advancement of Colored People. Despite the accolades and sales, the most moving moment in the process came before the book was published. Haley writes in the final chapter of *Roots,* "On September 29, 1967, I felt I should be nowhere else in the world except standing on a pier at Annapolis—and I was; it was two hundred years to the day after the *Lord Ligonier* had landed. Staring out to seaward across those waters over which my great-great-great-great grandfather had been brought, again I found myself weeping."

A BRIEF HISTORY OF TIME,
Stephen Hawking, 1988

❧

Today we still yearn to know why we are here and where we came from. Humanity's deepest desire for knowledge is justification enough for our continuing quest. And our goal is nothing less than a complete description of the universe we live in.

Although he was diagnosed with amyotrophic lateral sclerosis just after his twenty-first birthday and told he would not last three more years, Stephen Hawking's illness has never placed any boundaries on his extraordinary mind. In the 1980s he set about writing a book that explained briefly and in plain English how the universe works, partly to fund the cost of his own care. The surprise bestseller broke many publishing records and made the wheelchair-bound physicist an international celebrity. But before becoming a household name and appearing on popular television programs such as *Star Trek: The Next Generation* and *The Simpsons,* Hawking was a working scientist with a simple goal—in his own words that goal still is "a complete understanding of the universe, why it is as it is and why it exists at all."

Stephen William Hawking was always an exceptional and unusual human being. Born in Oxford, England, at the height of World War II in 1942, Stephen was a small, clumsy child who did not excel at school or sports. He could not read proficiently until the age of eight but instead spent a great deal of time trying to discover how things worked.

According to his biographer, Kristine Larson, Stephen liked nothing more than spending days disassembling radios and clocks and then attempting, often unsuccessfully, to put them back together. He also used to challenge himself with various logistical dilemmas. For instance, at one stage during his childhood Stephen made it his mission to find as many routes into and out of his house as possible without being discovered by his parents. He eventually discovered twelve covert avenues of escape and reentry.

Larson says Stephen surrounded himself with like-minded friends. As adolescents their favorite pastime was the creation of complex board games in the style of *Risk*. The boys constructed a manufacturing game, for instance, and the feudal game they invented was so detailed that each player had his or her own dynastic family tree. Stephen also enjoyed creating intricate alternative universes. A friend later commented that Stephen "loved the fact that he had created the world and then created the laws that governed it."

But after looking at Stephen's family, his behavior is not at all surprising. The Hawkings were fondly known in their St. Albans' neighborhood as eccentrics. Frank Hawking, a research biologist originating from Yorkshire, and his wife, Isobel, who had studied economics, philosophy, and politics at Oxford University in the 1930s (a remarkable accomplishment for a woman in those days), lived in a rundown house that Frank was always intending to renovate. But despite his best intentions, the house remained without the most basic of British real estate requirements, central heating. When his children complained of the cold, he simply told them to put on more clothes.

Although the family lacked material possessions, the one item the Hawkings were not short of was books—they were stacked two-deep on numerous bookshelves around the house. The children's friends thought it extremely odd, not to mention a little rude, when they were invited to tea and the entire family sat at the dinner table with their heads buried in books. Friends and locals nicknamed the strange way the family spoke as "Hawking-ese," due to the fact that Frank stuttered and the children spoke so quickly that they were constantly stumbling over their words. Further eccentricities were the family car, an old black cab, and the beehives in their basement.

When it came to their education, though, Frank wanted nothing less than the best for his only son. Frank's parents had been farmers who had stretched their limited means to send their son to Oxford, and now Frank found himself in a similar position. His hopes were to send Stephen to the prestigious Westminster School, but this dream depended on his son passing the scholarship exam. Unfortunately, though, on the day of the exam Stephen fell ill and Frank had to be content with his son remaining at St. Albans School. Stephen later said that at St. Albans he received as good an education, or better, than he would have at Westminster.

On his graduation from St. Albans in 1959, Stephen won a scholarship to study physics at University College, Oxford, but once at college his study habits were extremely poor. He didn't purchase all of the necessary books and he rarely took notes in lectures. In one particular examination his borderline score made an oral examination necessary. At twenty years of age he scraped through his final year and graduated with a degree in 1962. His physics tutor later explained to the *New York Times* that the oral examiners "were intelligent enough to realise they were talking to someone far more clever than most of themselves."

In the 1960s the debate raging in scientific circles concerned the Big Bang. There was no consensus about how the universe began, and it was in this environment that Hawking began, at Trinity Hall, Cambridge University, to begin postgraduate study in cosmology and astronomy. Even though cosmology was not highly regarded by the scientific community at the time, Hawking was determined to pursue this passion, along with his other interest, Einstein's theory of relativity. Hawking later remarked that these were neglected fields that were ripe for development at the time.

Hawking struggled through his first year at Cambridge. His background in mathematics was weak and, despite the urgings of his mentor Dennis Sciama to give up cosmology and general relativity and switch to astrophysics, Hawking battled on. But mathematics was not the only challenge Hawking was to face at Cambridge. A few weeks after his twenty-first birthday, in January 1963, Hawking fell while ice skating and was unable to get up. While studying at Oxford he had experienced a few strange symptoms such as clumsiness and slurred speech, which he chose to ignore. But his accident on the ice was altogether different, and Hawking was admitted to St. Bartholomew's Hospital.

After two weeks of medical tests and examinations, Hawking was diagnosed with amyotrophic lateral sclerosis (also known as Lou Gehrig's disease or Motor Neurone disease), a degenerative disease that attacks the central nervous system. Hawking was told by doctors that his time was limited, and his condition deteriorated quickly. Nevertheless, Hawking continued with his studies and explained, ". . . although there was a cloud hanging over my future, I found to my surprise that I was enjoying life in the present more than I had before. I began to make progress with my research . . ." Hawking said that he began working hard for the first time in his life after realizing that if he was going to marry the girl he'd fallen in love with, Jane Wilde, he was going to have to earn his degree and get a job. He was awarded his doctorate in 1966.

First a research fellow and then a professional fellow at Gonville and Caius College, Cambridge, Hawking decided in the early 1970s to supervise an undergraduate math course in the hope of improving his own ability with numbers. While working on his theories on black holes and general relativity, he became Professor of Gravitational Physics in 1977 and, two years later, was appointed Lucasian Professor of Mathematics, a distinguished position held more than three hundred years earlier by Sir Isaac Newton. But while his mind was exploring the outer reaches of quantum theory, his physical condition had deteriorated dramatically and the lack of resources for the handicapped in British universities was limiting his potential.

In 1982, having to rely on caregivers for all his needs, Hawking decided to write an accessible book on cosmology to help pay the costs. Within two years he had produced the first draft of *A Brief History of Time*. But the following year Hawking was to encounter another setback. "I was in Geneva . . . in the summer of 1985 . . . I caught pneumonia and was rushed to hospital," he recalled. "The hospital in Geneva suggested to my wife that it was not worth keeping the life support machine on. But she was having none of that. I was flown back to Addenbrooke's Hospital in Cambridge, where a surgeon called Roger Grey carried out a tracheotomy. That operation saved my life but took away my voice."

After being given a computer that allowed him the ability to speak, Hawking revised the final draft of *A Brief History of Time* and the book was published in 1988. Hawking used the book to explain to the general public a range of subjects in cosmology, including black holes and the Big Bang. In order to keep complex theories simple the author included diagrams and illustrations. On the advice of his publisher, who explained that for every equation the book contained the readership would halve, Hawking included only one equation, $E=mc^2$.

Criticized as being an unread bestseller, *A Brief History of Time* sold nine million copies by 2002 and appeared in the *Sunday Times* bestseller list for a record 237 weeks. The paperback, released on April 6, 1995, reached the list's number-one position within three days.

FURTHER READING

PRIDE AND PREJUDICE
The Jane Austen Society of Australia: www.jasa.net.au.
Jane Austen Society of North America: www.jasna.org.
Knox-Shaw, Peter. *Jane Austen and the Enlightenment.* Cambridge: Cambridge University Press, 2004.
Tomalin, Claire. *Jane Austen, A Life.* London: Penguin Books, 1998.

FRANKENSTEIN
Garrett, Martin. *Mary Shelley.* London: British Library, 2002.
St. Clair, William. *The Godwins and the Shelleys: The Biography of a Family.* London: Faber and Faber, 1989.
Seymour, Miranda. *Mary Shelley.* London: John Murray, 2000.

OLIVER TWIST
Ackroyd, Peter. *Dickens.* New York: Vintage, 2002.
Benson, Kenneth. "Charles Dickens: The Life of the Author." www.fathom.com.
Forster, John. *Life of Charles Dickens.* Limbricht, Netherlands: Uitgeverij Diderot, 2005.

JANE EYRE
Barker, Juliet. *The Brontës.* New York: St. Martin's Press, 1996.
Fraser, Rebecca. *Charlotte Brontë.* London: Vintage, 2003.

Gordon, Lyndall. *Charlotte Brontë: A Passionate Life*. New York: W.W. Norton & Company, Inc., 1996.

The Victorian Web: www.victorianweb.org.

VANITY FAIR

Ferris, Ina. *William Makepeace Thackeray*. Boston: Twayne Publishers, 1983.

Monsarrat, Ann. *An Uneasy Victorian: Thackeray the Man*. New York: Dodd, Mead, and Co., 1980.

Shillingsburg, Peter. *William Makepeace Thackeray: A Literary Life*. Basingstoke, UK: Palgrave, 2001.

CRIME AND PUNISHMENT

Bloom, Harold. *Fyodor Dostoevsky*. Bloom's Modern Critical Views. New York: Chelsea House Publications, 1989.

———. *Dostoevsky: The Miraculous Years, 1865–1871*. Princeton, N.J.: Princeton University Press, 1995.

Frank, Joseph. *Dostoevsky: The Seeds of Revolt, 1821–1849*. Princeton, N.J.: Princeton University Press, 1976.

———. *Dostoevsky: The Years of Ordeal, 1850–1859*. Princeton, N.J.: Princeton University Press, 1987.

Leatherbarrow, W. J., ed. *The Cambridge Companion to Dostoevskii*. Cambridge Companions to Literature. Cambridge: Cambridge University Press, 2002.

WAR AND PEACE

Bayley, John. *Leo Tolstoy*. Jackson, Miss.: University Press of Mississippi, 1997.

Jones, Malcolm. *New Essays on Tolstoy*. Cambridge: Cambridge University Press, 1978.

Masterpiece Theater Web site for *Anna Karenina* (featuring a Tolstoy timeline): www.pbs.org/wgbh/masterpiece/anna/timeline.html.

Troyat, Henri. *Tolstoy*. Trans. Nancy Amphoux. New York: Grove Press, 2001.

Wilson, A. N. *Tolstoy*. New York: Ballantine Books, 1989.

ADVENTURES OF HUCKLEBERRY FINN

Emerson, Everett. *Mark Twain: A Literary Life.* Philadelphia: University of Pennsylvania Press, 2000.

Kaplan, Fred. *The Singular Mark Twain: A Biography.* New York: Doubleday, 2003.

The Mark Twain House and Museum: www.marktwainhouse.org.

THE WAR OF THE WORLDS

Coren, Michael. *The Invisible Man: The Life and Liberties of H. G. Wells.* New York: Atheneum, 1993.

Ferguson, Niall. "H. G. Wells warned us of how it would feel to fight a 'War of the World,'" *Telegraph,* July 24, 2005, www.telegraph.co.uk/opinion/main.jhtml?xml=opinion/2005/07/24/do2402.xml.

Gomme, A.W. *Mr. Wells as Historian.* Glasgow: MacLehose, Jackson, and Co., 1921.

Murray, Brian. *H. G. Wells.* New York: Continuum International Publishing Group, 1990.

Perry, Mike. "C. S. Lewis, H. G. Wells, and the Evolutionary Myth," July 1, 1998, www.discovery.org/scripts/viewDB/index.php?command=view&id=516.

Rabindranath, Tagore, and H. G. Wells in Geneva, 1930. "Rabindranath Tagore: In Conversation with H. G. Wells," Excerpt from *A Tagore Reader,* Amiya Chakravarty, ed., www.schoolofwisdom.com/tagore-wells.html.

THE HOUND OF THE BASKERVILLES

The official Web site of the Sir Arthur Conan Doyle Literary Estate: www.sherlockholmesonline.org.

Sir Arthur Conan Doyle—His Life, All His Works and More: http://sirconandoyle.com/.

PETER PAN

Birkin, Andrew. *J. M. Barrie and the Lost Boys.* New Haven: Yale University Press, 2003.

Lane, Anthony. "Lost Boys: Why J. M. Barrie Created Peter Pan," *The New Yorker,* November, 2004.

THE GREAT GATSBY

Donaldson, Scott. *Fool for Love.* New York: Congdon & Weed, 1983.

Koblas, John J. *F. Scott Fitzgerald in Minnesota: His Homes and Haunts.* St. Paul: Minn.: Minnesota Historical Society Press, 1978.

LeVot, Andre. *F. Scott Fitzgerald.* New York: Doubleday, 1983.

PBS's American Storytellers: www.pbs.org/kteh/amstorytellers/bios.html.

Turnbull, Andrew. *Scott Fitzgerald.* New York: Scribners, 1962.

University of South Carolina Web site: www.sc.edu/fitzgerald/index.html.

WINNIE-THE-POOH

Crews, Frederick. *The Pooh Perplex.* Chicago: University of Chicago Press, 2003.

————. *Postmodern Pooh.* New York: North Point Press, Pooh Corner Web site: www.pooh-corner.com.

Thwaite, Ann. *A. A. Milne: His Life.* New York: Random House, 1990.

Wullschlager, Jackie. *Inventing Wonderland: The Lives and Fantasies of Lewis Carroll, Edward Lear, J. M. Barrie, Kenneth Grahame and A. A. Milne.* New York: The Free Press, 1996.

ALL QUIET ON THE WESTERN FRONT

Firda, Richard Arthur. *All Quiet on the Western Front: Literary Analysis and Cultural Context.* New York: Twayne Publishers, 1993.

O'Neill, Terry, ed. *Readings on All Quiet on the Western Front.* San Diego, Calif.: Greenhaven Press, 1999.

GONE WITH THE WIND

Margaret Mitchell House & Museum: www.gwtw.org/.

Margaret Mitchell Web site: www.geocities.com/Athens/6098/index.html.

"Miss Mitchell, 49, Dead of Injuries," *The New York Times,* August 1949, page 23.

THE HOBBIT

Carpenter, Humphrey. *J. R. R. Tolkien: A Biography.* New York: Houghton Mifflin Company, 2000.

HarperCollins's Tolkien Web site: www.tolkien.co.uk.

Pearce, Joseph. *Tolkien: Man and Myth.* London: HarperCollins Publishers, 1998.

Shippey, Tom. *J. R. R. Tolkien—Author of the Century.* New York: Houghton Mifflin Company, 2000.

Tolkien Society Web site: www.tolkiensociety.org.

THE GRAPES OF WRATH

Benson, Jackson J. *John Steinbeck, Writer: A Biography.* New York: Penguin Books, 1990.

Steinbeck, Elaine, ed. *Steinbeck: A Life in Letters.* New York: Penguin Books, 1989.

FOR WHOM THE BELL TOLLS

Allen, Jamie. "Hemingway Biography: From Illinois to International Celebrity," in *A Hemingway Retrospective,* www.cnn.com/SPECIALS/books/1999/hemingway/.

"Hemingway's Prize-Winning Works Reflected Preoccupation With Life and Death," *The New York Times,* July 1961, page 6.

NINETEEN EIGHTY-FOUR

Bowker, Gordon. *Inside George Orwell.* Hampshire, UK: Palgrave Macmillan, 2003.

Crick, Bernard. *George Orwell: A Life.* New York: Penguin Books, 1982.

Orwell, George. "Why I Write," www.orwell.ru/library/essays/
wiw/english/e_wiw.

Taylor, J. D. *Orwell: The Life*. New York: Henry Holt and
Company, 2003.

THE CATCHER IN THE RYE

Dead Caulfields Web site: www.geocities.com/deadcaulfields/
DCHome.html.

Yardley, Jonathan. "J. D. Salinger's Holden Caulfield, Aging
Gracelessly," *The Washington Post,* October 18, 2004,
page C01, www.washingtonpost.com/wp-dyn/articles/
A43680-2004Oct18.html.

FROM HERE TO ETERNITY

Aldrich, Nelson. "The Art of Fiction No. 22." *The Paris
Review,* Issue 20, Autumn–Winter, 1958–1959.

CASINO ROYALE

Ian Fleming Centre Web site: www.ianflemingcentre.com.

Lycett, Andrew. *Ian Fleming*. London: Orion Books, 1996.

Pearson, John. *The Life of Ian Fleming: The Man Who Created
James Bond*. London: Aurum Press, Ltd., 2003.

LORD OF THE FLIES

Golding family Web site: www.william-golding.co.uk.

Lambert, Bruce. "William Golding Is Dead at 81; The Author
of 'Lord of the Flies,'" *The New York Times,* June 1993,
section 1, page 38.

LOLITA

Boyd, Brian, *Vladimir Nabokov: The American Years*. Princeton,
N.J.: Princeton University Press, 1991.

———. *Vladimir Nabokov: The Russian Years*. Princeton, N.J.:
Princeton University Press, 1993.

Edmunds, Jeff. " 'Lolita': complex, often tricky and 'a
hard sell,' " April 9, 1999, www.cnn.com/SPECIALS/
books/1999/nabokov/lolita.sociological.essay.

Haven, Cynthia. "The Lolita Question," *Stanford Magazine,* May/June, 2006.

CAT IN THE HAT
Dr. Seuss National Memorial Web site: www.catinthehat.org/.

Morgan, Judith, and Neil Morgan. *Dr. Seuss & Mr. Geisel: A Biography.* New York: Da Capo Press, 1996.

Nel, Philip. *Dr. Seuss: American Icon.* New York: Continuum International Publishing Group, 2005.

DOCTOR ZHIVAGO
The American Academy of Poets Web site: www.poets.org.

Carlisle, Olga. "The Art of Fiction No. 25." *The Paris Review,* Issue 24, Summer–Fall, 1960.

Clowes, Edith W., ed. *Doctor Zhivago: A Critical Companion.* Evanston, Ill.: Northwestern University Press, 1995.

Fleishman, Lazar. *Boris Pasternak: The Poet and His Politics.* Cambridge, Mass.: Cambridge University Press, 1990.

"From Lyric Poet to Epic Novelist: Boris Pasternak (1890–1960)," www.pbs.org/wgbh/masterpiece/zhivago/ ei_pasternak.html.

Hingley, Ronald. *Pasternak: A Biography.* New York: Knopf, 1983.

The Nobel Prize Web site: http://nobelprize.org/nobel_prizes/ literature/laureates/1958/press.html.

"Pasternak Letters Tell of Work on 'Zhivago,'" *The Boston Globe,* April 1987, page 20.

TO KILL A MOCKINGBIRD
Article on Harper Lee at future Web site of the Encyclopedia of Alabama: www.encyclopediaofalabama.org/samples/ sample03.html.

Bloom, Harold, ed. *Harper Lee's To Kill a Mockingbird.* Contemporary Literary Views Series. New York: Chelsea House, 1996.

Harper Lee Web site: www.harperlee.com/.

Author interview by Roy Newquist. *Counterpoint*. Skokie, Ill.: Rand McNally, 1964.

Johnson, Claudia Durst. *To Kill a Mockingbird: Threatening Boundaries*. Twayne's Masterwork Studies Series, no. 139. New York: Twayne Publishers, 1994.

THE SPY WHO CAME IN FROM THE COLD

Author biography at www.randomhouse.com.

Bruccoli, Michael Joseph, and Judith S. Baughman, eds. *Conversations with John Le Carré*. Jackson: University Press of Mississippi, 2004.

Cobbs, John. L. *Understanding John Le Carré*. Columbia: University of South Carolina Press, 1998.

Interview by Kerry O'Brien on *The 7.30 Report*: www.abc.net.au/7.30/stories/s252445.htm.

VALLEY OF THE DOLLS

"All Hail the Bitch Goddess," (Discussion between Camille Paglia and Glenn Belverio.) www.salon.com/feature/1997/12/cov_19feature.html.

www.swinginchicks.com/.

THE GODFATHER

Author interview at http://us.penguingroup.com/static/rguides/us/essential_godfather.html.

Author interview on *Larry King Live,* August 2, 1996.

"'Godfather' author Mario Puzo dies," July 2, 1999, www.cnn.com/books/news/9907/02/obit.puzo.01/.

"Godfather creator dies," Saturday, July 3, 1999, http://news.bbc.co.uk/1/hi/world/americas/384624.stm.

THE DAY OF THE JACKAL

Author interview on *Larry King Live,* April 15, 2000.

Author interview on Radio Prague. www.radio.cz/en.

Author interview at www.spiegel.de/international.

CARRIE

King, Stephen. *On Writing: A Memoir of the Craft*. New York: Scribner, 2000.

Nashawaty, Chris. "Shock Ending." *Who,* October, 2002, page 54.

The Official Stephen King Web site: www.stephenking.com.

Raworth, Ben. "The Horror Author." *FHM,* December, 1998, page 92.

JAWS

Bauder, David. "Peter Benchley Wouldn't Write Same 'Jaws' Today." *The Trentonian,* April, 2000.

Dowling, Stephen. "The book that spawned a monster," http://news.bbc.co.uk/1/hi/entertainment/arts/3400291.stm.

"Jaws author Peter Benchley dies," http://news.bbc.co.uk/1/hi/world/americas/4707576.stm.

The Peter Benchley Web site: www.peterbenchley.com.

MIDNIGHT'S CHILDREN

Kadzis, Peter. "Salman Speaks," *The Boston Phoenix,* June 21, 2007, http://thephoenix.com/Article.aspx?id=42212&page=1.

Richards, Linda L. "Salman Rushdie," *January Magazine,* http://januarymagazine.com/profiles/rushdie2002.html.

"Rushdie's Courage." *The Boston Phoenix,* June 20, 2007, http://thephoenix.com/article_ektid42241.aspx.

THE COLOR PURPLE

Dieke, Ikenna, ed. *Critical Essays on Alice Walker*. Westport, Conn.: Greenwood Press, 1999.

Gates, Henry Louis, and K. A. Appiah, eds. *Alice Walker: Critical Perspectives Past and Present*. New York: Amistad Press, 1993.

Haisty Winchell, Donna. *Alice Walker*. New York: Twayne Publishers, 1992.

Interview by Jenni Murray. *Woman's Hour,* April 24, 1998, Radio 4, www.bbc.co.uk/bbcfour/audiointerviews/profilepages/walkera1.shtml.

Interview by Sue MacGregor. *Woman's Hour,* May 15, 1985, Radio 4, www.bbc.co.uk/bbcfour/audiointerviews/profile pages/walkera1.shtml.

Lauret, Maria. *Alice Walker.* Modern Novelists Series. New York: St. Martin's Press, 2000.

White, Evelyn. *Alice Walker: A Life.* New York: W.W. Norton & Company, Inc., 2004.

Whitted, Qiana. www.georgiaencyclopedia.org. www.gale.com.

HOLLYWOOD WIVES

Bardin, Brantley. "Oh, Jackie!" *Premiere,* July 2001.

Foulkas, Nick. "A Tale of Two Sisters," *New Idea*, July 2002.

The Jackie Collins Web site: www.jackiecollins.com.

BRIDGET JONES'S DIARY

The Bridget Jones Online Archive: www.bridgetarchive. altervista.org.

HARRY POTTER AND THE SORCERER'S STONE

Author interview. www.kidsread.com/HP07/content/rowling. asp.

Gibb, Eddie. "Tales From a Single Mother," *The Sunday Times* (London), June 29, 1997, www.accio-quote.org/articles/ 1997/0697-sundaytimes-gibb.html.

Glaister, Dan. "Debut Author and Single Mother Sells Children's Book for £100,000," *The Guardian*, July 8, 1997, www.accio-quote.org/articles/19970797-guardian-glaister-htm.

Goring, Rosemary. "Harry's Fame," *Scotland on Sunday*, January 17, 1999, www.accio-quote.org/articles/1999/ 0199-scotlandsunday-goring.html.

Johnstone, Anne. "Happy Ending, and That's for Beginners," *The Herald,* June 24, 1997, www.accio-quote.org/ articles/1997/0697-herald-johnstone.html.

McGinty, Stephen. "The JK Rowling Story," *The Scotsman,* June 16, 2003, http://news.scotsman.com/topics. cfm?id=662772003&tid=3.

Reynolds, Nigel. "$100,000 Success Story for Penniless Mother," *The Telegraph,* July 7, 1997, www.accio-quote. org/articles/1997/spring97-telegraph-reynolds.htm.

Williams, Rhys. "The Spotty Schoolboy and Single Mother Taking the Mantle from Roald Dahl," *The Independent* (London), January 29, 1999, www. accio-quote.org/articles/1999/0199-independent-williams.html.

True History of the Kelly Gang

"Carey on Dickens, the Queen and Ned Kelly," *The Sydney Morning Herald,* May 6, 1998, page 13.

Contemporary Writers in the UK Web site: www. contemporarywriters.com.

Interview by Cathy Border at www.uqp.uq.edu.au/carey/txt/inv.htm.

Ned Kelly Web site: www.ironoutlaw.com/.

The Da Vinci Code

Author interview at www.danbrown.com.

Button, James. "Da Vinci Author Finds His Marriage on Trial," *The Age,* March 16, 2006, www.theage.com.au/news/world/da-vinci-author-finds-his-marriage-on-trial/2006/03/15/1142098528960.html?page=2#.

"Decoding the Da Vinci Code Author," April 7, 2006, http://news.bbc.co.uk/2/hi/entertainment/3541342.stm.

Moses, Alexa, and Julian Lee. "Cracking the Hollywood Code," *The Sydney Morning Herald,* May 13, 2006, page 8.

Smith, David. "Veni Vida Da Vinci," *The Guardian,* December 12, 2004, http://books.guardian.co.uk/. departments/generalfiction/story/0,6000,1372682,00.html.

Walters, Joanna, and Alice O'Keefe. "How Dan Brown's Wife Unlocked the Code to Bestseller Success," *Guardian*

Unlimited, March 12, 2006. http://observer.guardian.co.uk/
uk_news/story/0,,1729079,00.html.

THE ENGLISH DICTIONARY

Green, Jonathon. *Chasing the Sun: Dictionary Makers and the
Dictionaries They Made.* London: Jonathon Cape, 1996.

Mugglestone, Lynda. *Lost for Words: The Hidden History of
the Oxford English Dictionary.* New Haven: Yale University
Press, 2005.

Willinsky, John. *Empire of Words: The Reign of the Oxford English
Dictionary.* Princeton, N.J.: Princeton University Press, 1995.

Winchester, Simon. *The Meaning of Everything: The Story of the
Oxford English Dictionary.* Oxford: Oxford University Press,
2003.

ENCYCLOPAEDIA BRITANNICA

Einbinder, Harvey. *The Myth of the Britannica.* New York:
Grove Press, 1964.

Encyclopaedia Britannica Online: www.britannica.com.

Jacobs, Arnold Stephen, Jr. *The Know-It-All: One Man's
Humble Quest to Become the Smartest Person in the World.*
New York: Simon & Schuster, 2004.

Kogan, Herman. *The Great EB: The Story of the Encyclopædia
Britannica.* Chicago: University of Chicago Press, 1958.

THE ORIGIN OF SPECIES

Allen, Grant. *Charles Darwin.* Whitefish, MT: Kessinger
Publishing, 2004.

The Life & Times of Charles Darwin: www.aboutdarwin.com.

SCOUTING FOR BOYS

Boy Scouts of America National Council Web site: www.
scouting.org.

Drewery, Mary. *Baden-Powell.* London: Hodder and Stoughton,
1975.

Interview with Baden-Powell. "Be Prepared," *Listener,* 1937,
reproduced at www.pinetreeweb.com/bp=listener.htm.

Jeal, Tim. *The Boy-Man: The Life of Lord Baden-Powell.* New York: William Morrow & Co, 1990.

Peterson, Robert. "Marching to a Different Drummer," *Scouting Magazine,* October 2003.

Scouts Australia Web site: www.scouts.com.au.

Etiquette in Business, in Society, in Politics and at Home
The Emily Post Institute: www.emilypost.com.

"Emily Post Is Dead Here at 86; Writer Was Arbiter of Etiquette," *The New York Times,* September 1960, page 1.

Post, Edwin. *Truly Emily Post.* New York: Funk & Wagnalls, 1961.

Guinness World Records
Guinness World Records Web site: www. guinnessworldrecords.com.

"1975: TV Presenter Ross McWhirter Shot Dead," http://news.bbc.co.uk/onthisday/hi/dates/stories/november/27/newsid_2528000/2528787.

Watson, Bruce. "World's Unlikeliest Bestseller," *Smithsonian,* August 2005, pp. 76–81.

In Cold Blood
Carr, David. "Cold-blooded Tellers of Tales," *The Age,* August 6, 2005, www.theage.com.au/news/film/.coldblooded-tellers-of-tales/2005/08/04/1123125842281.html.

Krebs, Albin. "Truman Capote is Dead at 59; Novelist of Style and Clarity," *The New York Times,* August 26, 1984.

Mass, Mark H. "Capote's Legacy: The Challenge of Creativity and Credibility in Literary Journalism." Paper presented for competition in the Cultural and Critical Studies Division, Association for Education in Journalism and Mass Communication, Annual Convention, Phoenix, Ariz., August 2000.

PBS's *American Masters* Web site: www.pbs.org/wnet/americanmasters/database/capote_t.html.

Truman Capote Web site: www.capotebio.com/.

ALL THE PRESIDENT'S MEN

Jensen Carl. *Stories that Changed America: Muckrakers of the 20th Century*. New York: Seven Stories Press, 2000.

Satter, James. *Journalists Who Made History*. Minneapolis: The Oliver Press, Inc., 1998.

ROOTS

Alex Haley biography: www.gale.com/freeresources/bhm/bio/haley_a.htm.

Cashill, Jack. *Hoodwinked: How Intellectual Hucksters Have Hijacked American Culture*. Nashville: Thomas Nelson, 2005.

Crowley, Anne S. "Research Help Supplies Backbone for Haley's Book," *Chicago Tribune,* October 24, 1985, page 10H.

A BRIEF HISTORY OF TIME

Boslough, John. *Stephen Hawking's Universe*. New York: Avon Books, 1985.

Ferguson, Kitty. *Stephen Hawking: Quest for a Theory of Everything*. London: Franklin Watts, 1991.

Larson, Kristine. *Stephen Hawking: A Biography*. Westport, Conn.: Greenwood Press, 2005.

GENERAL LITERATURE

Books and Writers: www.kirjasto.sci.fi.

The Paris Review: www.parisreview.com.

Literary Encyclopedia: www.litencyc.com.